APOCALYPSE 91

REVOLUTION NEVER SLEEPS

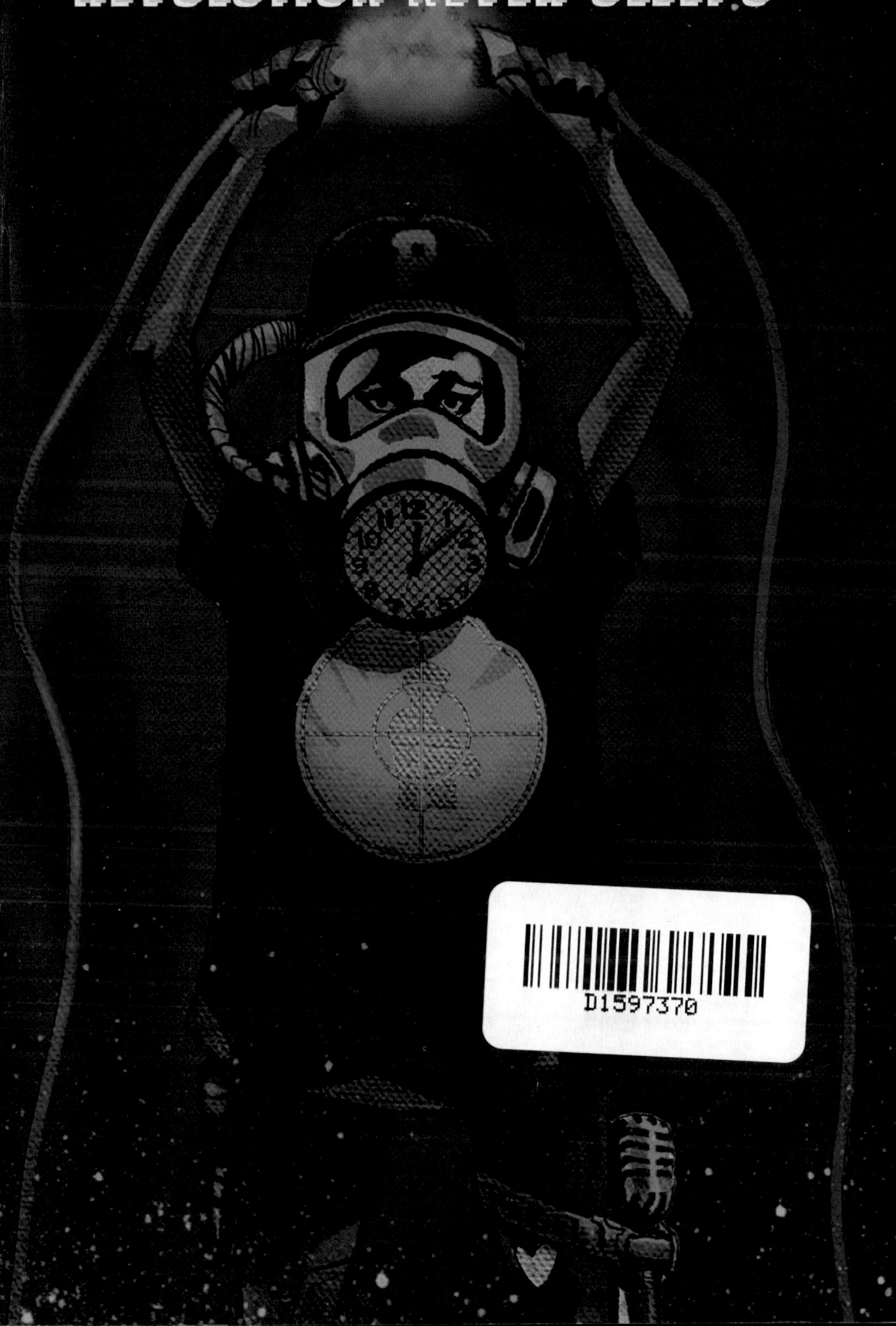

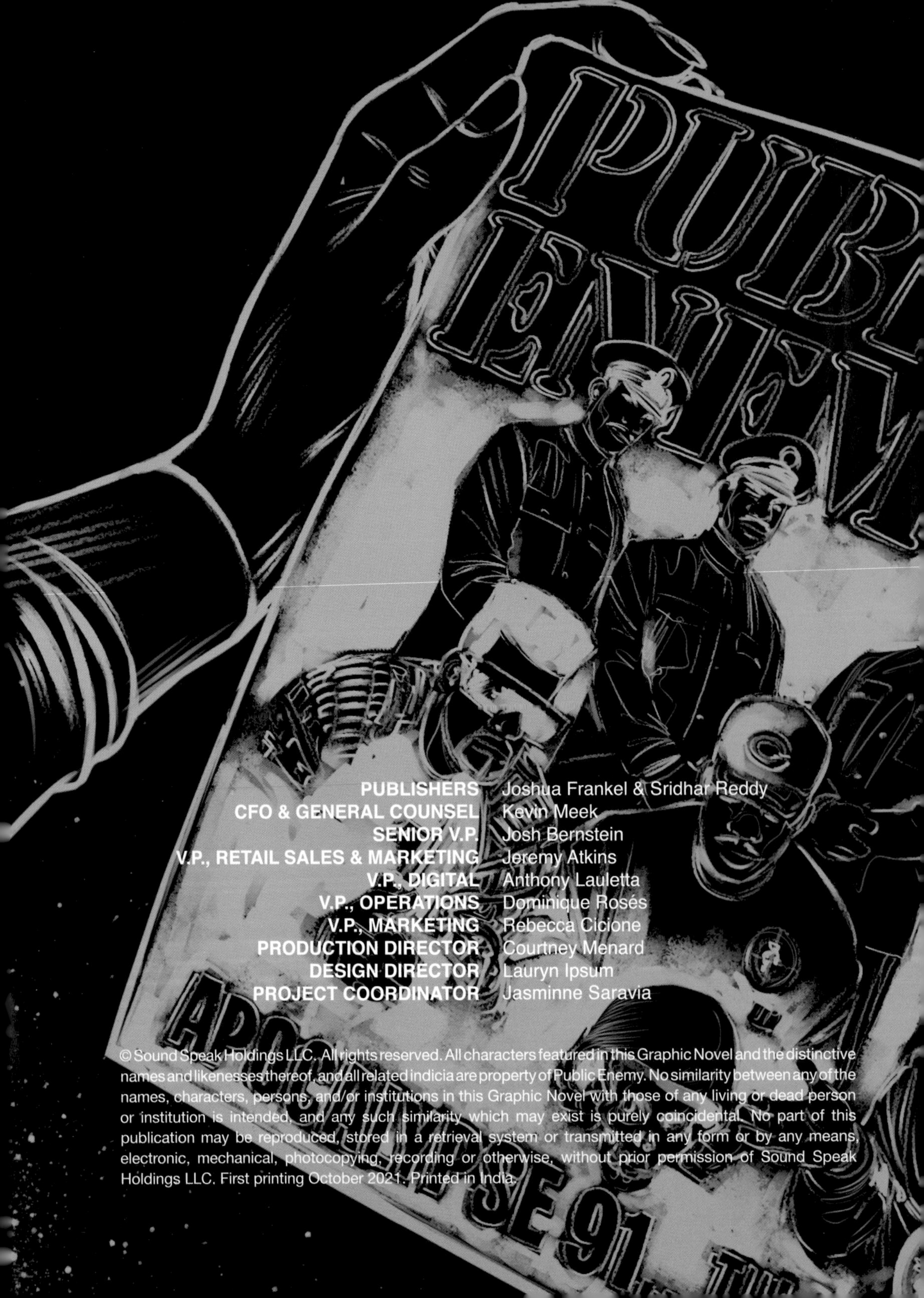

PUBLISHERS Joshua Frankel & Sridhar Reddy
CFO & GENERAL COUNSEL Kevin Meek
SENIOR V.P. Josh Bernstein
V.P., RETAIL SALES & MARKETING Jeremy Atkins
V.P., DIGITAL Anthony Lauletta
V.P., OPERATIONS Dominique Rosés
V.P., MARKETING Rebecca Cicione
PRODUCTION DIRECTOR Courtney Menard
DESIGN DIRECTOR Lauryn Ipsum
PROJECT COORDINATOR Jasminne Saravia

ILLUSTRATORS
Chuck D, Koi Turnbull,
Carlos Olivares, & Butch Mapa

WRITERS
Chuck D & Troy-Jeffrey Allen, Regine Sawyer,
Che Grayson, & Evan Narcisse

EDITOR
Chris Robinson

COVER ARTIST
Mike del Mundo

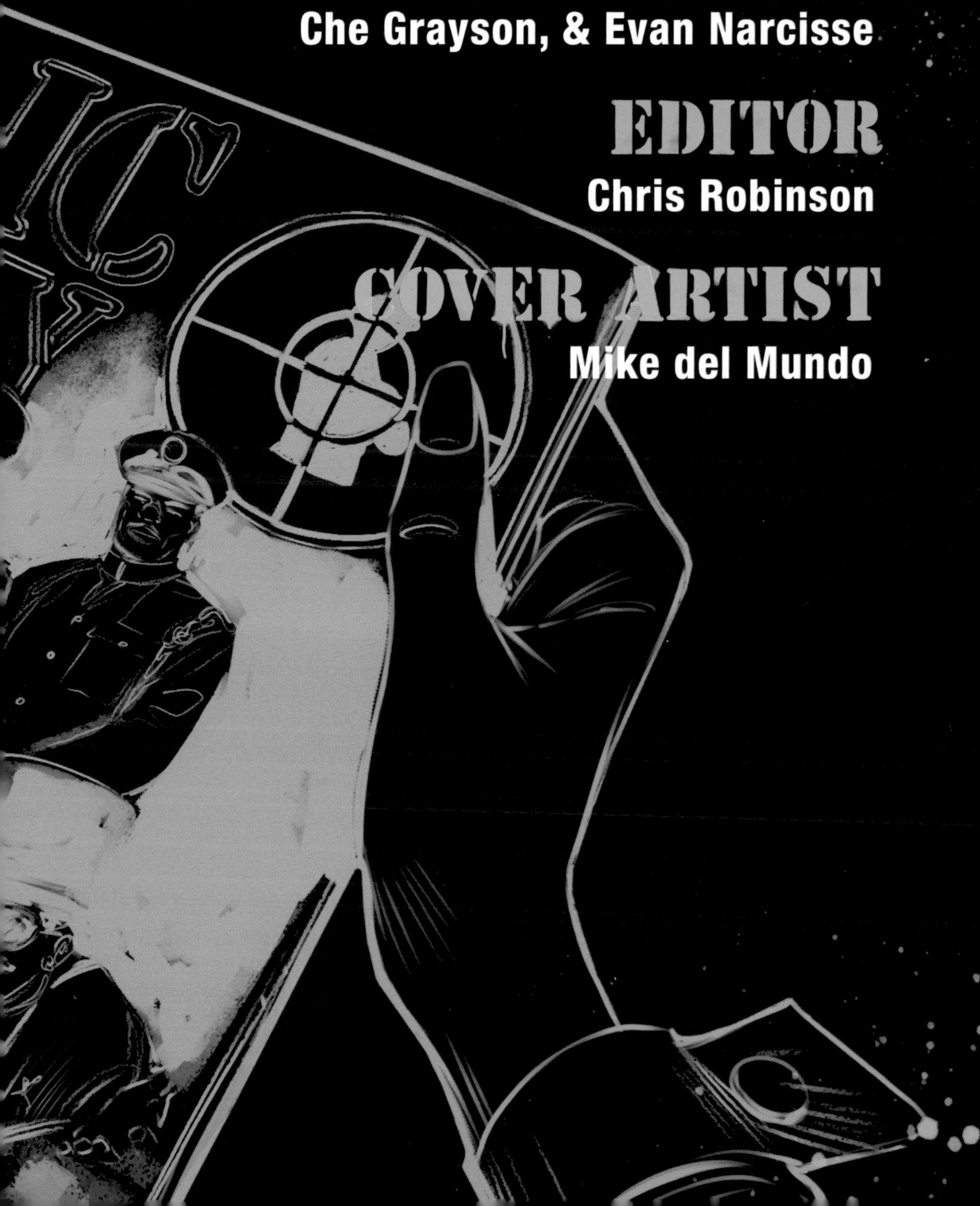

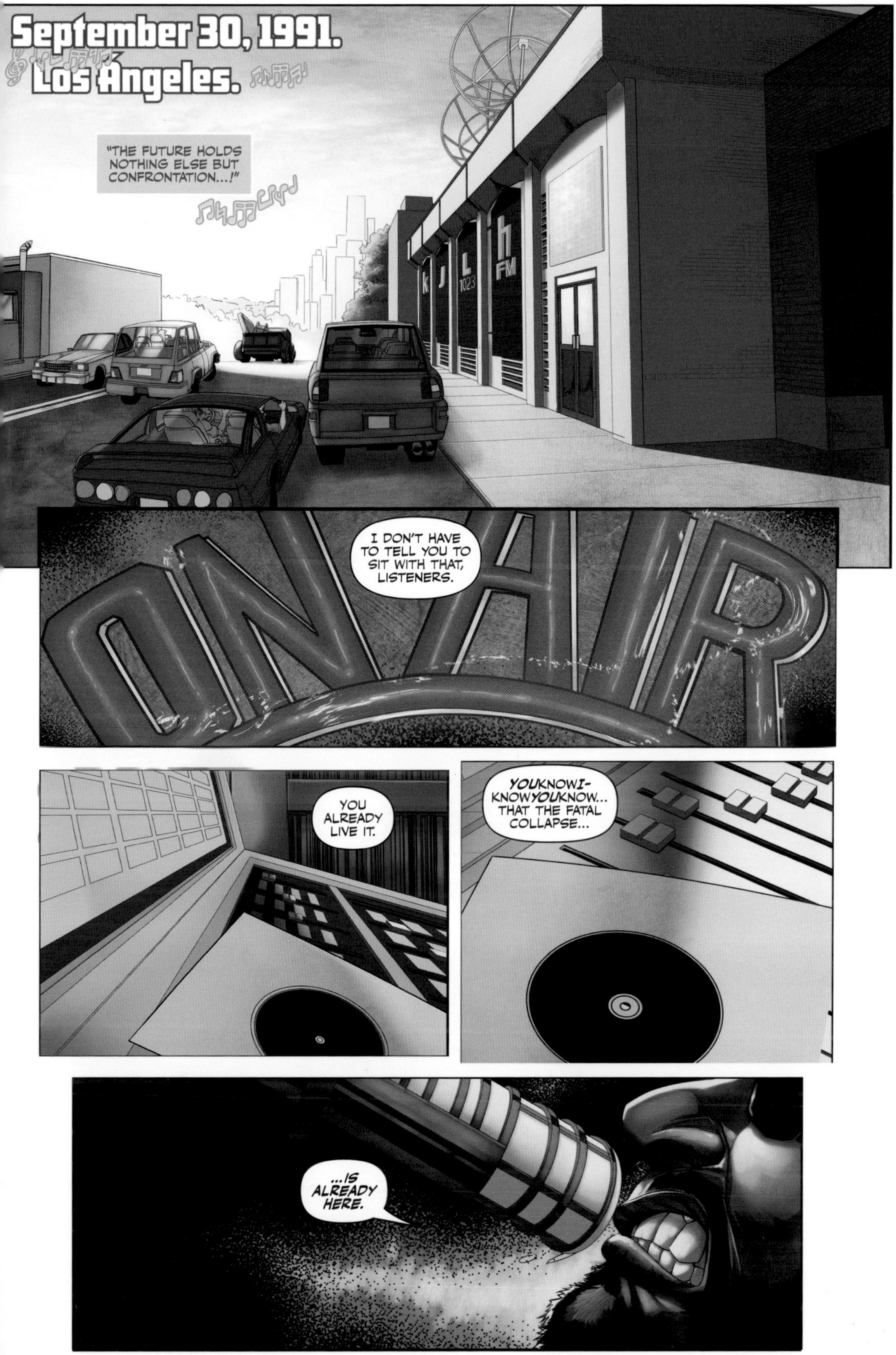
September 30, 1991.
Los Angeles.
"THE FUTURE HOLDS NOTHING ELSE BUT CONFRONTATION...!"
KJLH 102.3 FM
ON AIR
I DON'T HAVE TO TELL YOU TO SIT WITH THAT, LISTENERS.
YOU ALREADY LIVE IT.
YOU KNOW I-KNOW YOU KNOW... THAT THE FATAL COLLAPSE...
...IS ALREADY HERE.

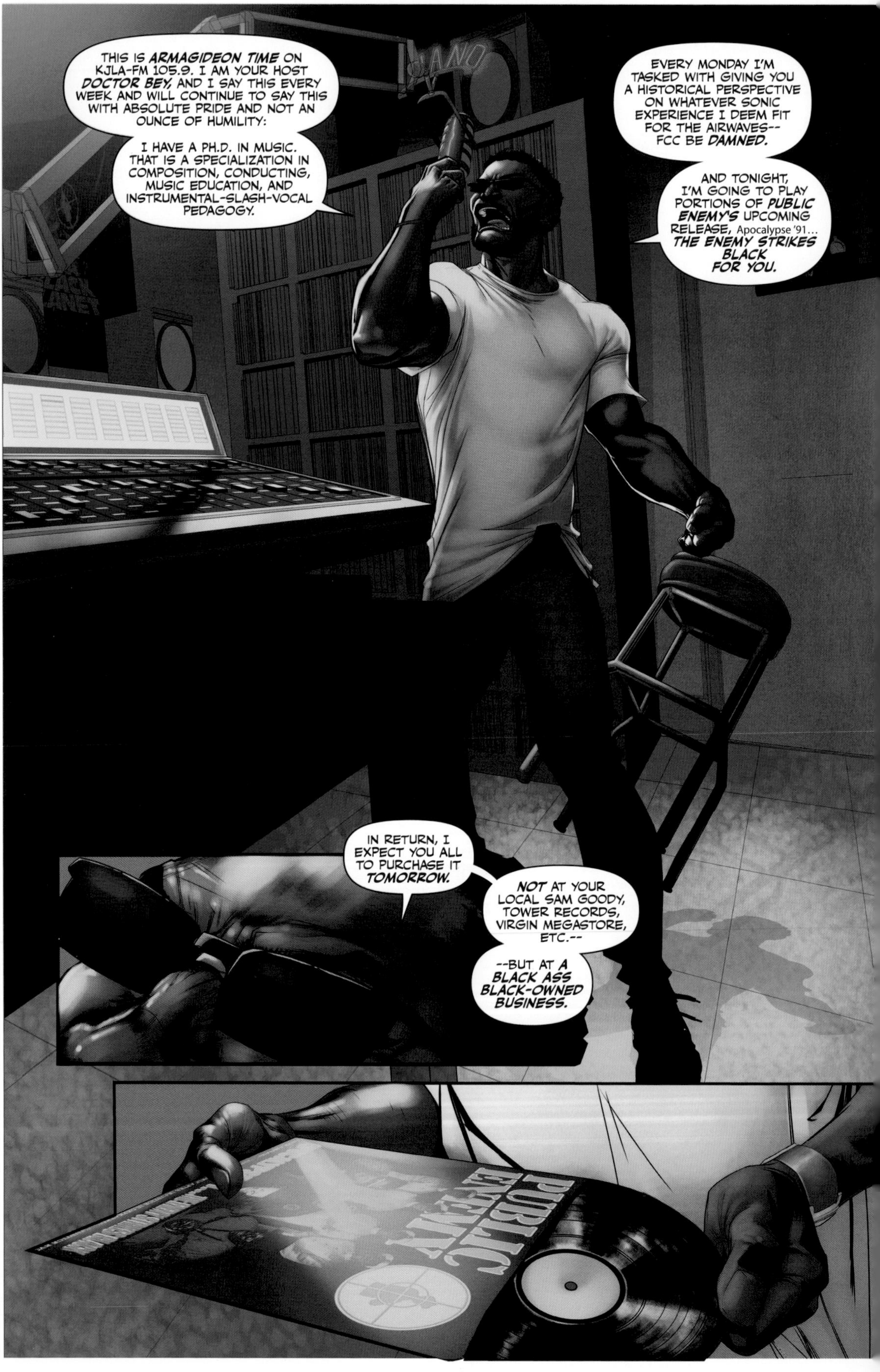

THIS IS ARMAGIDEON TIME ON KJLA-FM 105.9. I AM YOUR HOST DOCTOR BEY, AND I SAY THIS EVERY WEEK AND WILL CONTINUE TO SAY THIS WITH ABSOLUTE PRIDE AND NOT AN OUNCE OF HUMILITY:
I HAVE A PH.D. IN MUSIC. THAT IS A SPECIALIZATION IN COMPOSITION, CONDUCTING, MUSIC EDUCATION, AND INSTRUMENTAL-SLASH-VOCAL PEDAGOGY.
EVERY MONDAY I'M TASKED WITH GIVING YOU A HISTORICAL PERSPECTIVE ON WHATEVER SONIC EXPERIENCE I DEEM FIT FOR THE AIRWAVES-- FCC BE DAMNED.
AND TONIGHT, I'M GOING TO PLAY PORTIONS OF PUBLIC ENEMY'S UPCOMING RELEASE, Apocalypse '91... THE ENEMY STRIKES BLACK FOR YOU.
IN RETURN, I EXPECT YOU ALL TO PURCHASE IT TOMORROW.
NOT AT YOUR LOCAL SAM GOODY, TOWER RECORDS, VIRGIN MEGASTORE, ETC.--
--BUT AT A BLACK ASS BLACK-OWNED BUSINESS.
PUBLIC ENEMY

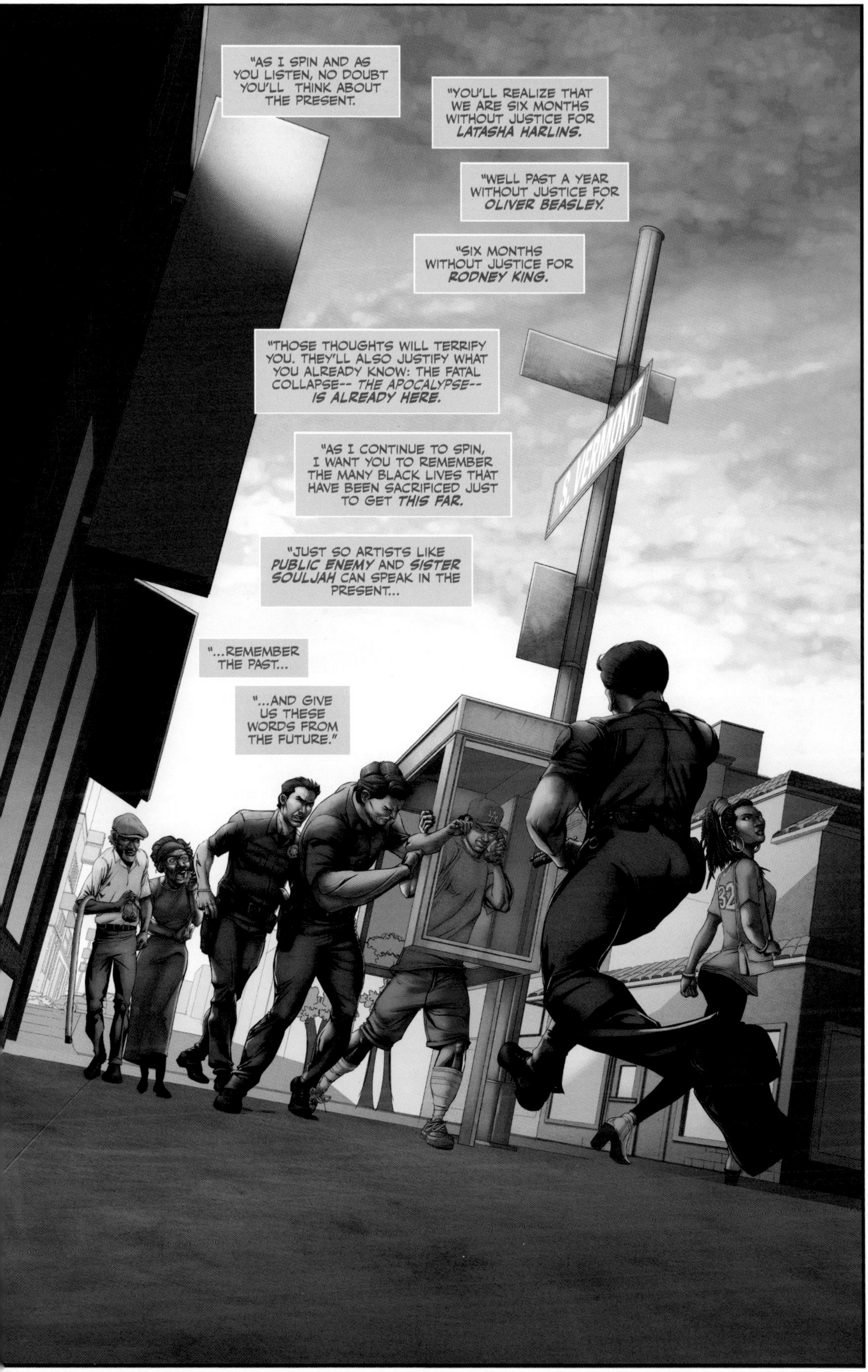

"AS I SPIN AND AS YOU LISTEN, NO DOUBT YOU'LL THINK ABOUT THE PRESENT.
"YOU'LL REALIZE THAT WE ARE SIX MONTHS WITHOUT JUSTICE FOR LATASHA HARLINS.
"WELL PAST A YEAR WITHOUT JUSTICE FOR OLIVER BEASLEY.
"SIX MONTHS WITHOUT JUSTICE FOR RODNEY KING.
"THOSE THOUGHTS WILL TERRIFY YOU. THEY'LL ALSO JUSTIFY WHAT YOU ALREADY KNOW: THE FATAL COLLAPSE-- THE APOCALYPSE-- IS ALREADY HERE.
"AS I CONTINUE TO SPIN, I WANT YOU TO REMEMBER THE MANY BLACK LIVES THAT HAVE BEEN SACRIFICED JUST TO GET THIS FAR.
"JUST SO ARTISTS LIKE PUBLIC ENEMY AND SISTER SOULJAH CAN SPEAK IN THE PRESENT...
"...REMEMBER THE PAST...
"...AND GIVE US THESE WORDS FROM THE FUTURE."
S. VERMONT

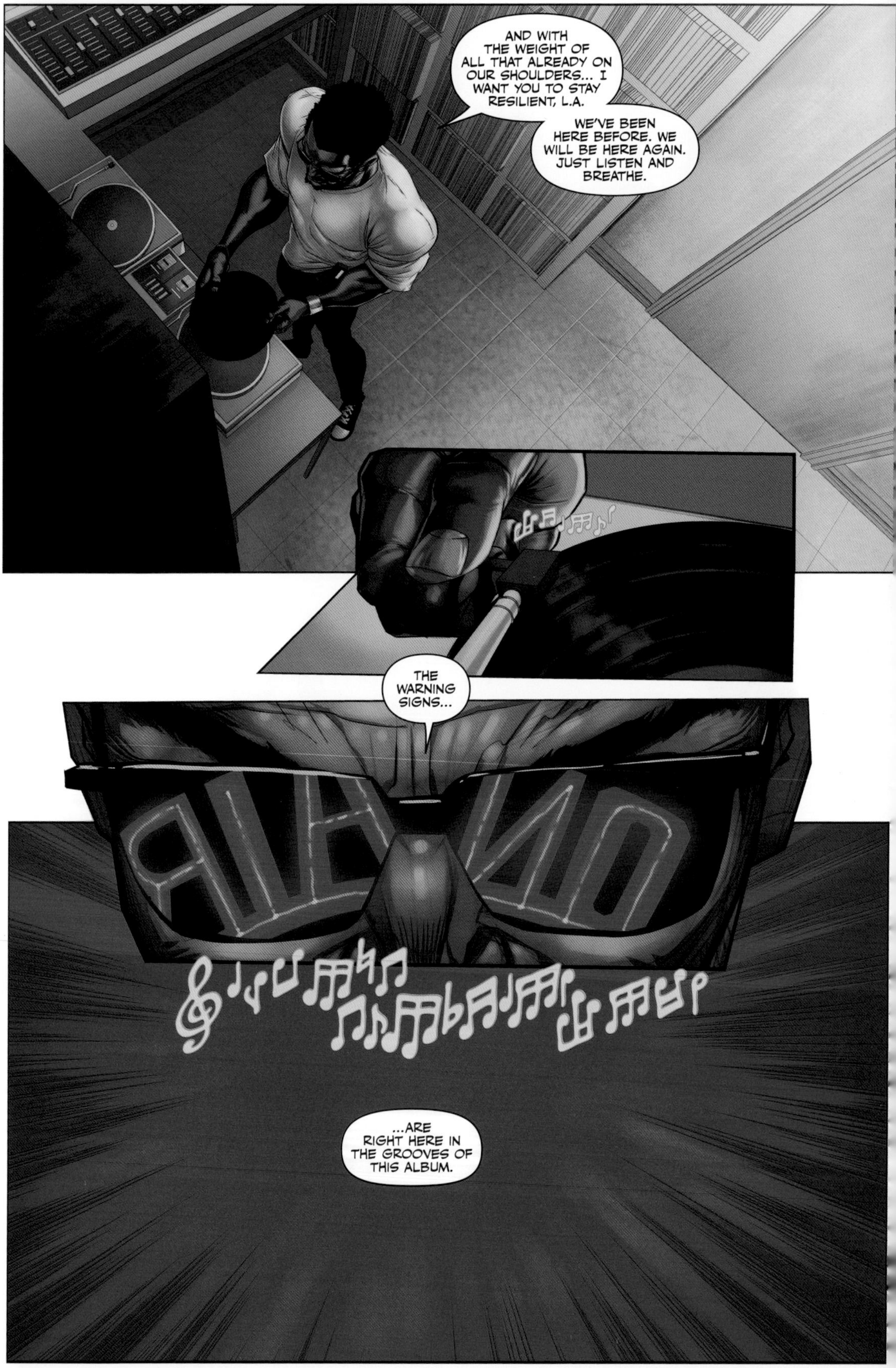
AND WITH THE WEIGHT OF ALL THAT ALREADY ON OUR SHOULDERS... I WANT YOU TO STAY RESILIENT, L.A.
WE'VE BEEN HERE BEFORE. WE WILL BE HERE AGAIN. JUST LISTEN AND BREATHE.
THE WARNING SIGNS...
...ARE RIGHT HERE IN THE GROOVES OF THIS ALBUM.

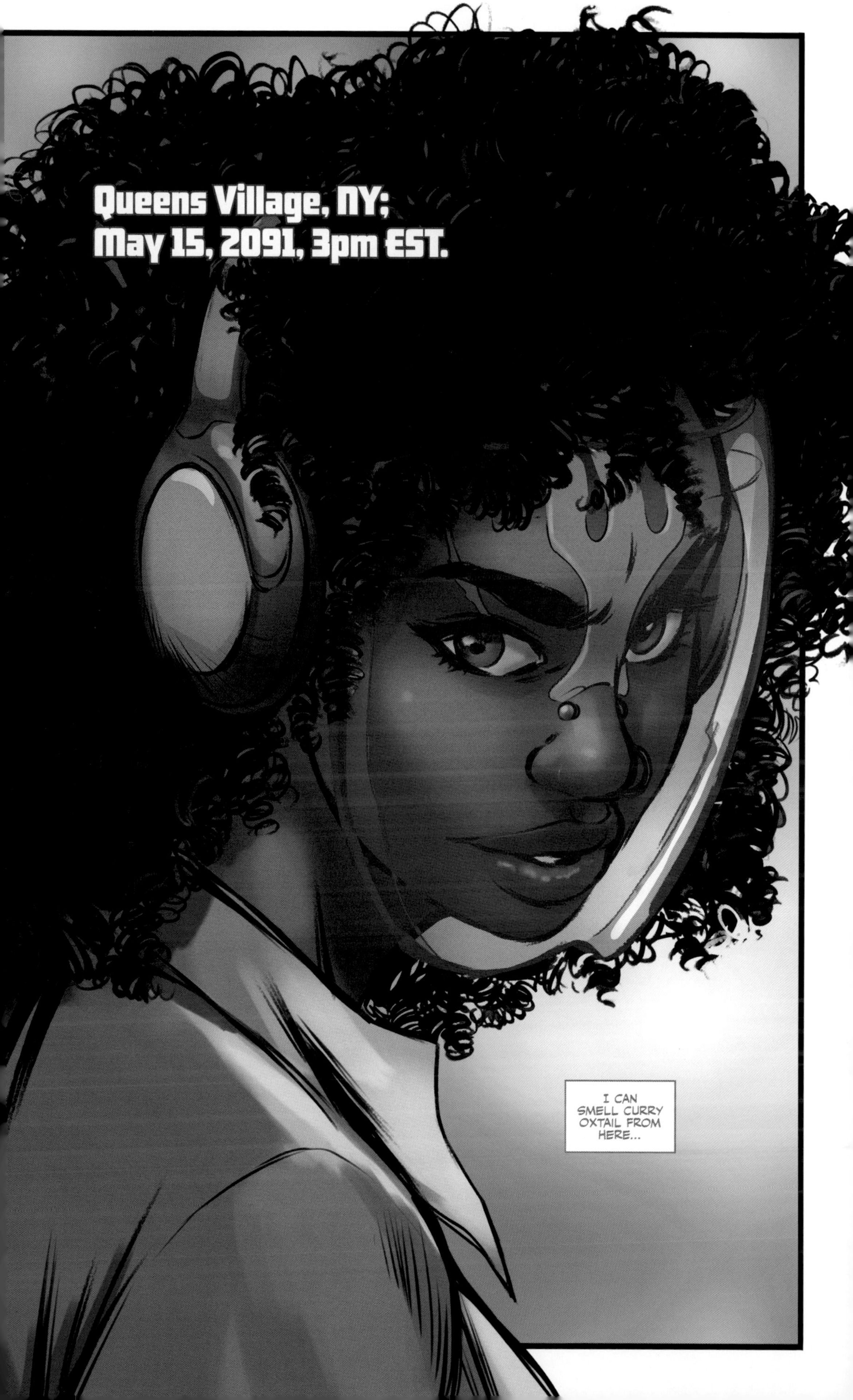
Queens Village, NY;
May 15, 2091, 3pm EST.
I CAN SMELL CURRY OXTAIL FROM HERE...

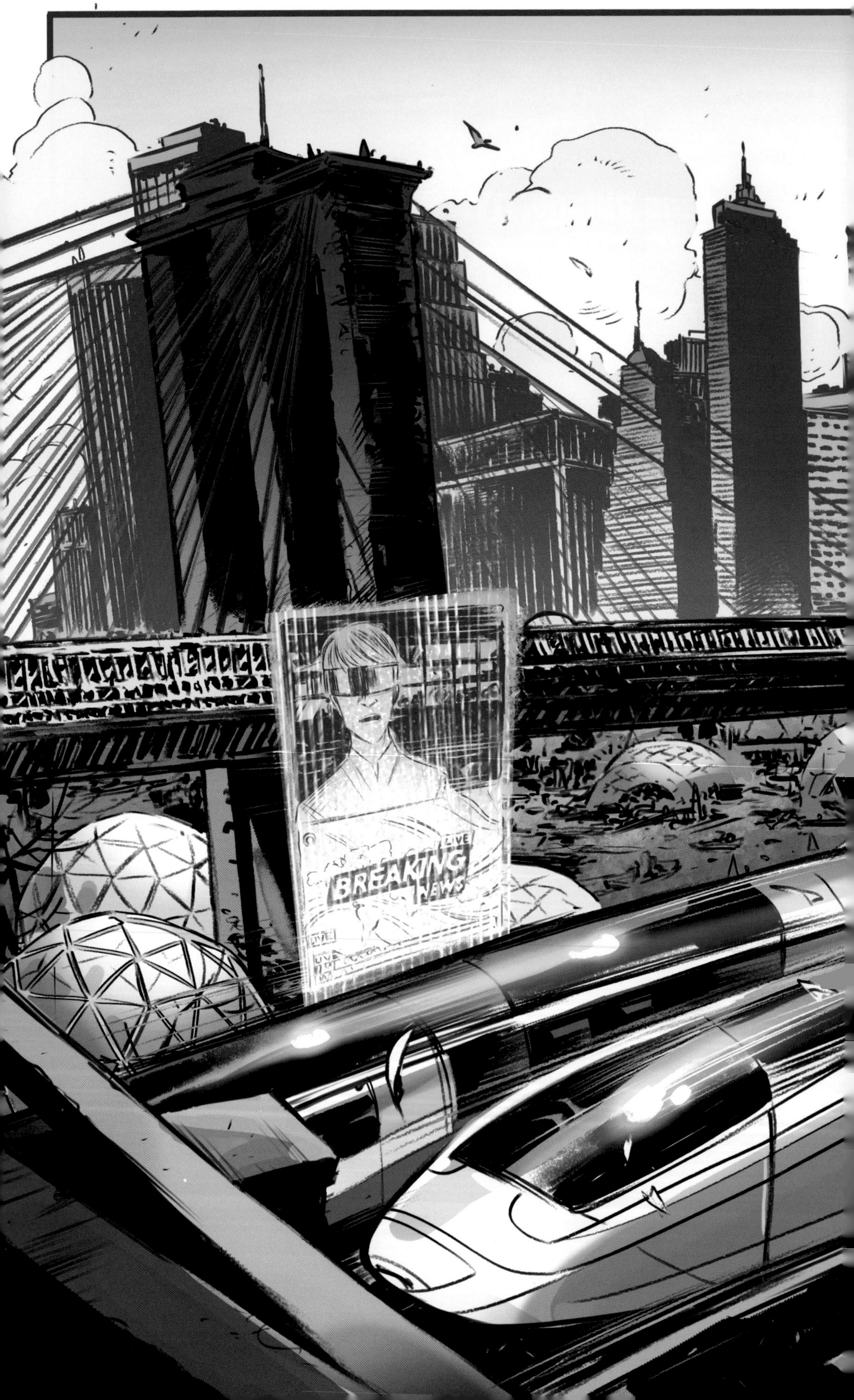
LIVE
BREAKING NEWS

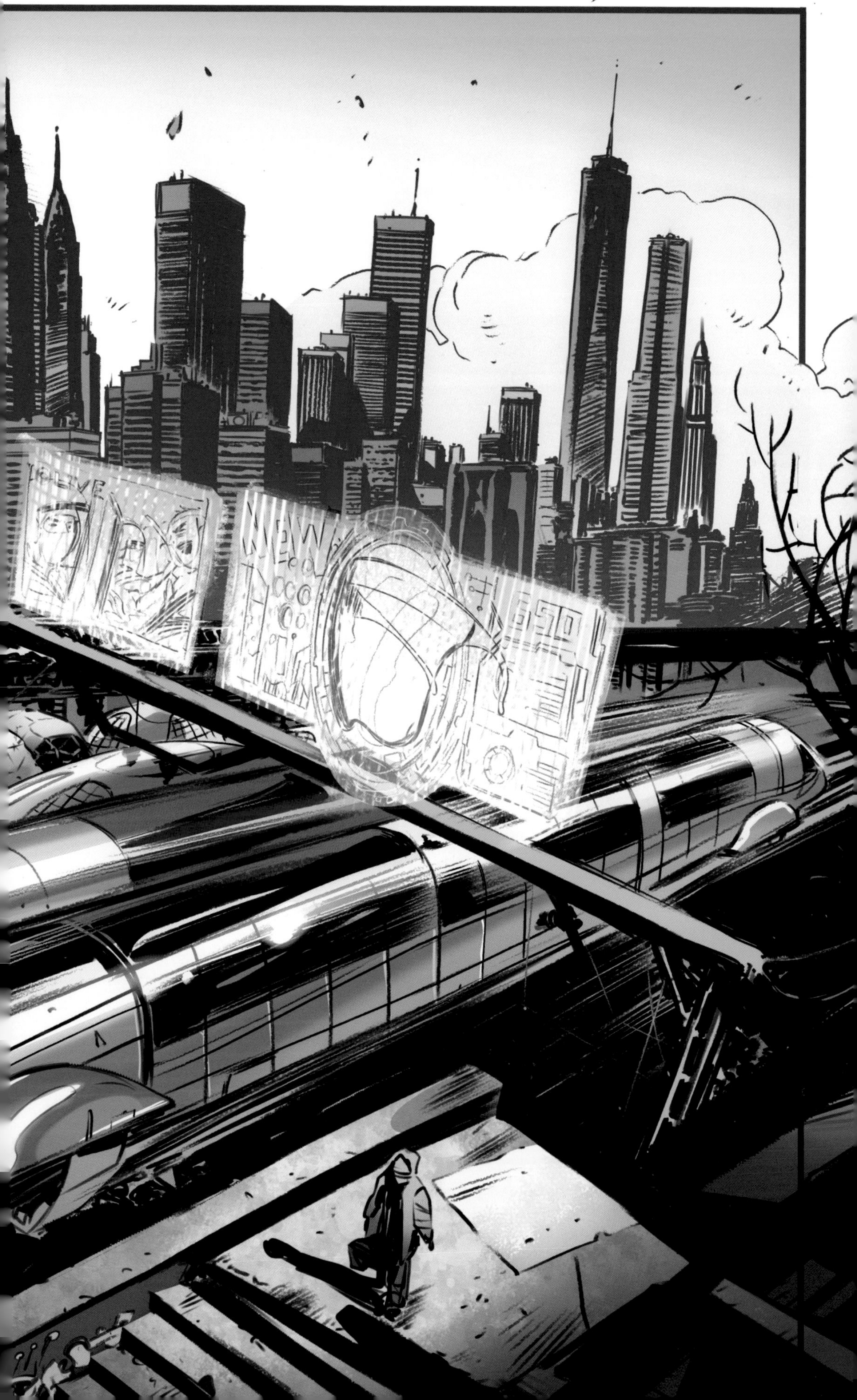
LIVE
NEW

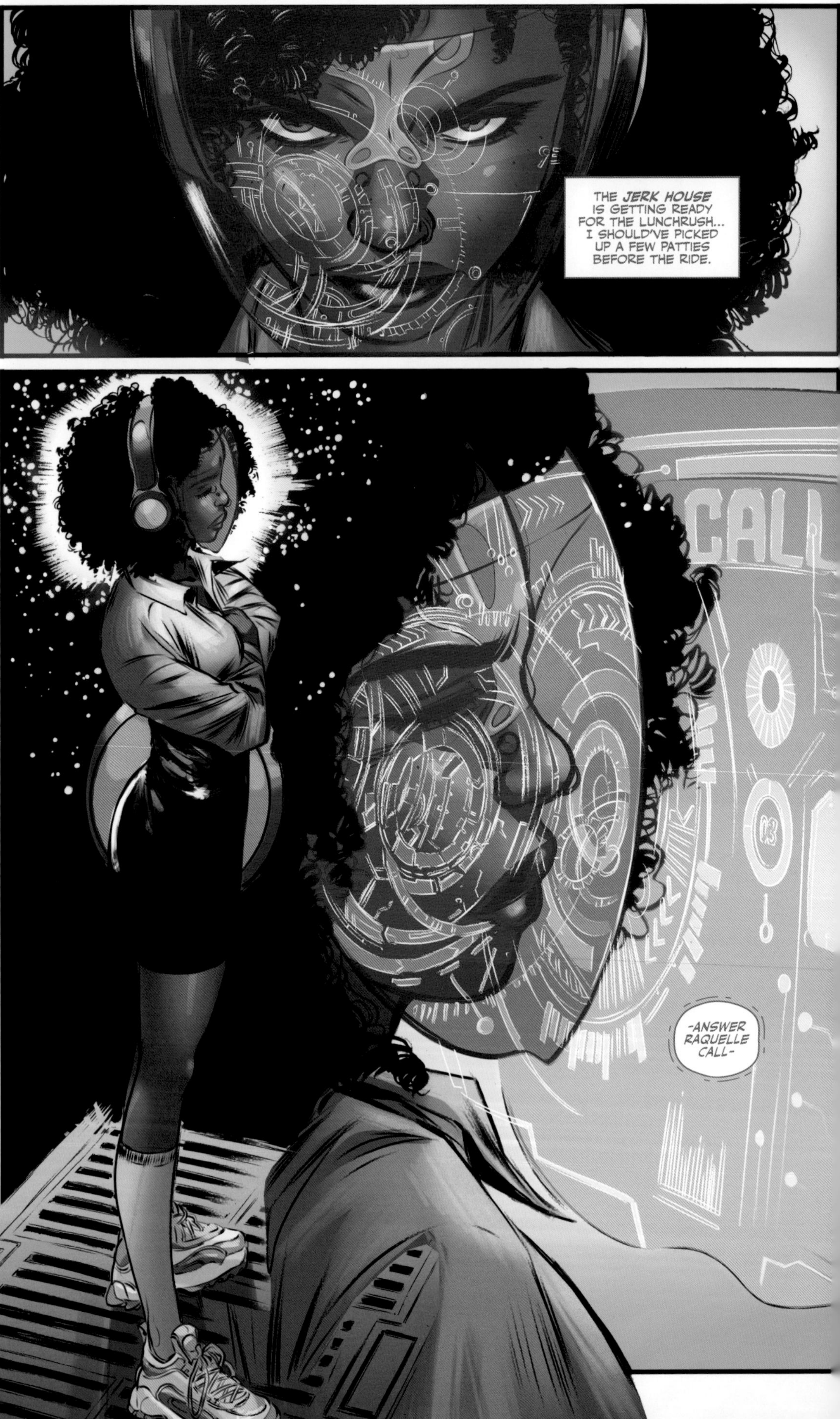
THE *JERK HOUSE* IS GETTING READY FOR THE LUNCHRUSH... I SHOULD'VE PICKED UP A FEW PATTIES BEFORE THE RIDE.
-ANSWER RAQUELLE CALL-

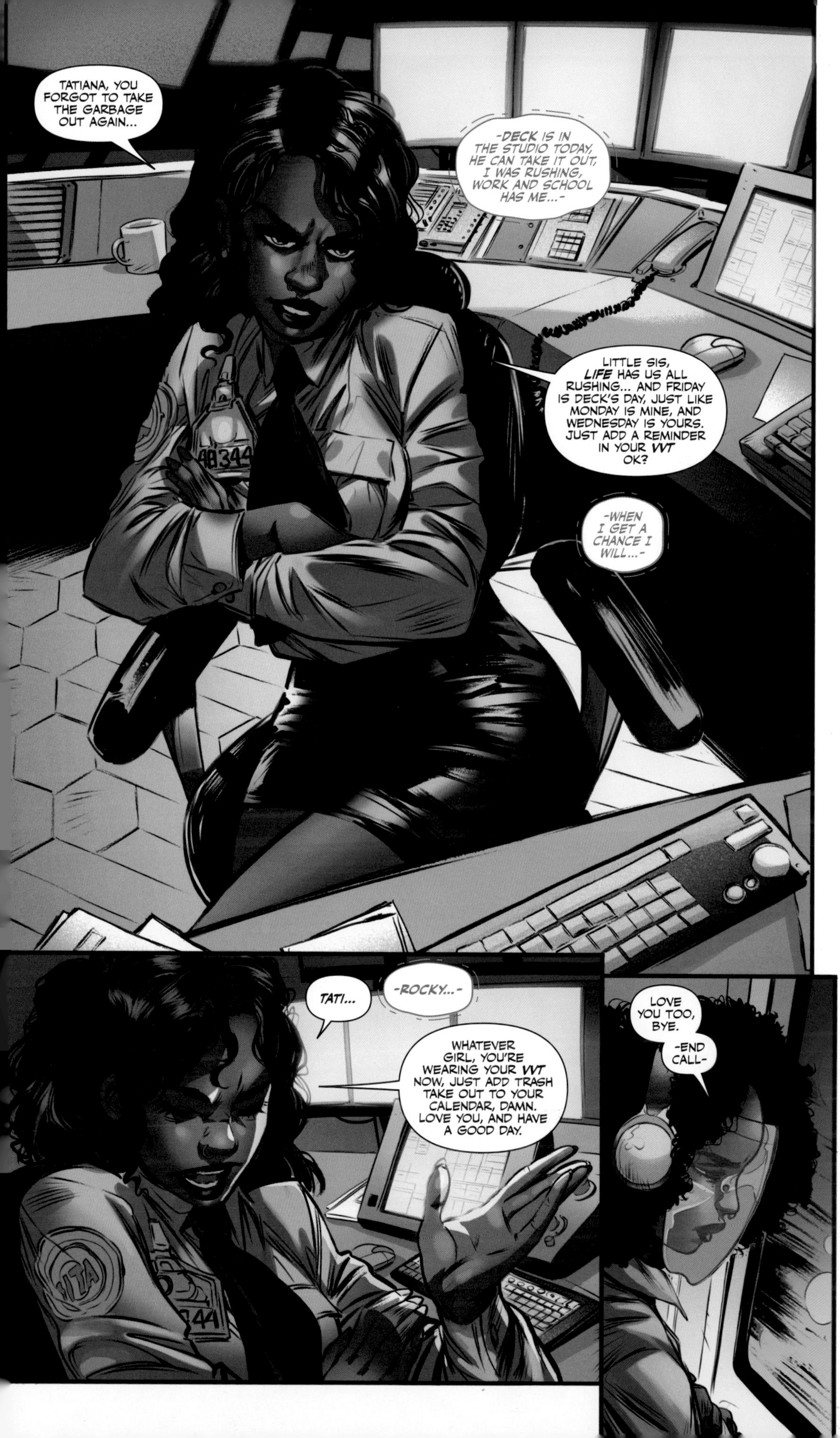
TATIANA, YOU FORGOT TO TAKE THE GARBAGE OUT AGAIN...
-DECK IS IN THE STUDIO TODAY, HE CAN TAKE IT OUT, I WAS RUSHING, WORK AND SCHOOL HAS ME...-
LITTLE SIS, LIFE HAS US ALL RUSHING... AND FRIDAY IS DECK'S DAY, JUST LIKE MONDAY IS MINE, AND WEDNESDAY IS YOURS. JUST ADD A REMINDER IN YOUR VVT OK?
-WHEN I GET A CHANCE I WILL...-
TATI...
-ROCKY...-
WHATEVER GIRL, YOU'RE WEARING YOUR VVT NOW, JUST ADD TRASH TAKE OUT TO YOUR CALENDAR, DAMN. LOVE YOU, AND HAVE A GOOD DAY.
LOVE YOU TOO, BYE.
-END CALL-

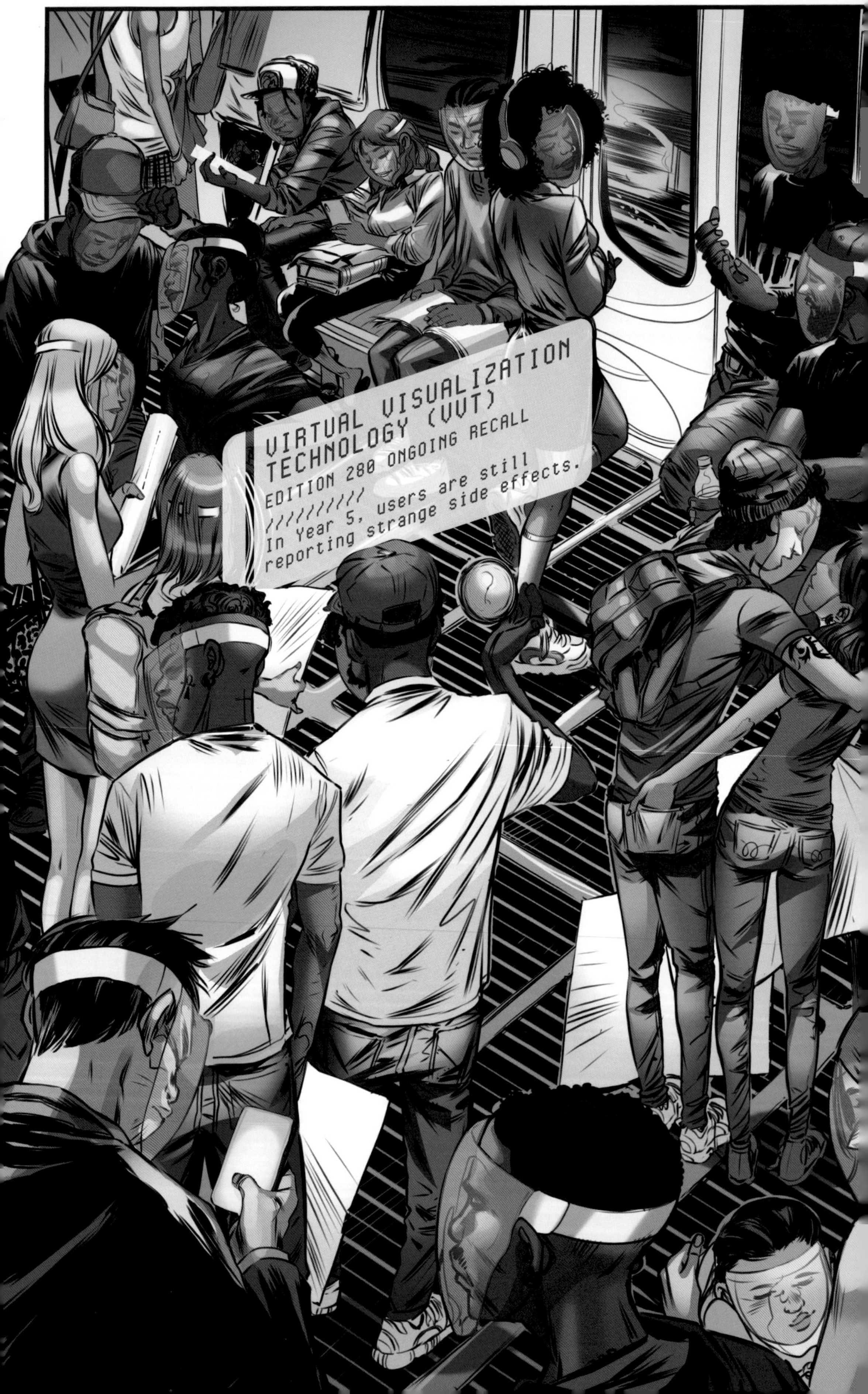
VIRTUAL VISUALIZATION
TECHNOLOGY (VVT)
EDITION 280 ONGOING RECALL
//////////
In Year 5, users are still
reporting strange side effects.

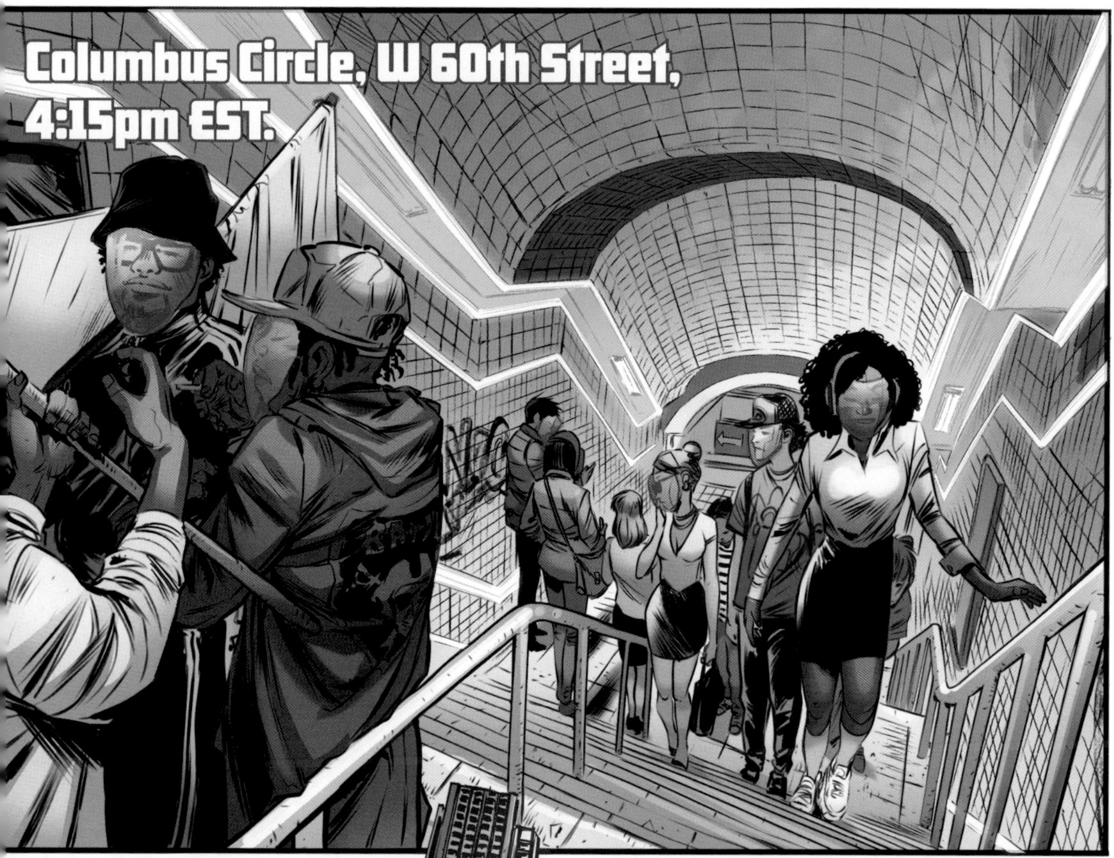
Columbus Circle, W 60th Street,
4:15pm EST.

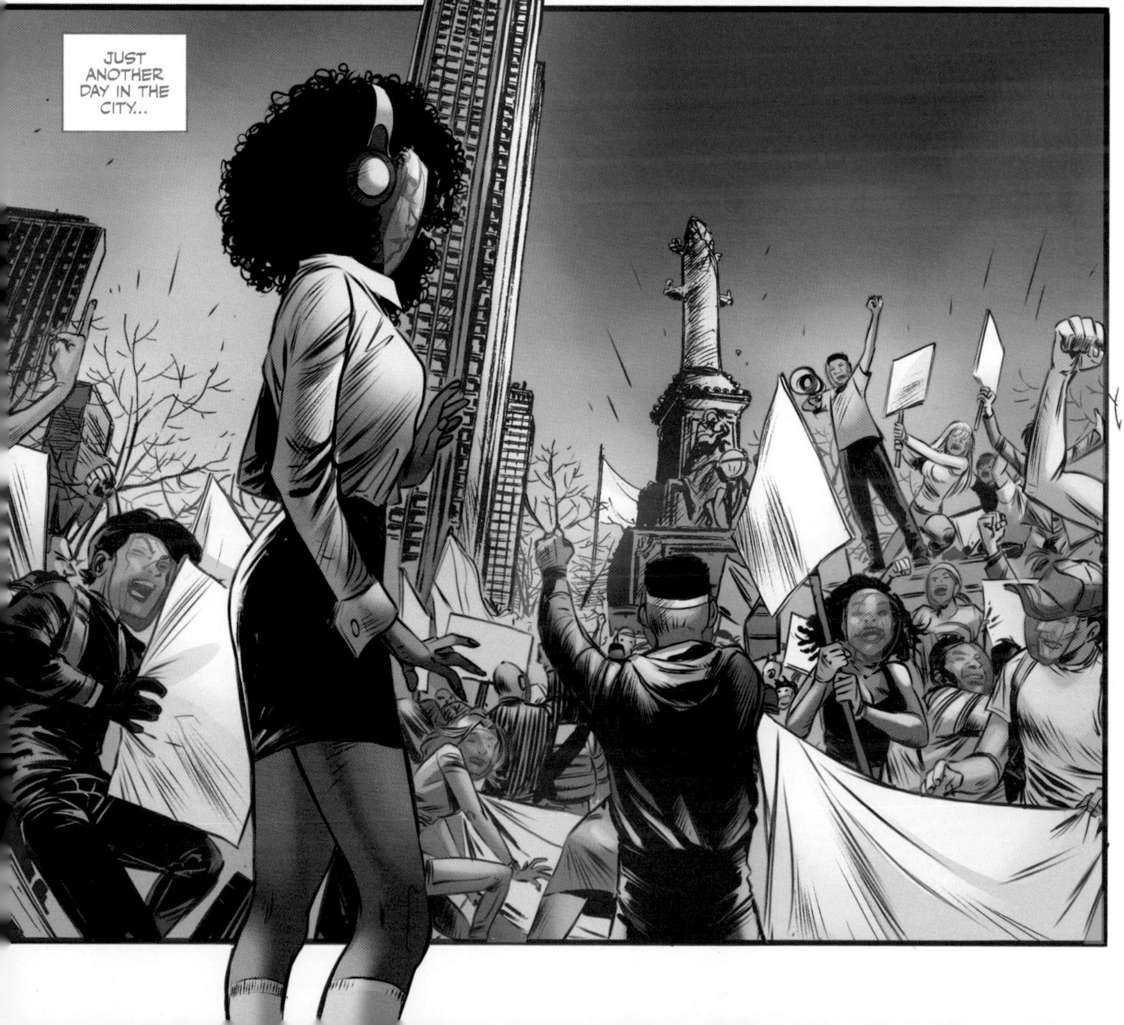
JUST ANOTHER DAY IN THE CITY...

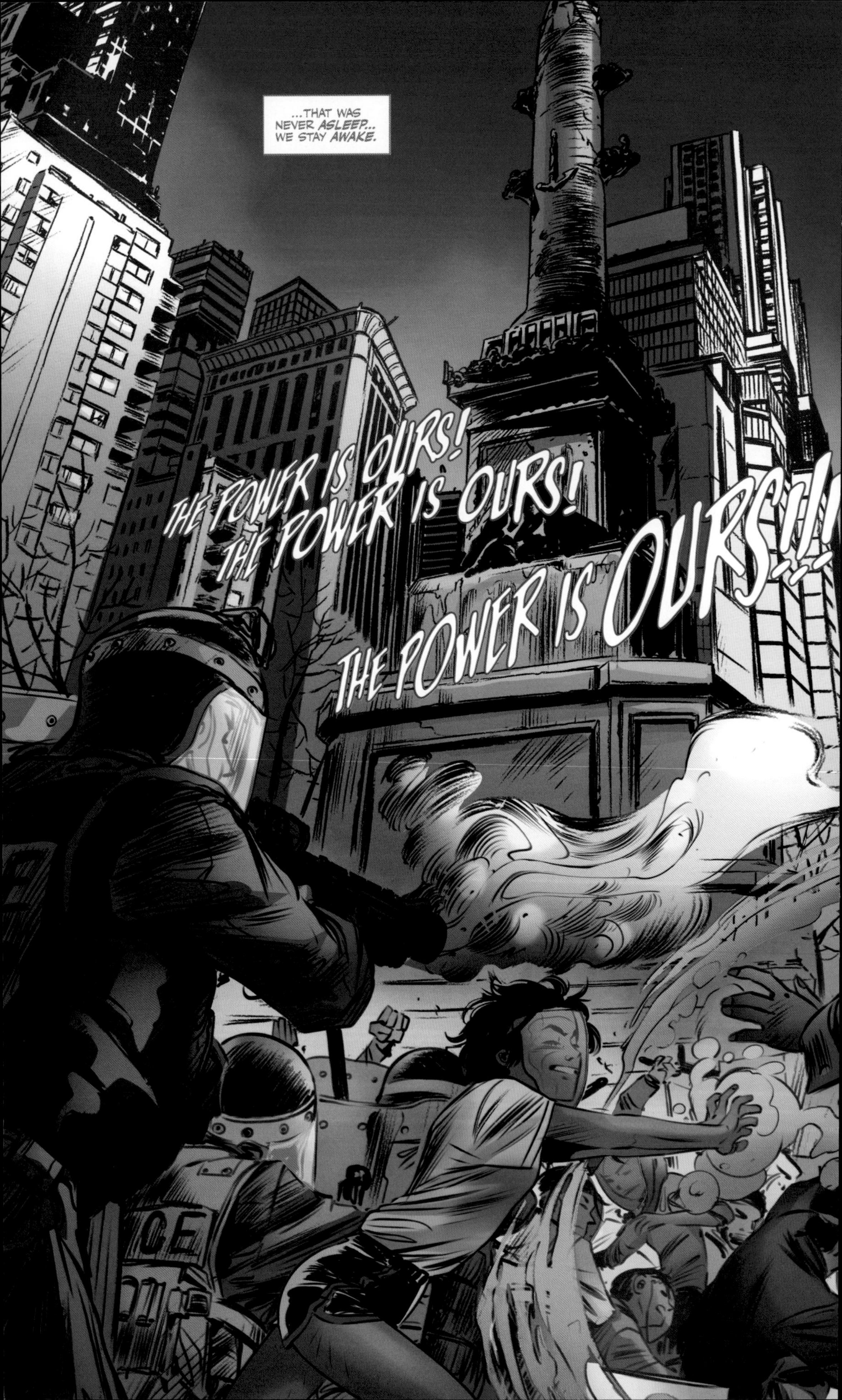
...THAT WAS NEVER ASLEEP... WE STAY AWAKE.
THE POWER IS OURS!
THE POWER IS OURS!
THE POWER IS OURS!!!

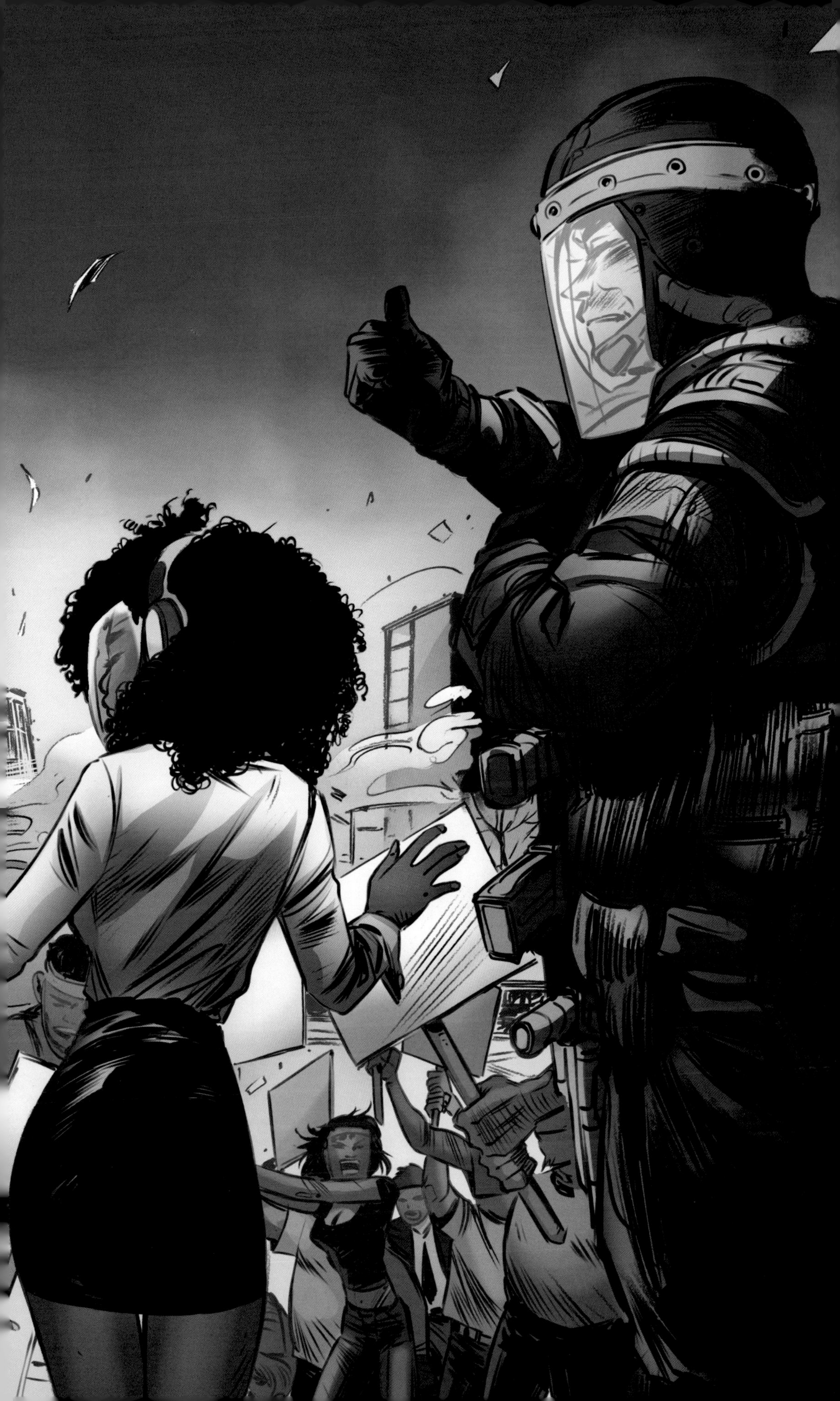

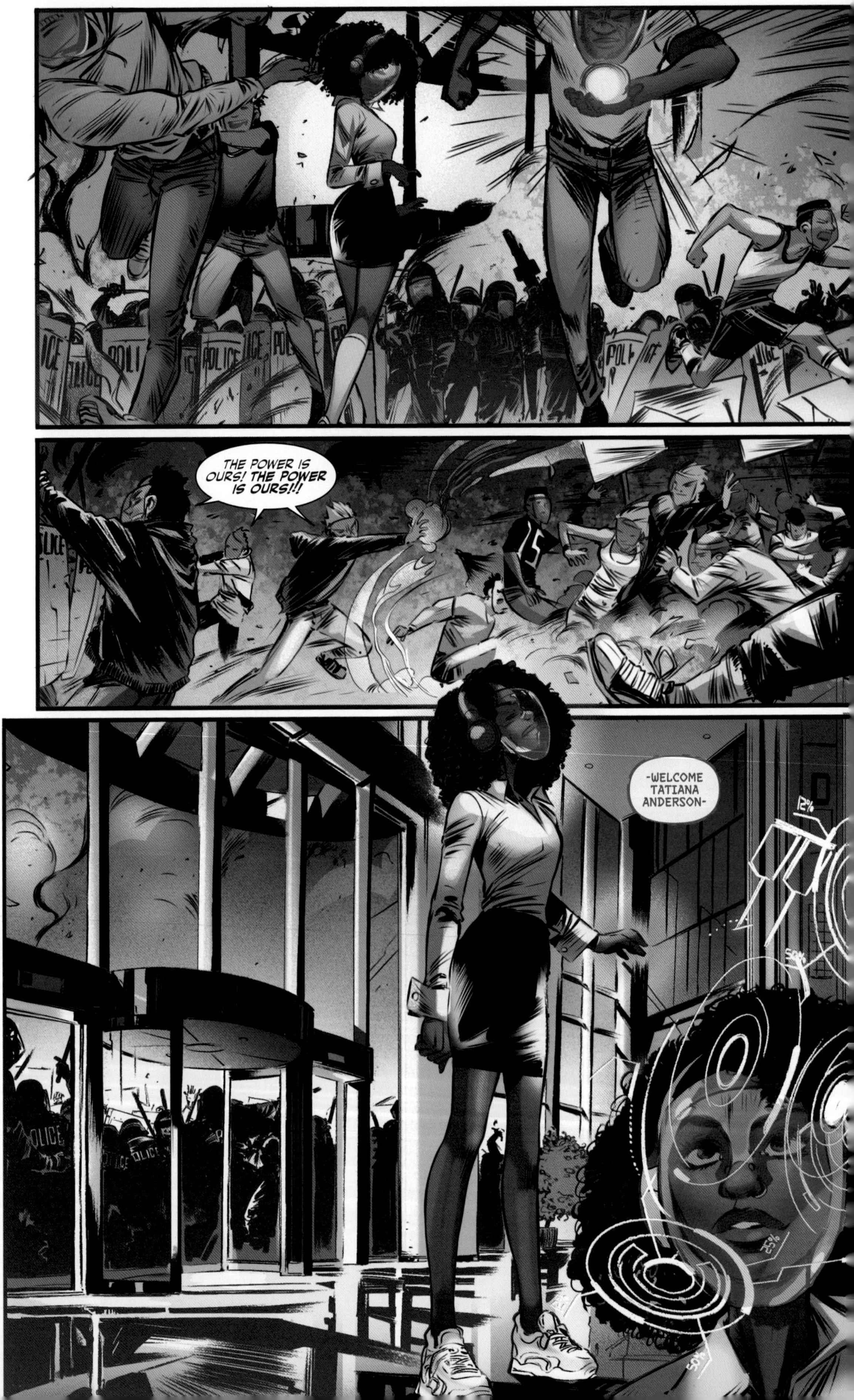
POLICE
THE POWER IS OURS! THE POWER IS OURS!!
-WELCOME TATIANA ANDERSON-
12%
50%
75%

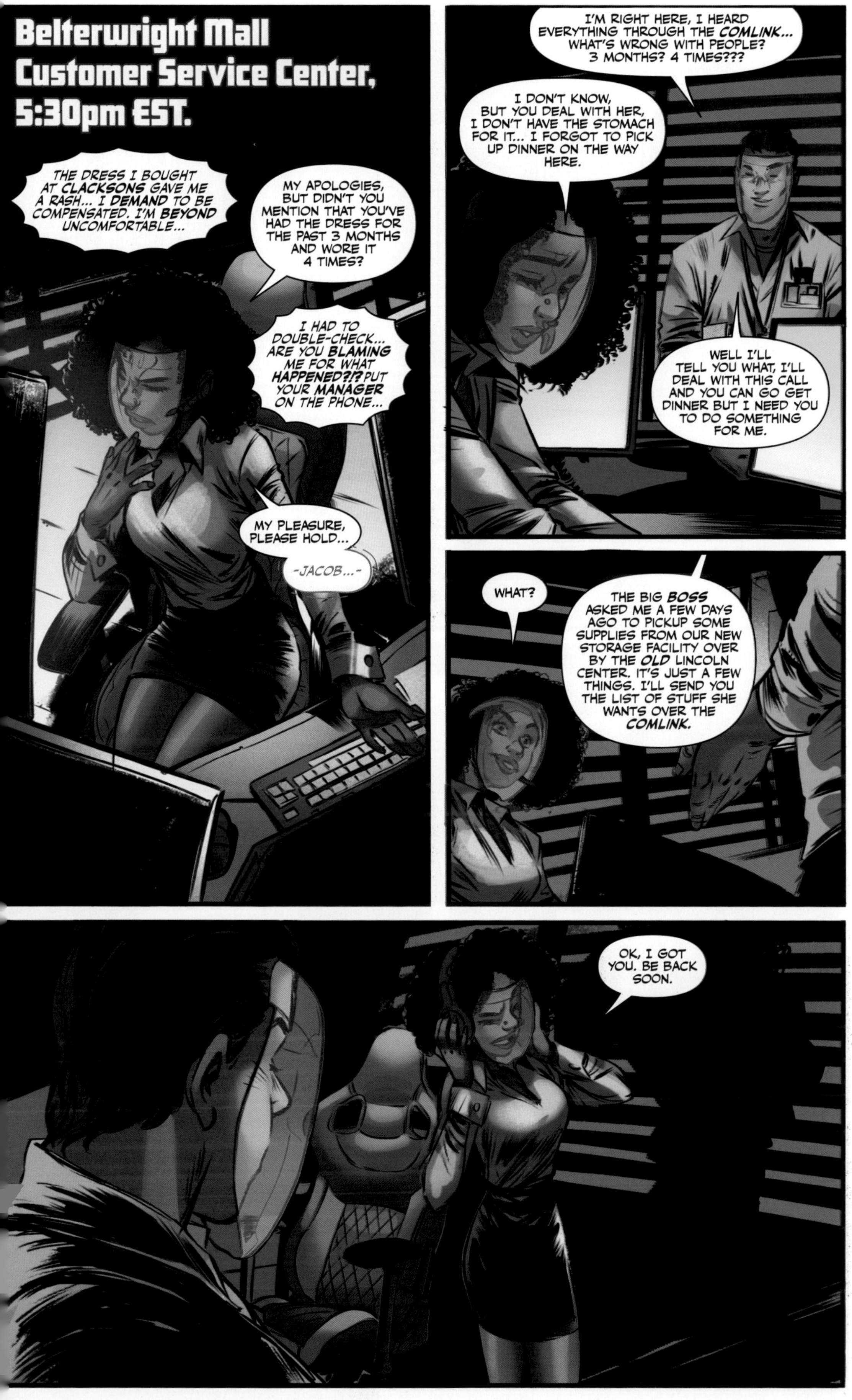
Belterwright Mall
Customer Service Center,
5:30pm EST.
THE DRESS I BOUGHT AT CLACKSONS GAVE ME A RASH... I DEMAND TO BE COMPENSATED. I'M BEYOND UNCOMFORTABLE...
MY APOLOGIES, BUT DIDN'T YOU MENTION THAT YOU'VE HAD THE DRESS FOR THE PAST 3 MONTHS AND WORE IT 4 TIMES?
I HAD TO DOUBLE-CHECK... ARE YOU BLAMING ME FOR WHAT HAPPENED?!? PUT YOUR MANAGER ON THE PHONE...
MY PLEASURE, PLEASE HOLD...
-JACOB...-
I'M RIGHT HERE, I HEARD EVERYTHING THROUGH THE COMLINK... WHAT'S WRONG WITH PEOPLE? 3 MONTHS? 4 TIMES???
I DON'T KNOW, BUT YOU DEAL WITH HER, I DON'T HAVE THE STOMACH FOR IT... I FORGOT TO PICK UP DINNER ON THE WAY HERE.
WELL I'LL TELL YOU WHAT, I'LL DEAL WITH THIS CALL AND YOU CAN GO GET DINNER BUT I NEED YOU TO DO SOMETHING FOR ME.
WHAT?
THE BIG BOSS ASKED ME A FEW DAYS AGO TO PICKUP SOME SUPPLIES FROM OUR NEW STORAGE FACILITY OVER BY THE OLD LINCOLN CENTER. IT'S JUST A FEW THINGS. I'LL SEND YOU THE LIST OF STUFF SHE WANTS OVER THE COMLINK.
OK, I GOT YOU. BE BACK SOON.

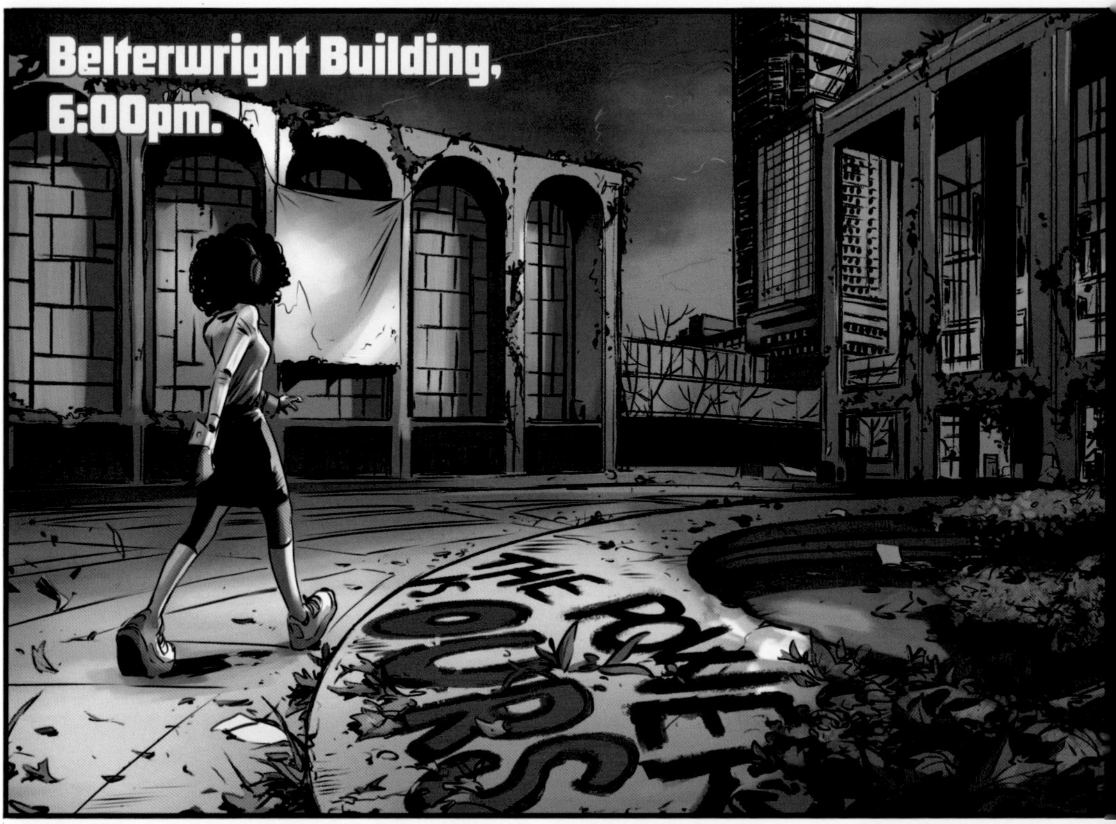

Belterwright Building,
6:00pm.

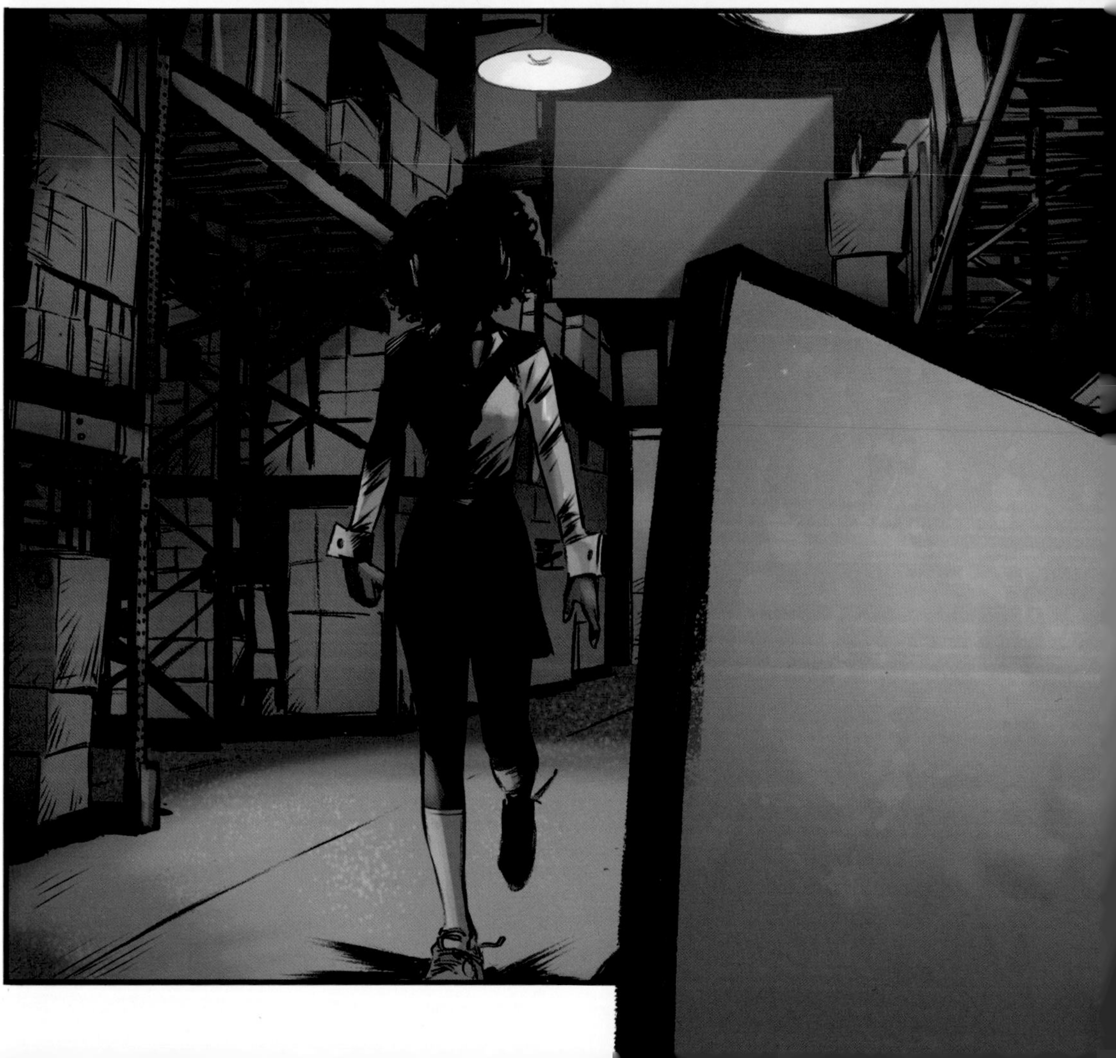

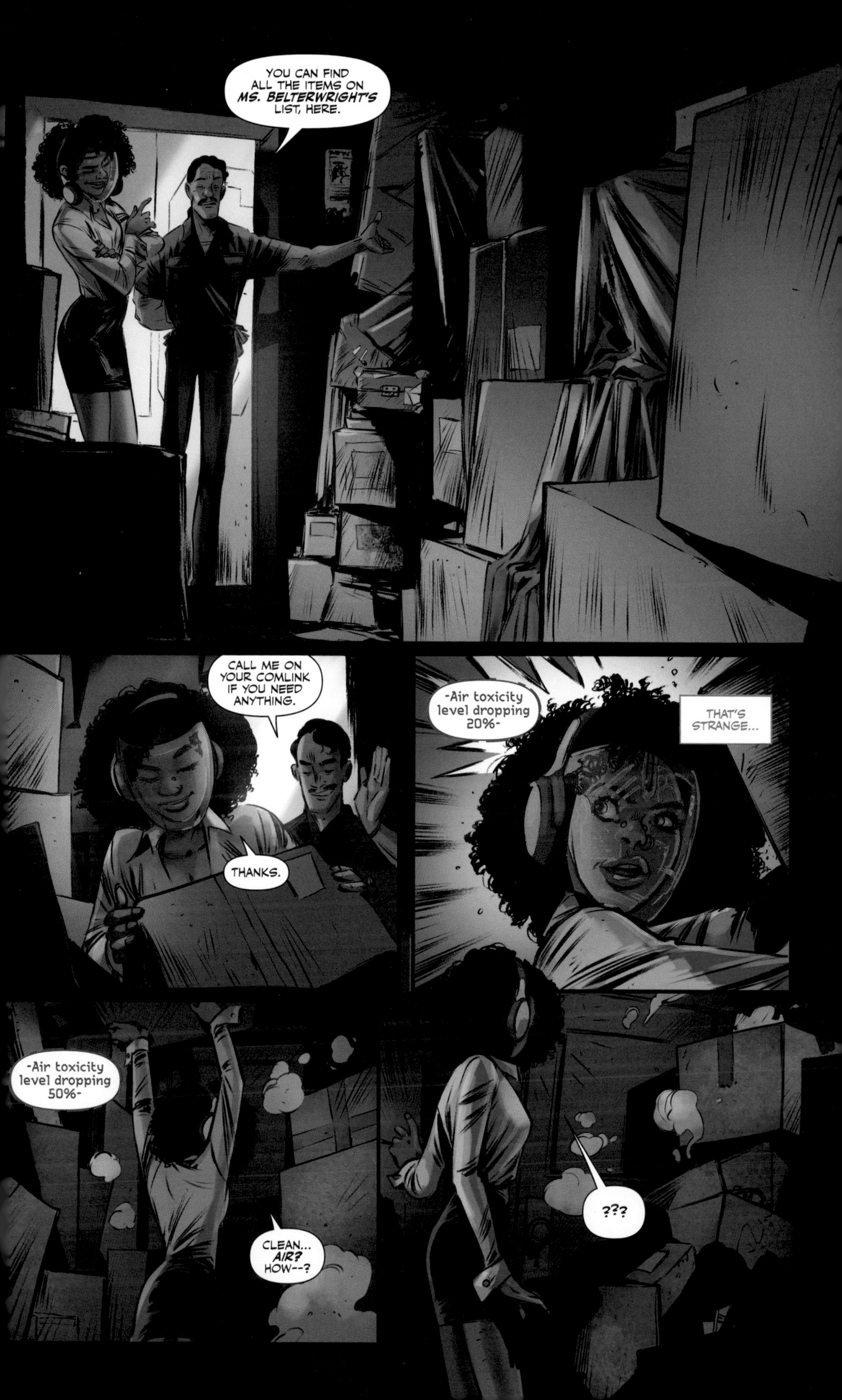
YOU CAN FIND ALL THE ITEMS ON MS. BELTERWRIGHT'S LIST, HERE.
CALL ME ON YOUR COMLINK IF YOU NEED ANYTHING.
THANKS.
-Air toxicity level dropping 20%-
THAT'S STRANGE...
-Air toxicity level dropping 50%-
CLEAN... AIR? HOW--?
???

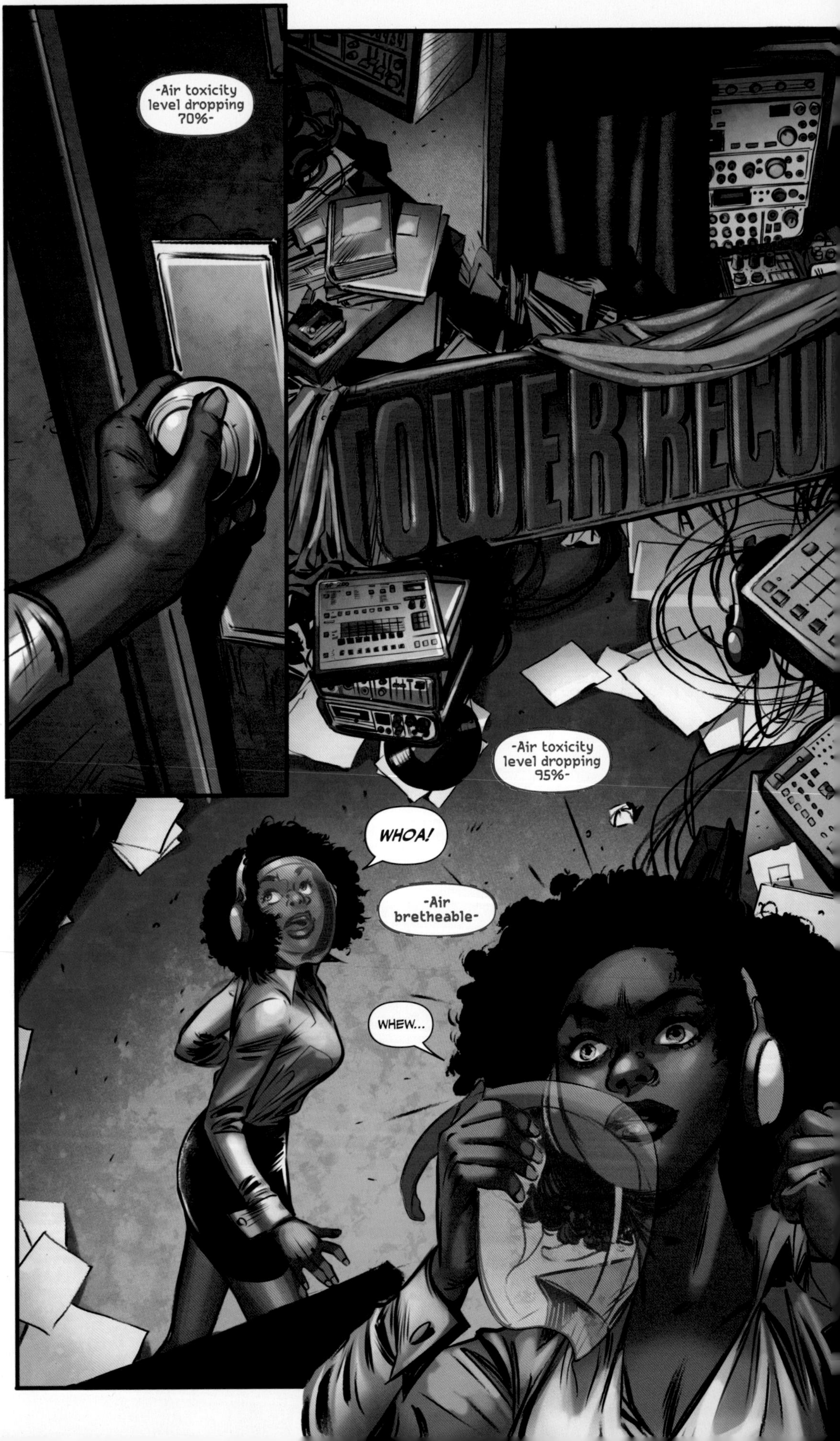
-Air toxicity level dropping 70%-
TOWER RECO
-Air toxicity level dropping 95%-
WHOA!
-Air bretheable-
WHEW...

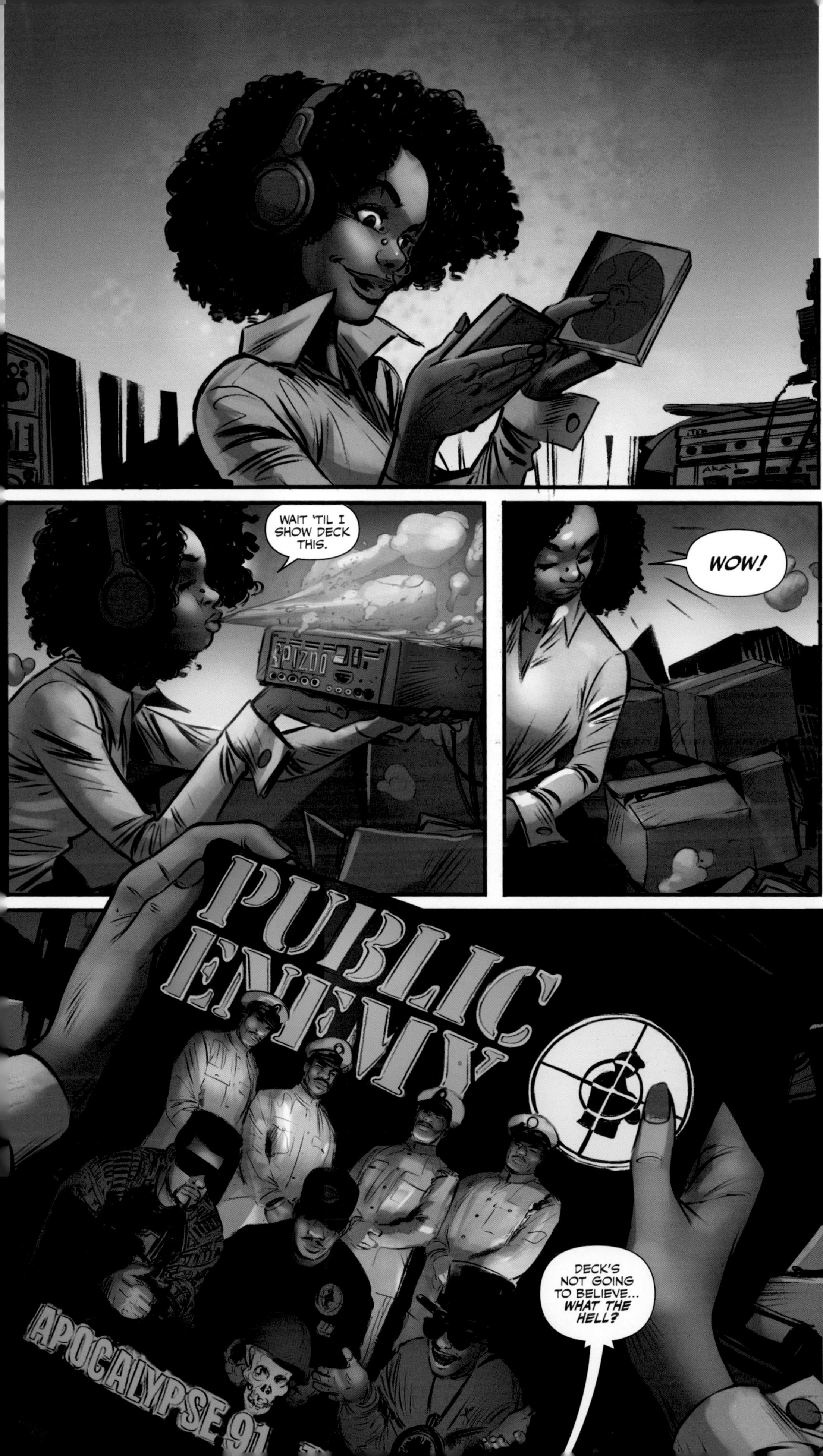

AKAI
WAIT 'TIL I SHOW DECK THIS.
SP1200
WOW!
PUBLIC ENEMY
APOCALYPSE 91
DECK'S NOT GOING TO BELIEVE... *WHAT THE HELL?*

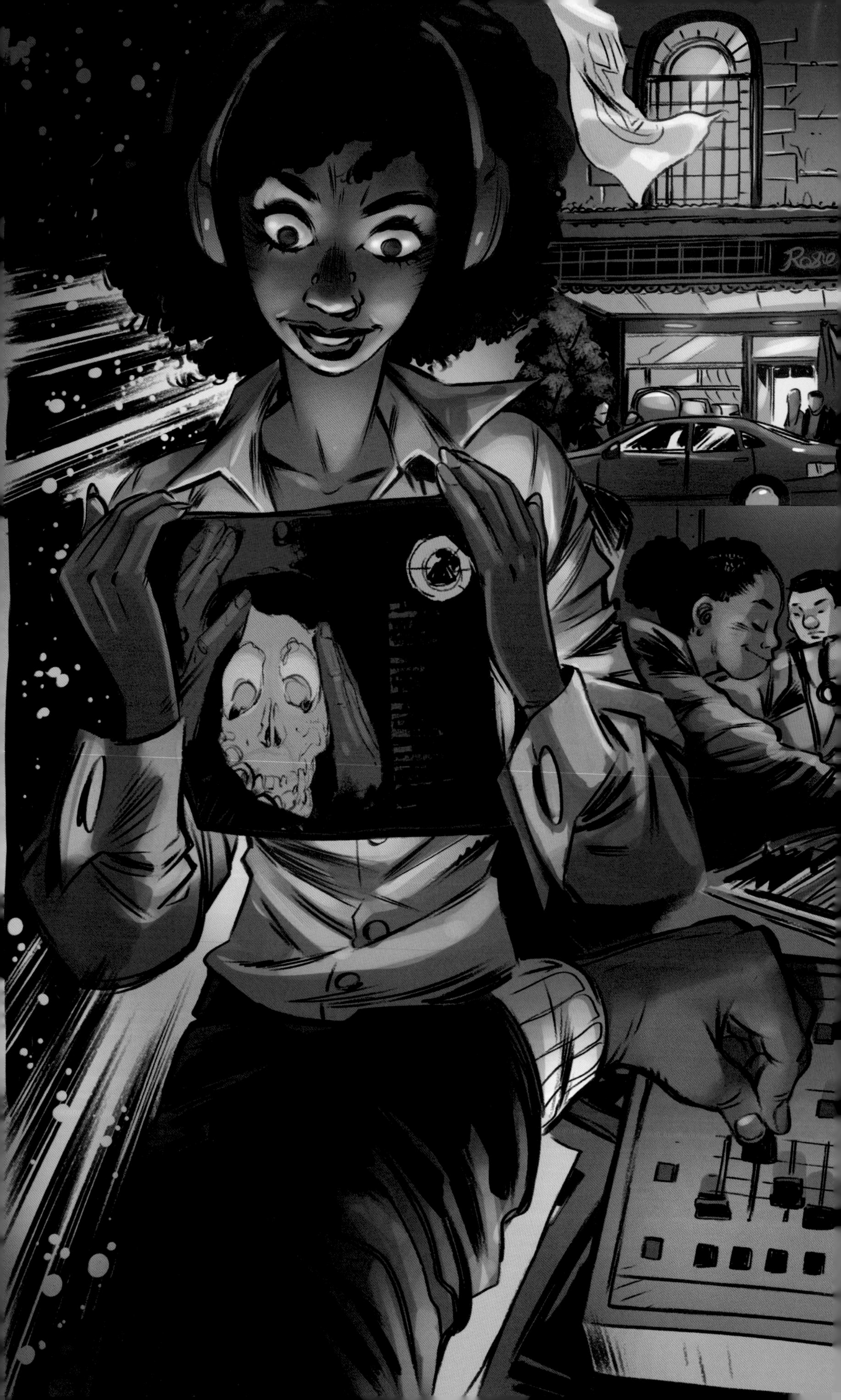

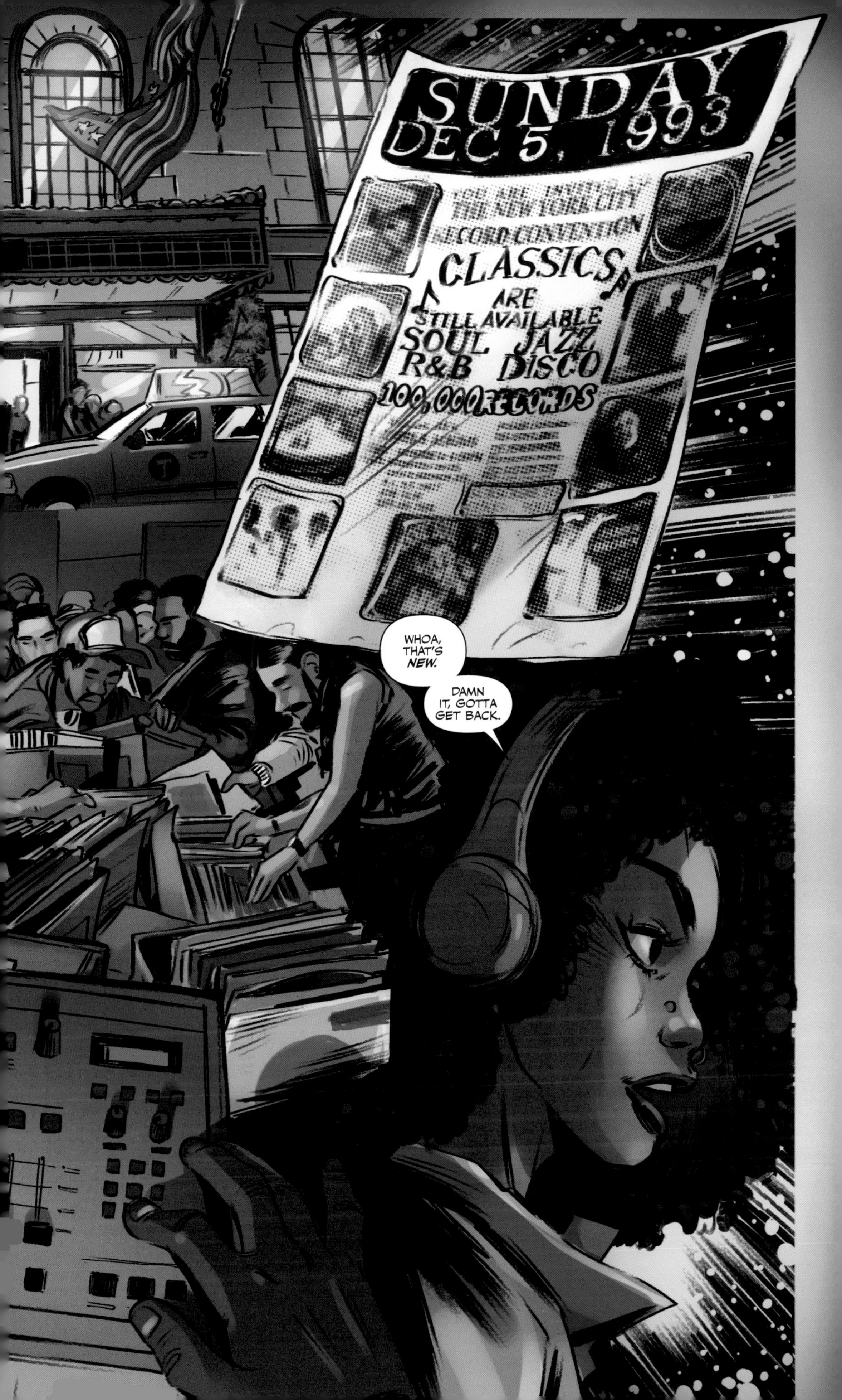

SUNDAY DEC 5, 1993
RECORD CONVENTION
CLASSICS ARE STILL AVAILABLE
SOUL JAZZ R&B DISCO
100,000 RECORDS
WHOA, THAT'S *NEW.*
DAMN IT, GOTTA GET BACK.

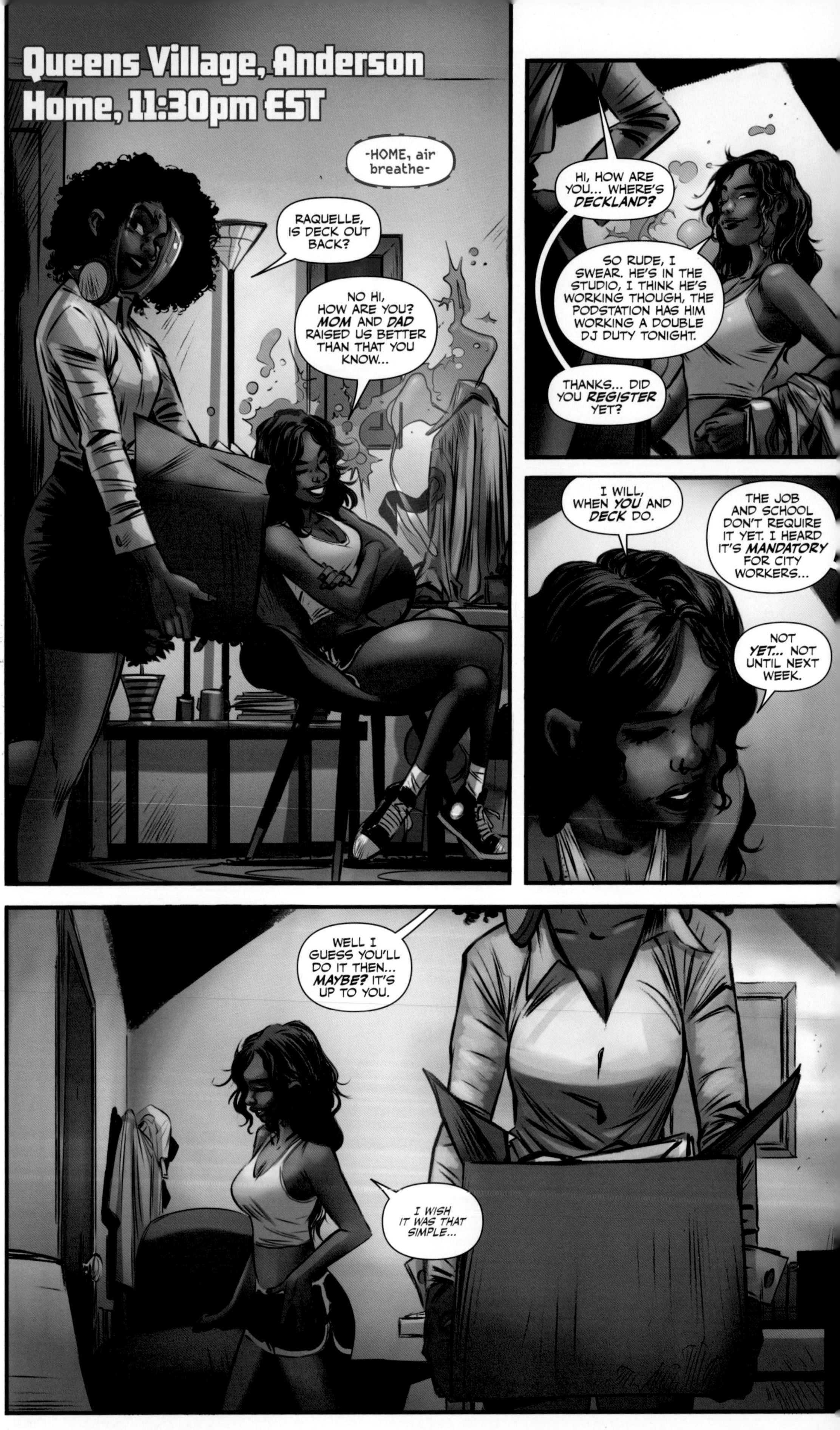
Queens Village, Anderson Home, 11:30pm EST
-HOME, air breathe-
RAQUELLE, IS DECK OUT BACK?
NO HI, HOW ARE YOU? MOM AND DAD RAISED US BETTER THAN THAT YOU KNOW...
HI, HOW ARE YOU... WHERE'S DECKLAND?
SO RUDE, I SWEAR. HE'S IN THE STUDIO, I THINK HE'S WORKING THOUGH, THE PODSTATION HAS HIM WORKING A DOUBLE DJ DUTY TONIGHT.
THANKS... DID YOU REGISTER YET?
I WILL, WHEN YOU AND DECK DO.
THE JOB AND SCHOOL DON'T REQUIRE IT YET. I HEARD IT'S MANDATORY FOR CITY WORKERS...
NOT YET... NOT UNTIL NEXT WEEK.
WELL I GUESS YOU'LL DO IT THEN... MAYBE? IT'S UP TO YOU.
I WISH IT WAS THAT SIMPLE...

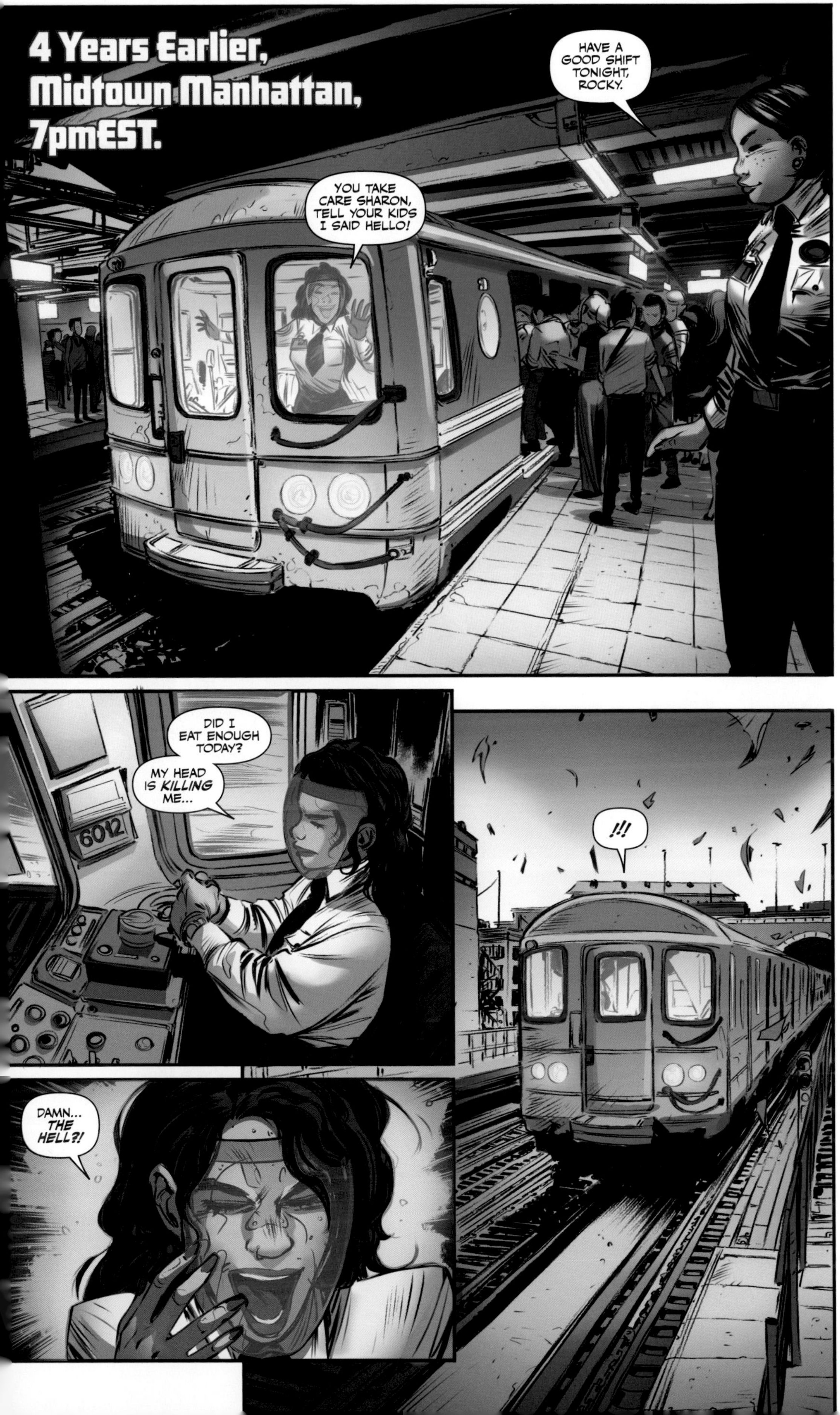
4 Years Earlier, Midtown Manhattan, 7pmEST.
HAVE A GOOD SHIFT TONIGHT, ROCKY.
YOU TAKE CARE SHARON, TELL YOUR KIDS I SAID HELLO!
DID I EAT ENOUGH TODAY?
MY HEAD IS KILLING ME...
6012
!!!
DAMN... THE HELL?!

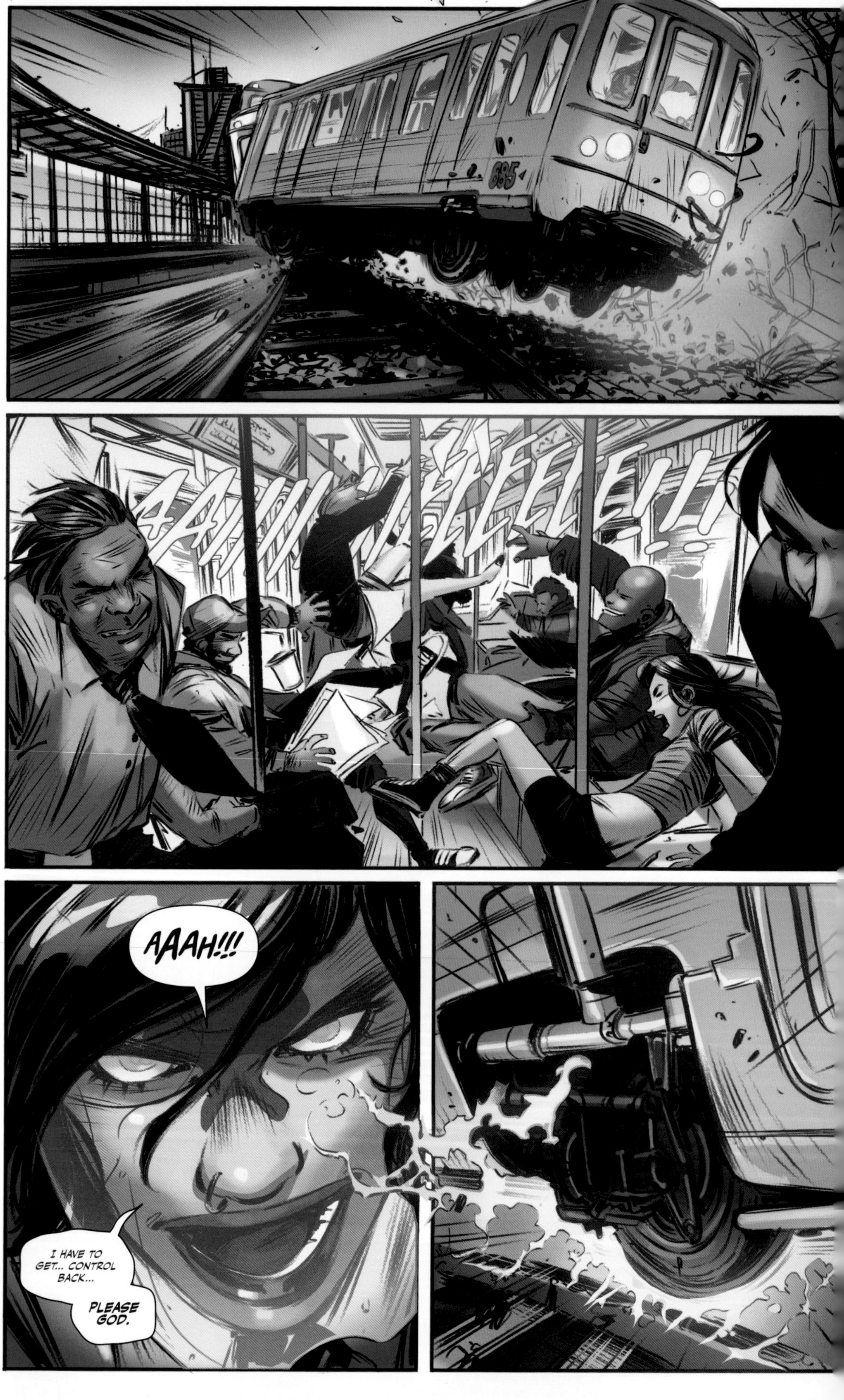
AAAH!!!
I HAVE TO GET... CONTROL BACK...
PLEASE GOD.

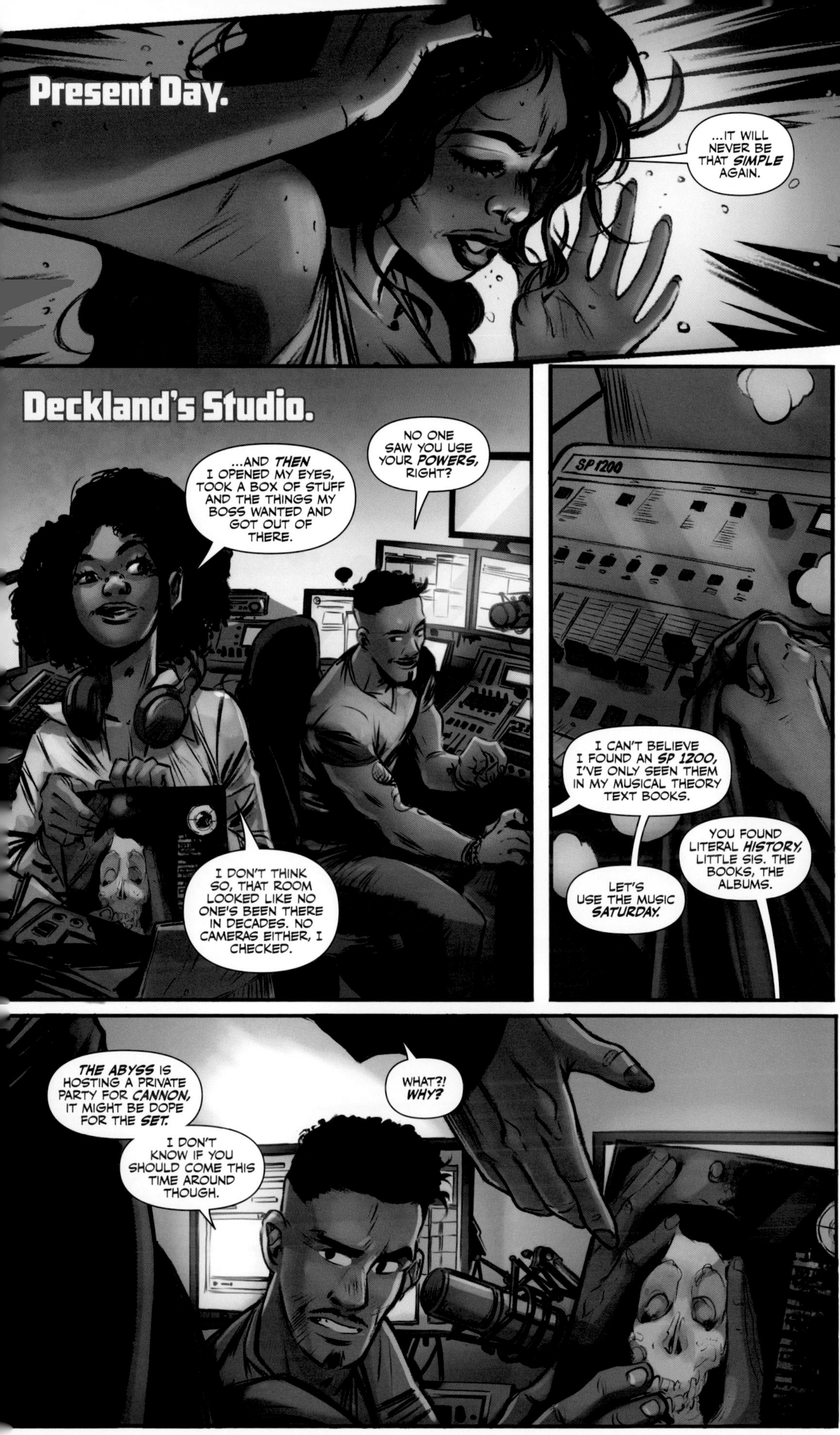
Present Day.
...IT WILL NEVER BE THAT SIMPLE AGAIN.
Deckland's Studio.
...AND THEN I OPENED MY EYES, TOOK A BOX OF STUFF AND THE THINGS MY BOSS WANTED AND GOT OUT OF THERE.
NO ONE SAW YOU USE YOUR POWERS, RIGHT?
I DON'T THINK SO, THAT ROOM LOOKED LIKE NO ONE'S BEEN THERE IN DECADES. NO CAMERAS EITHER, I CHECKED.
SP 1200
I CAN'T BELIEVE I FOUND AN SP 1200, I'VE ONLY SEEN THEM IN MY MUSICAL THEORY TEXT BOOKS.
LET'S USE THE MUSIC SATURDAY.
YOU FOUND LITERAL HISTORY, LITTLE SIS. THE BOOKS, THE ALBUMS.
THE ABYSS IS HOSTING A PRIVATE PARTY FOR CANNON, IT MIGHT BE DOPE FOR THE SET.
I DON'T KNOW IF YOU SHOULD COME THIS TIME AROUND THOUGH.
WHAT?! WHY?

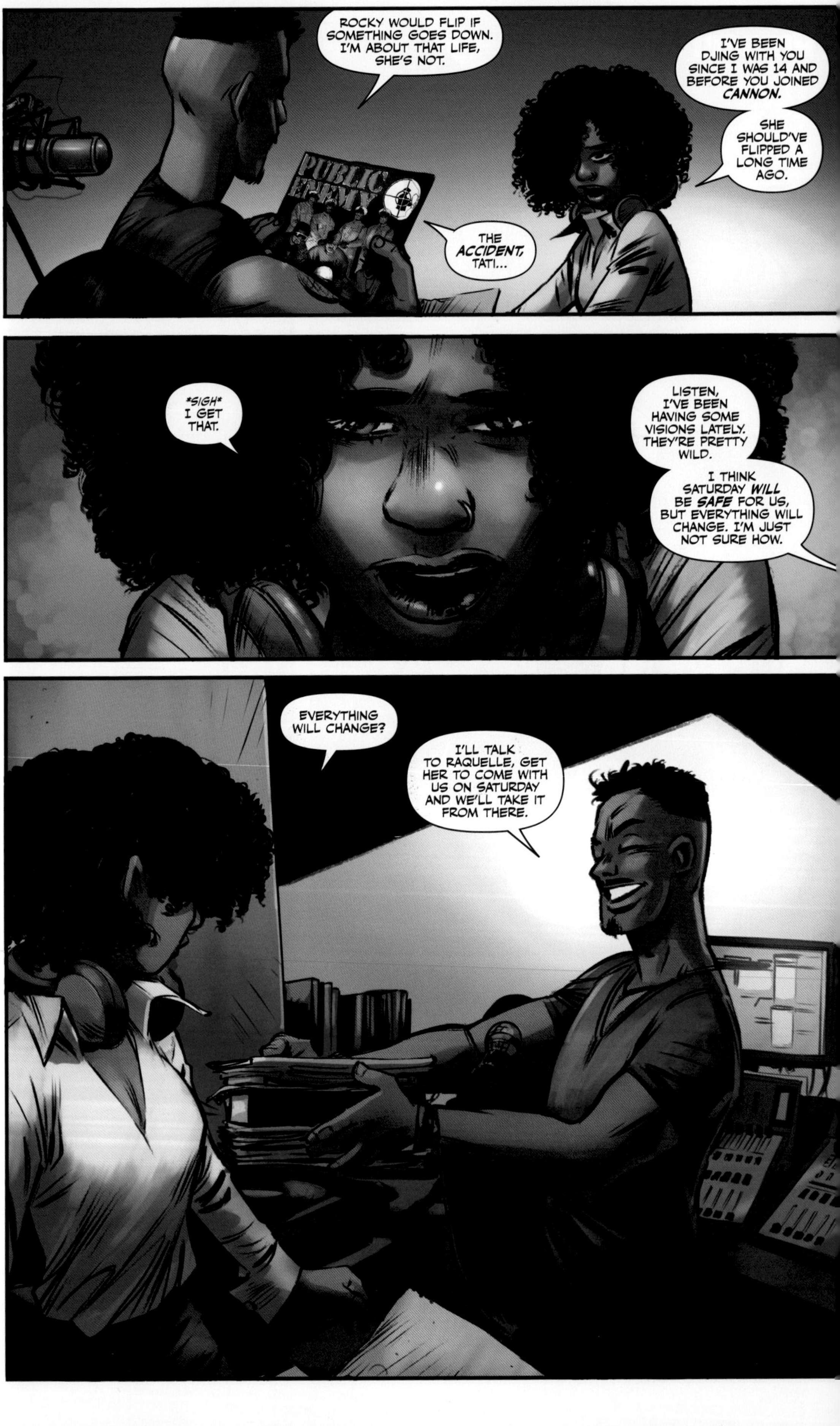
ROCKY WOULD FLIP IF SOMETHING GOES DOWN. I'M ABOUT THAT LIFE, SHE'S NOT.
I'VE BEEN DJING WITH YOU SINCE I WAS 14 AND BEFORE YOU JOINED *CANNON.*
SHE SHOULD'VE FLIPPED A LONG TIME AGO.
THE *ACCIDENT,* TATI...
PUBLIC ENEMY
SIGH I GET THAT.
LISTEN, I'VE BEEN HAVING SOME VISIONS LATELY. THEY'RE PRETTY WILD.
I THINK SATURDAY *WILL* BE *SAFE* FOR US, BUT EVERYTHING WILL CHANGE. I'M JUST NOT SURE HOW.
EVERYTHING WILL CHANGE?
I'LL TALK TO RAQUELLE, GET HER TO COME WITH US ON SATURDAY AND WE'LL TAKE IT FROM THERE.

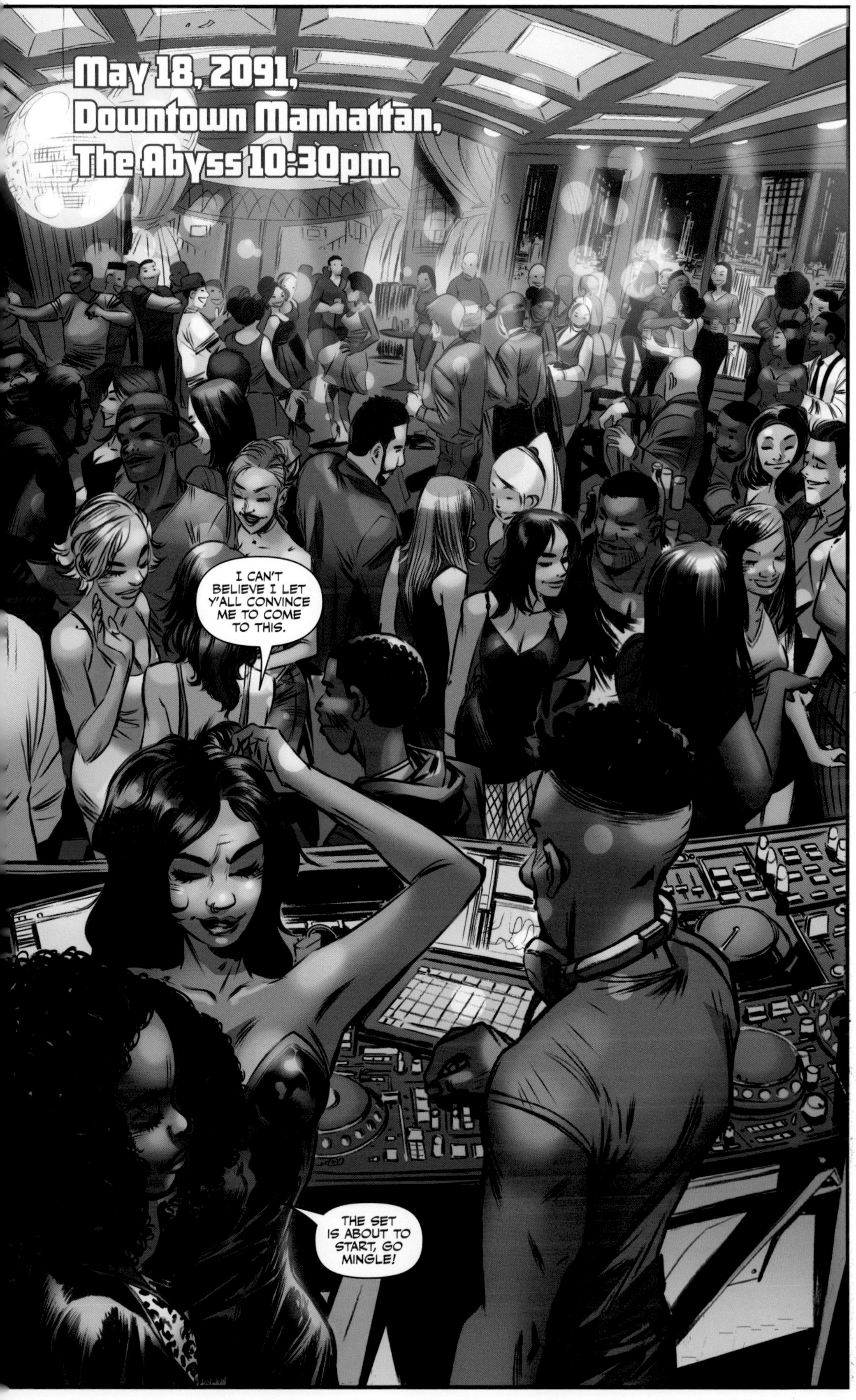

May 18, 2091,
Downtown Manhattan,
The Abyss 10:30pm.
I CAN'T BELIEVE I LET Y'ALL CONVINCE ME TO COME TO THIS.
THE SET IS ABOUT TO START, GO MINGLE!

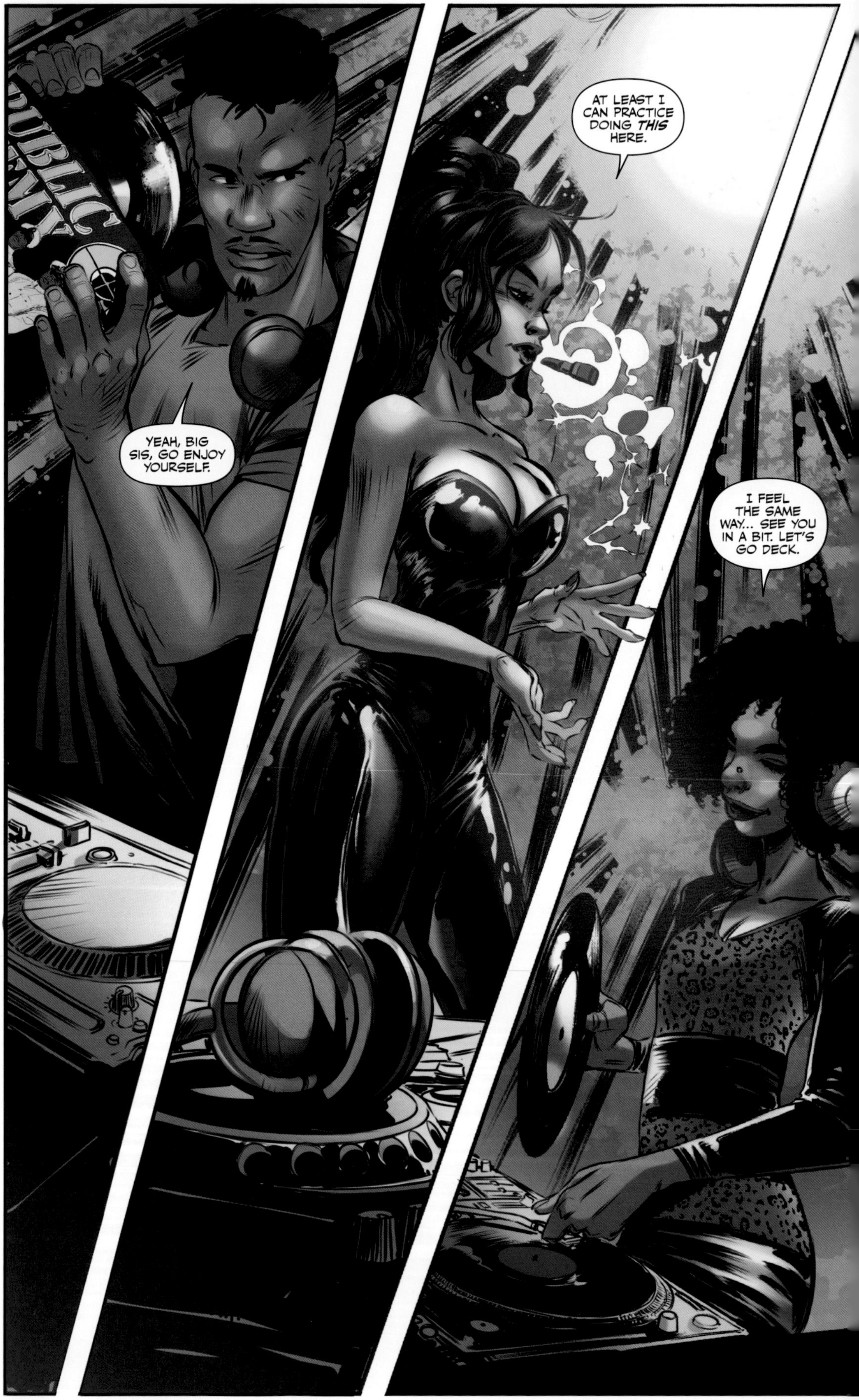

YEAH, BIG SIS, GO ENJOY YOURSELF.
AT LEAST I CAN PRACTICE DOING *THIS* HERE.
I FEEL THE SAME WAY... SEE YOU IN A BIT. LET'S GO DECK.

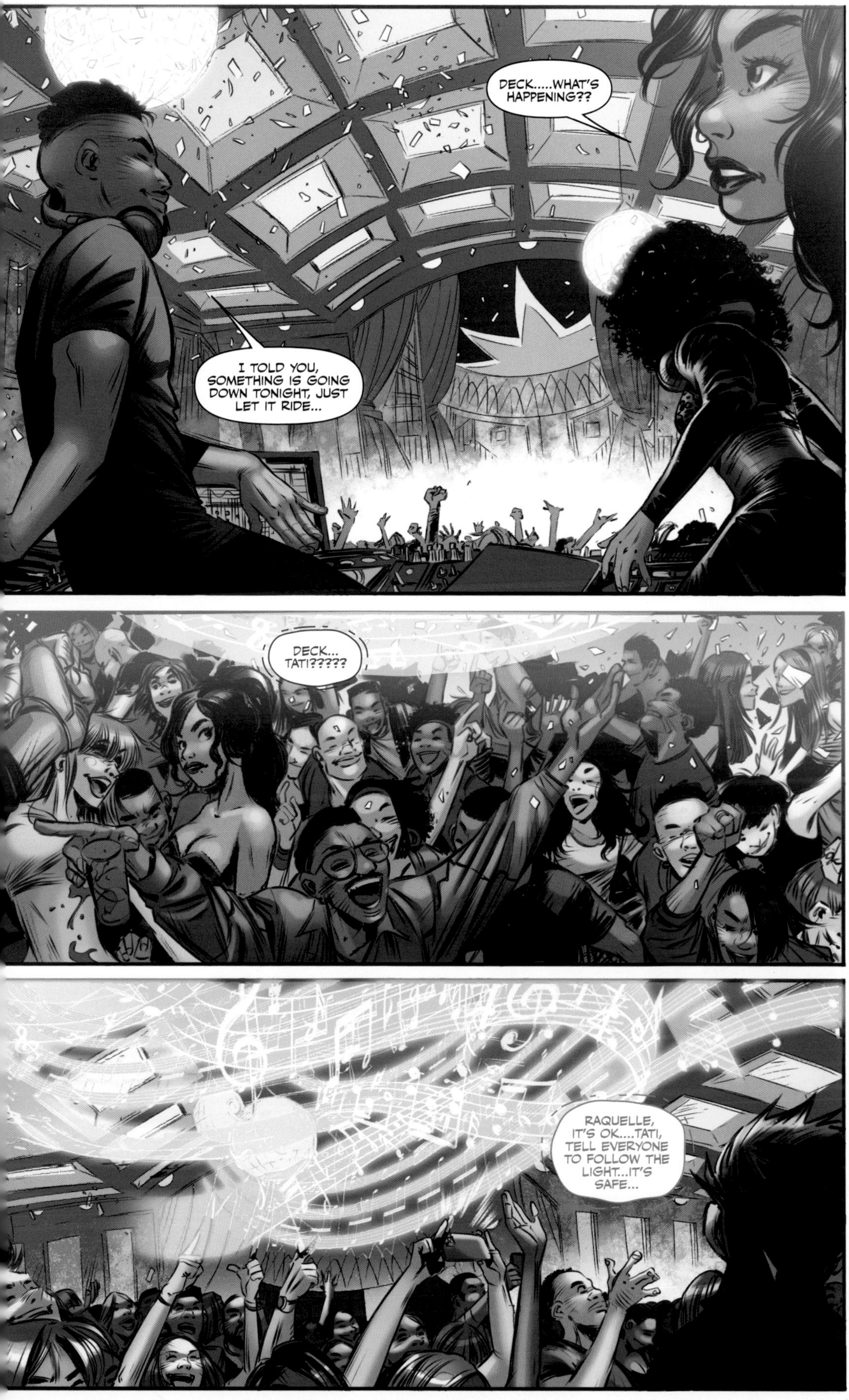
DECK.....WHAT'S HAPPENING??
I TOLD YOU, SOMETHING IS GOING DOWN TONIGHT, JUST LET IT RIDE...
DECK... TATI?????
RAQUELLE, IT'S OK....TATI, TELL EVERYONE TO FOLLOW THE LIGHT...IT'S SAFE...

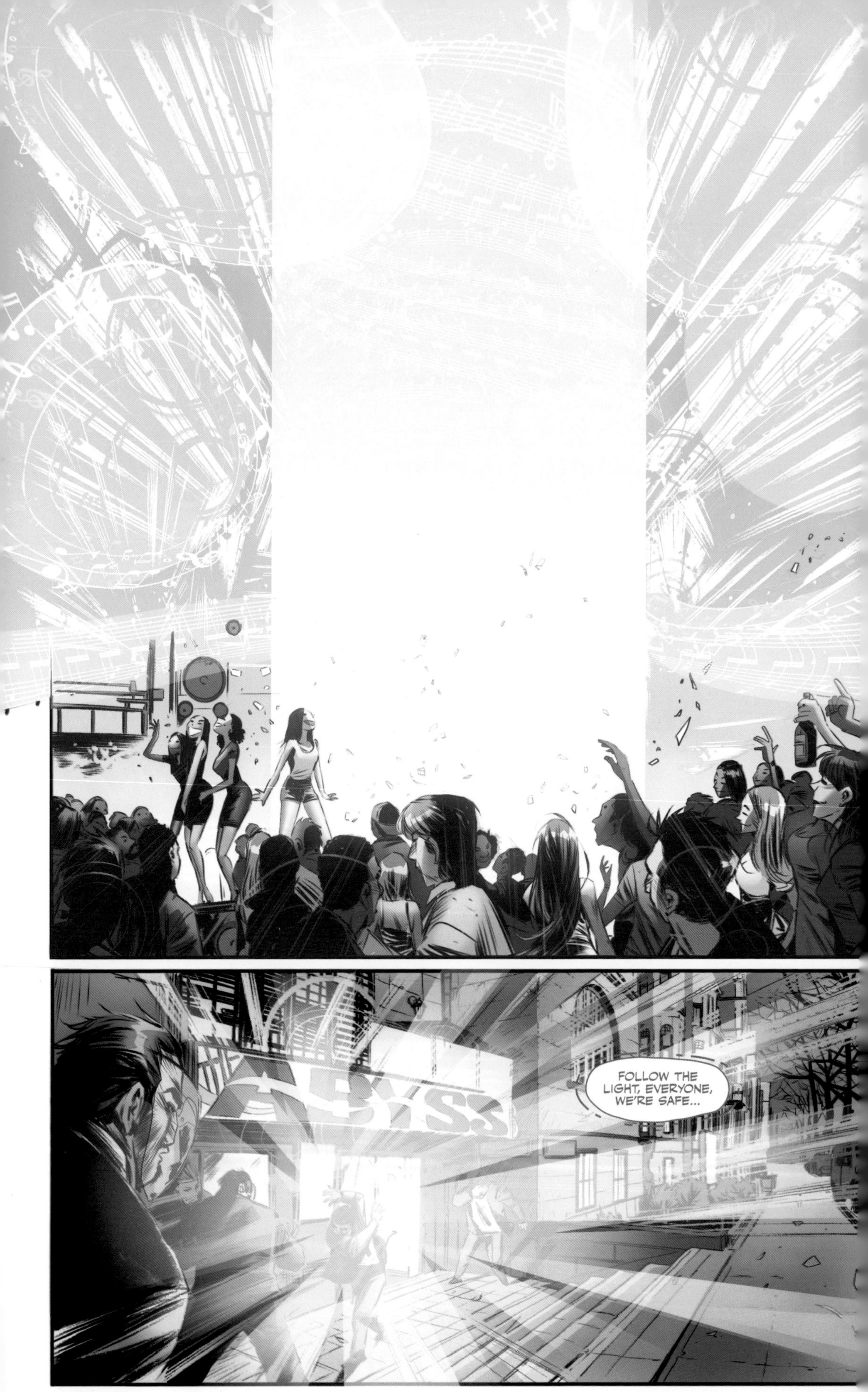
ABYSS
FOLLOW THE LIGHT, EVERYONE, WE'RE SAFE...

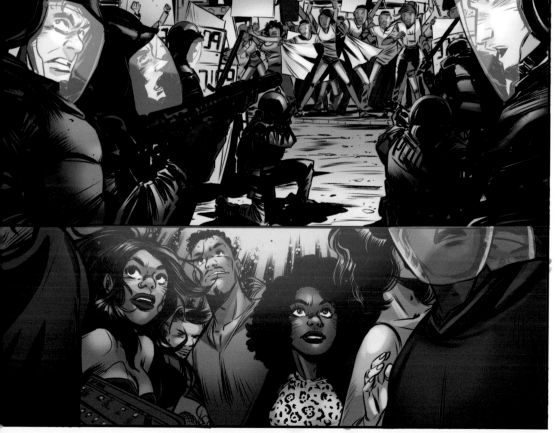

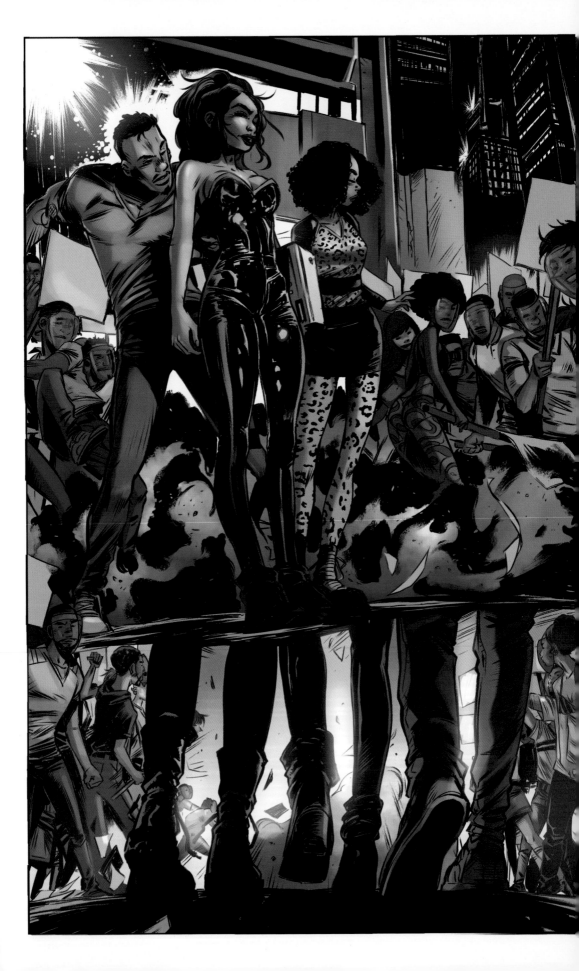

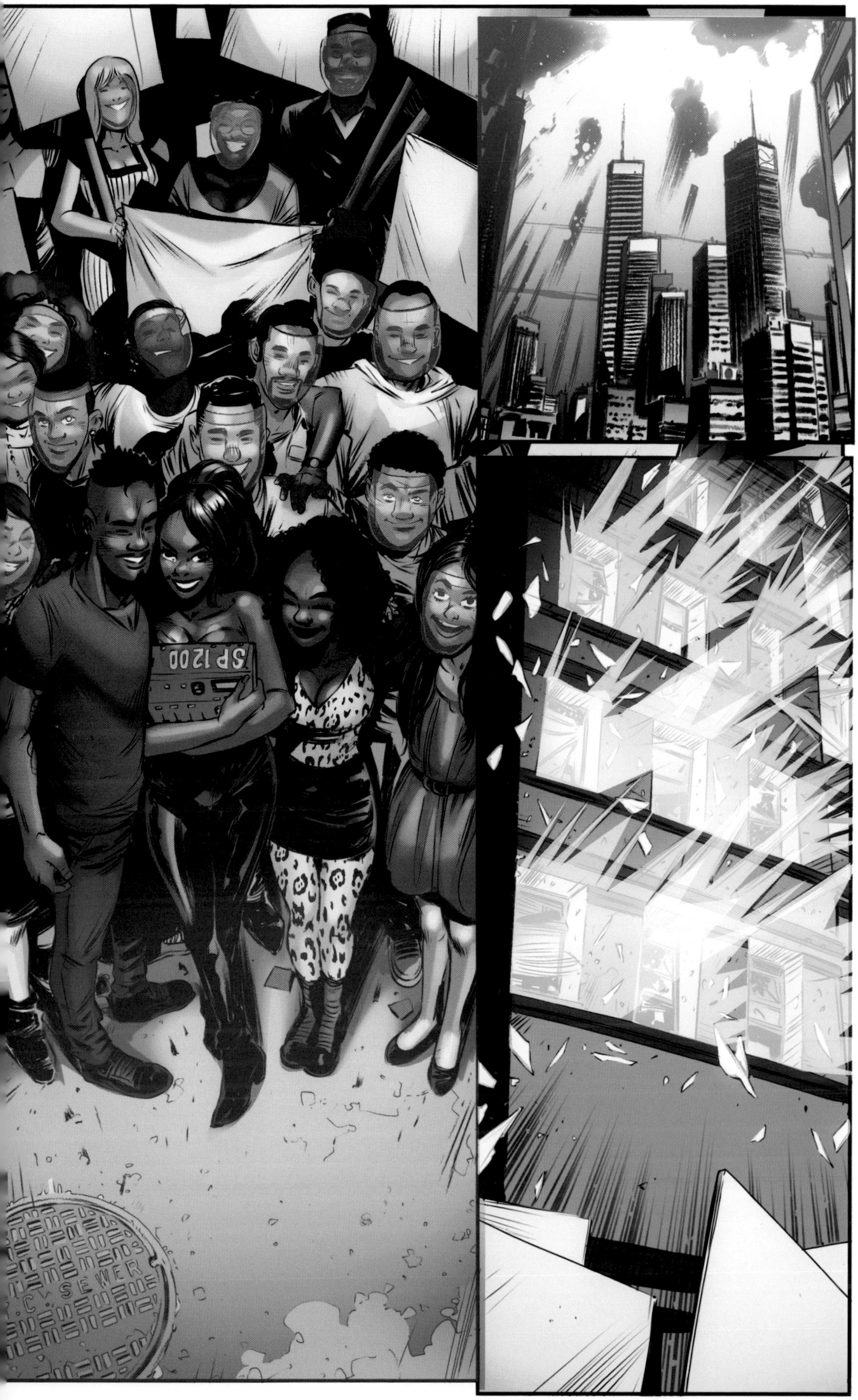
SP1200
SEWER

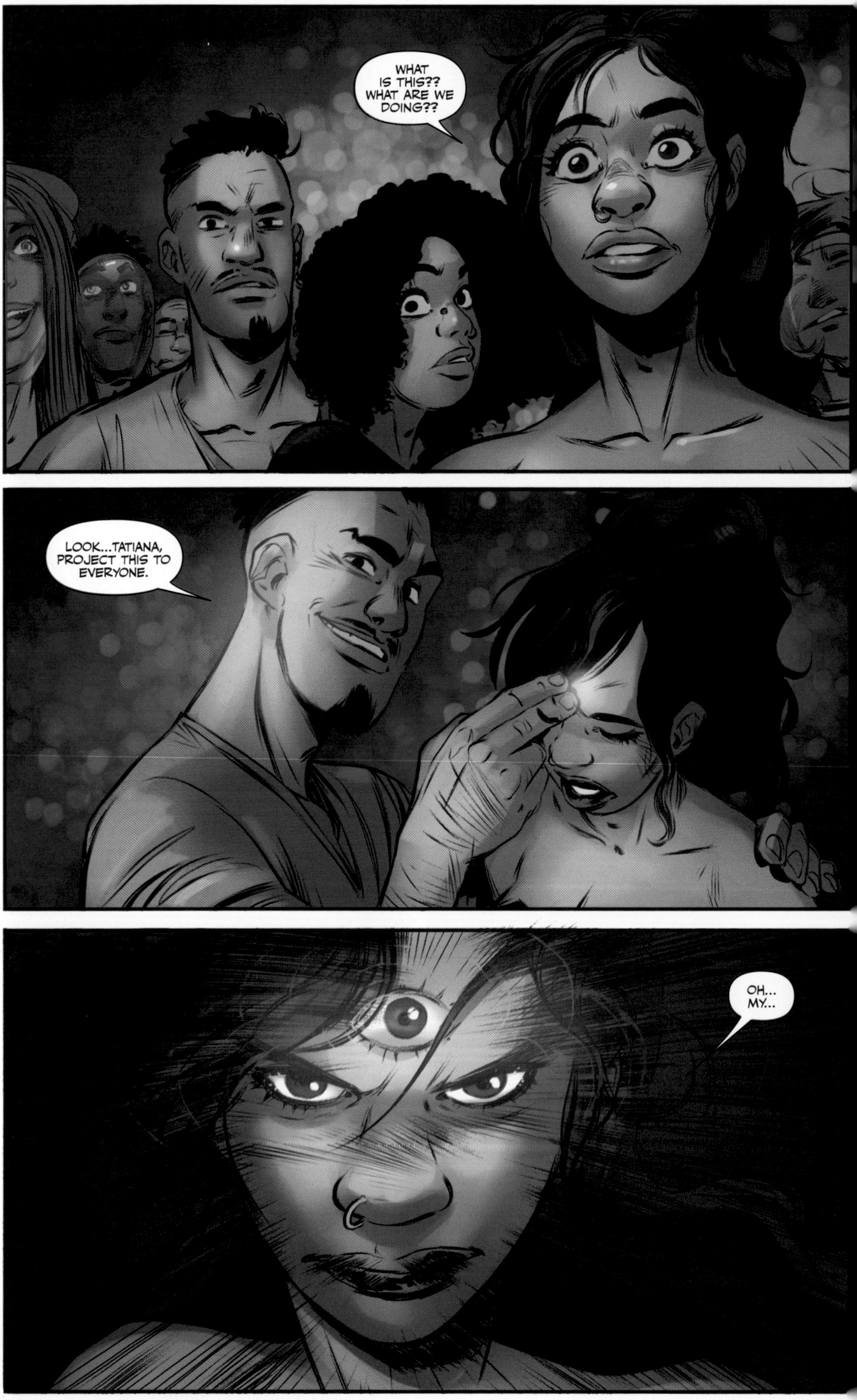
WHAT IS THIS?? WHAT ARE WE DOING??
LOOK...TATIANA, PROJECT THIS TO EVERYONE.
OH... MY...

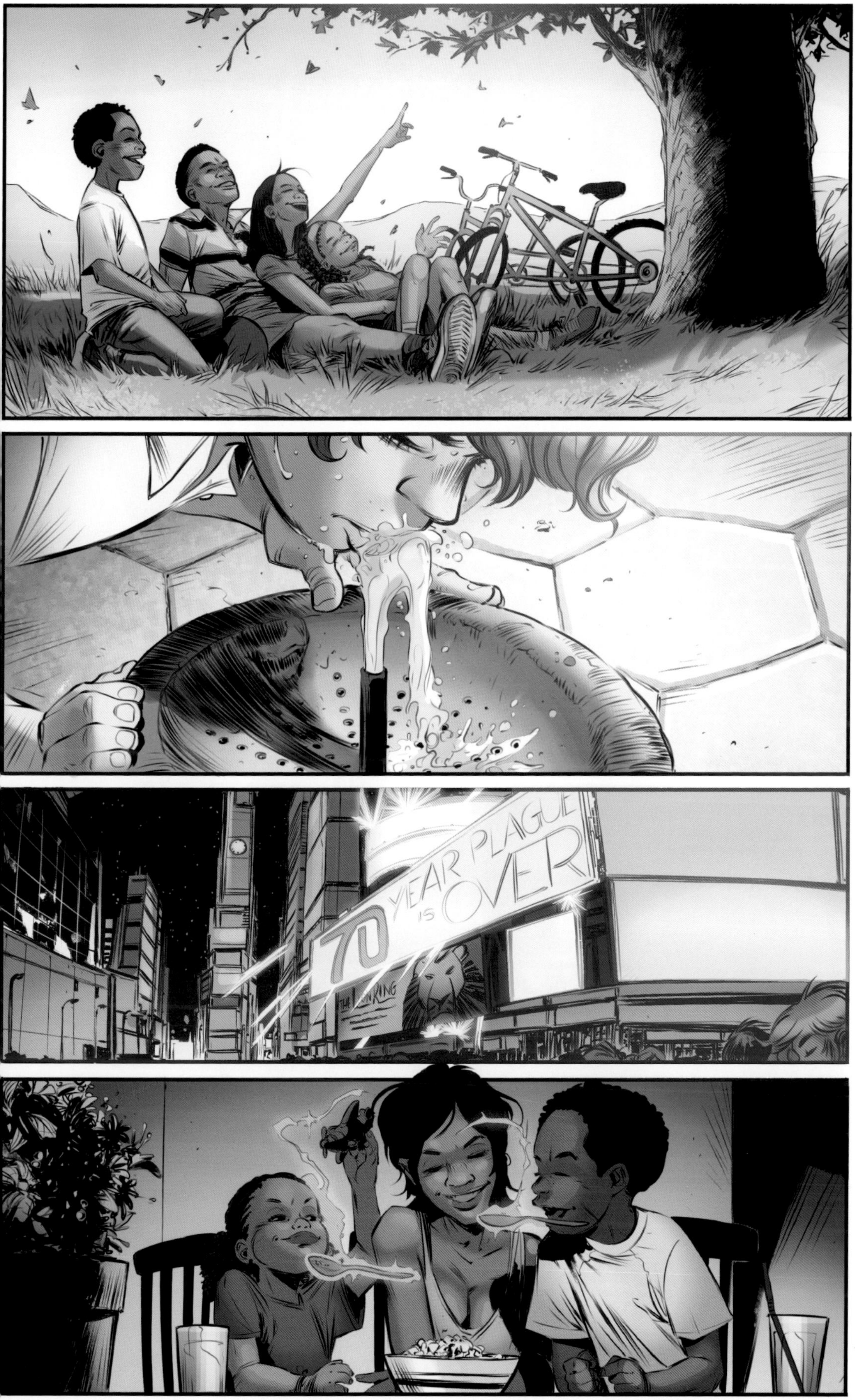
70 YEAR PLAGUE IS OVER

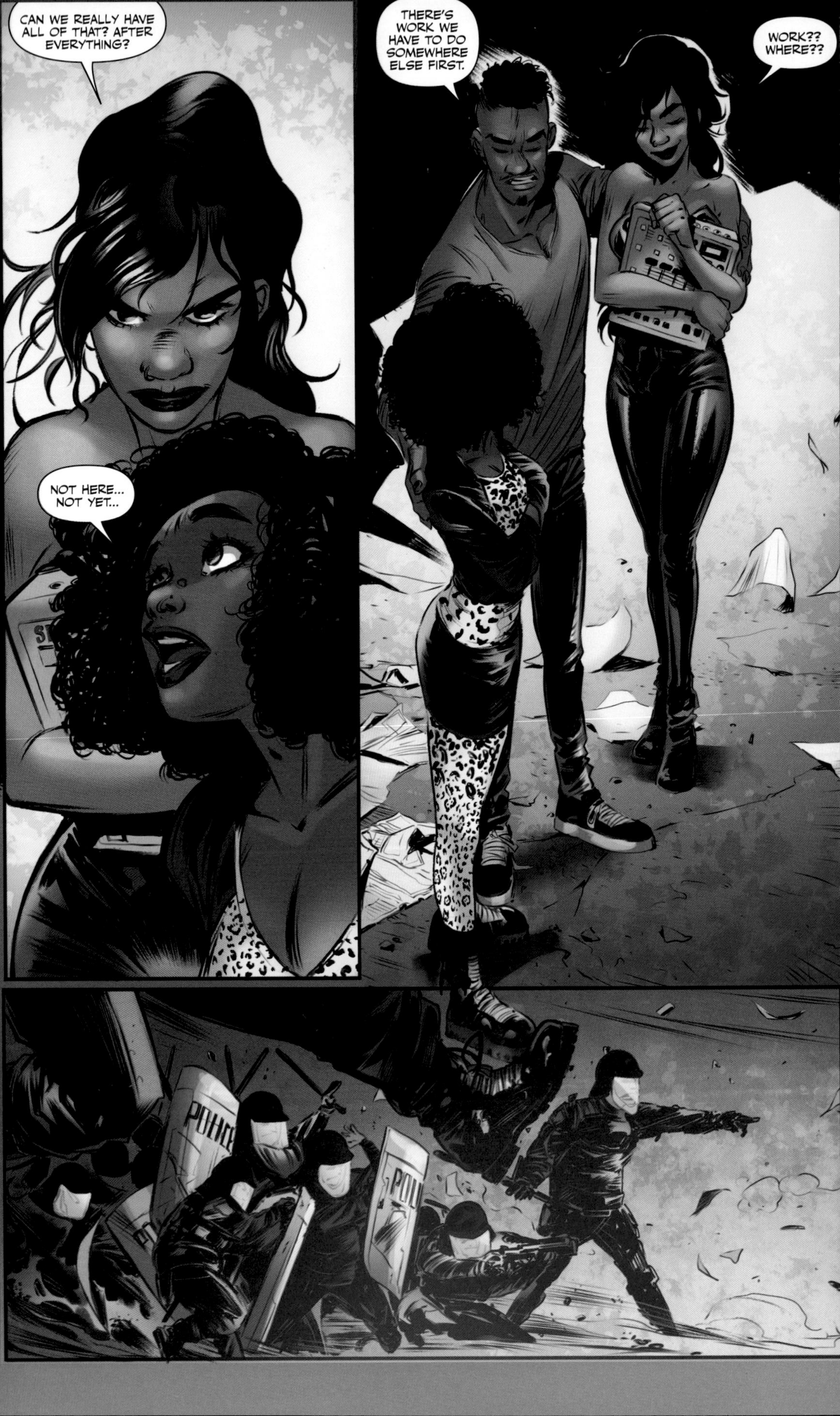
CAN WE REALLY HAVE ALL OF THAT? AFTER EVERYTHING?
NOT HERE... NOT YET...
THERE'S WORK WE HAVE TO DO SOMEWHERE ELSE FIRST.
WORK?? WHERE??
POLICE
POL

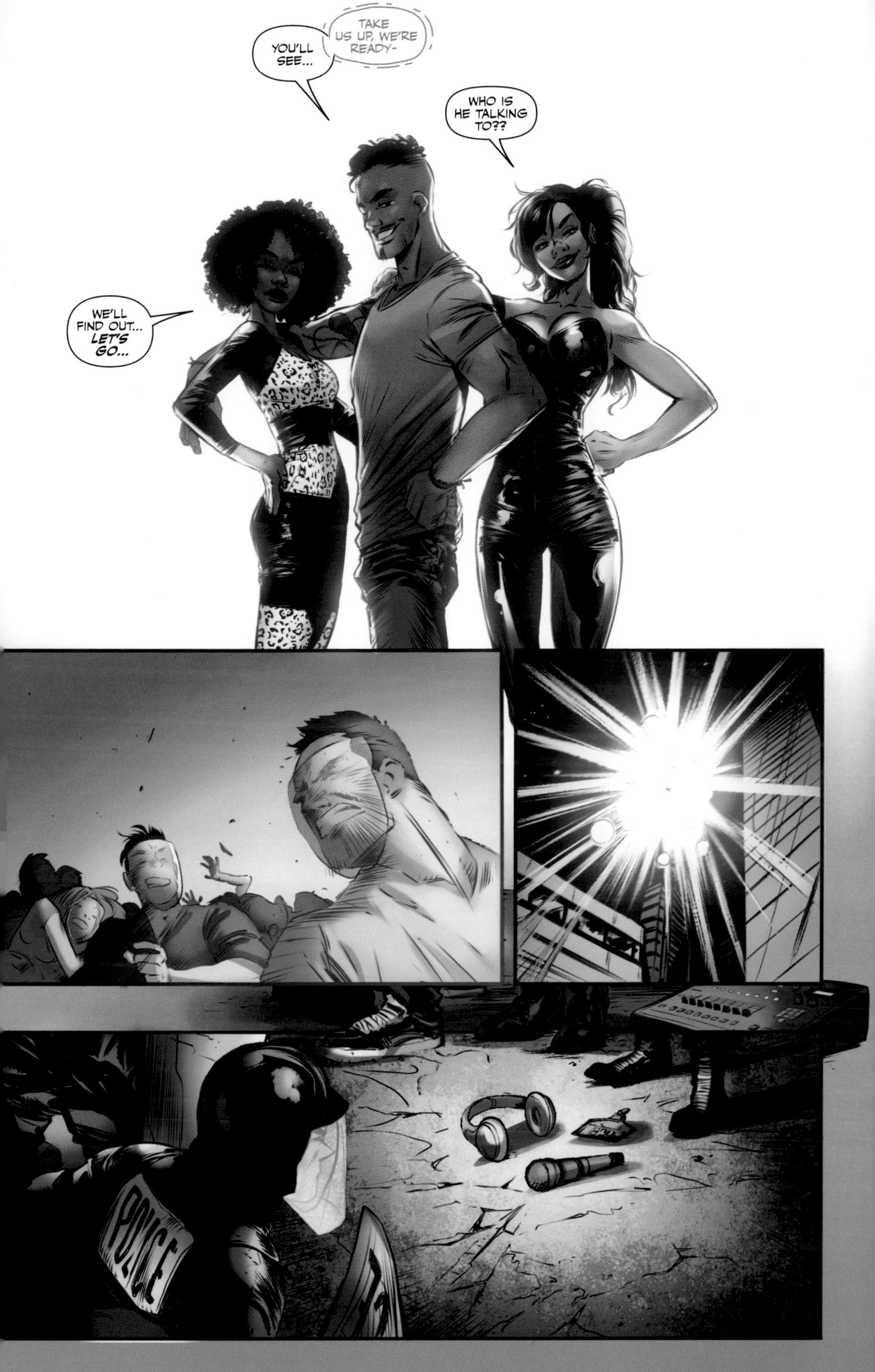
YOU'LL SEE...
TAKE US UP, WE'RE READY-
WHO IS HE TALKING TO??
WE'LL FIND OUT... LET'S GO...
POLICE

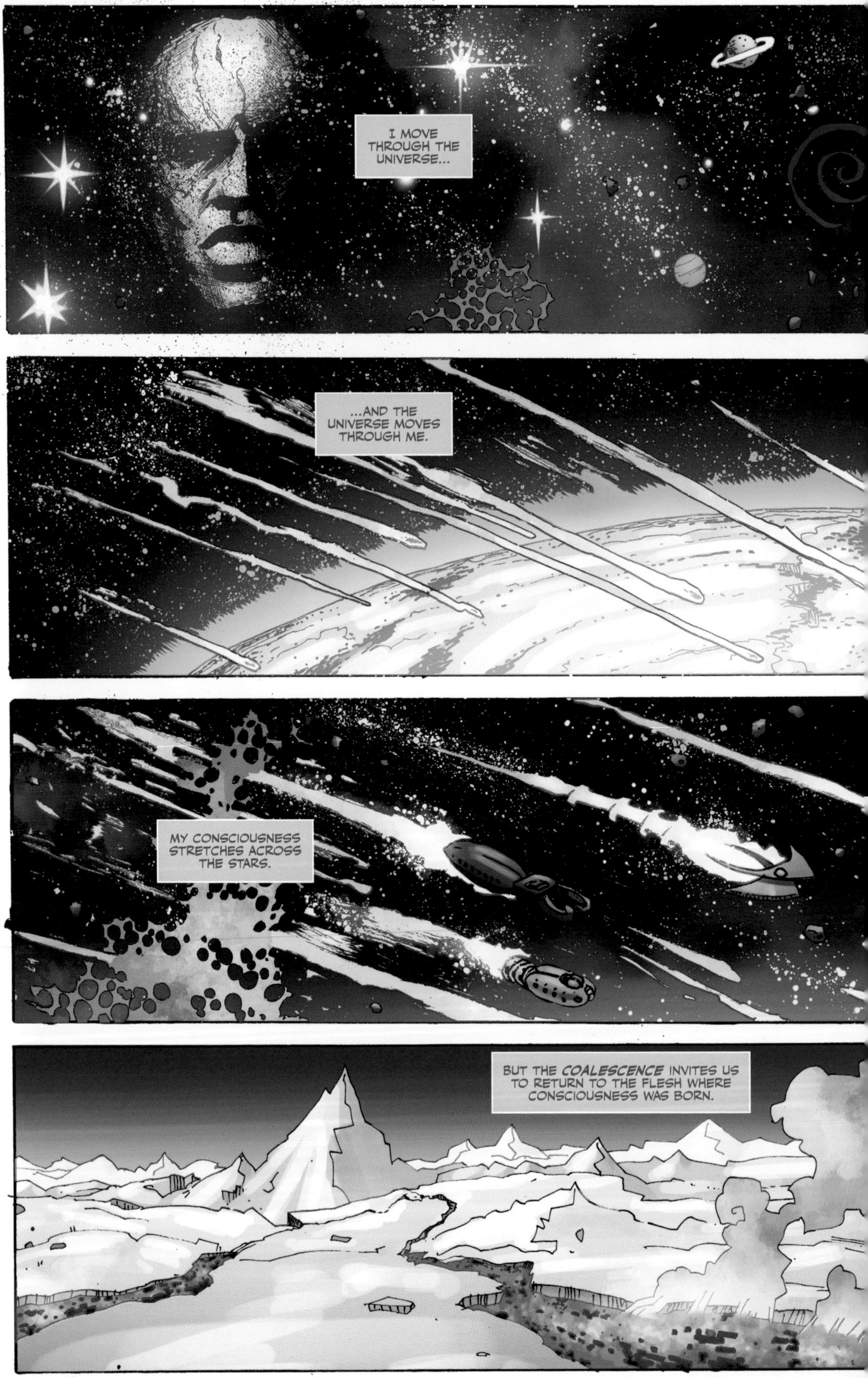

I MOVE THROUGH THE UNIVERSE...
...AND THE UNIVERSE MOVES THROUGH ME.
MY CONSCIOUSNESS STRETCHES ACROSS THE STARS.
BUT THE *COALESCENCE* INVITES US TO RETURN TO THE FLESH WHERE CONSCIOUSNESS WAS BORN.

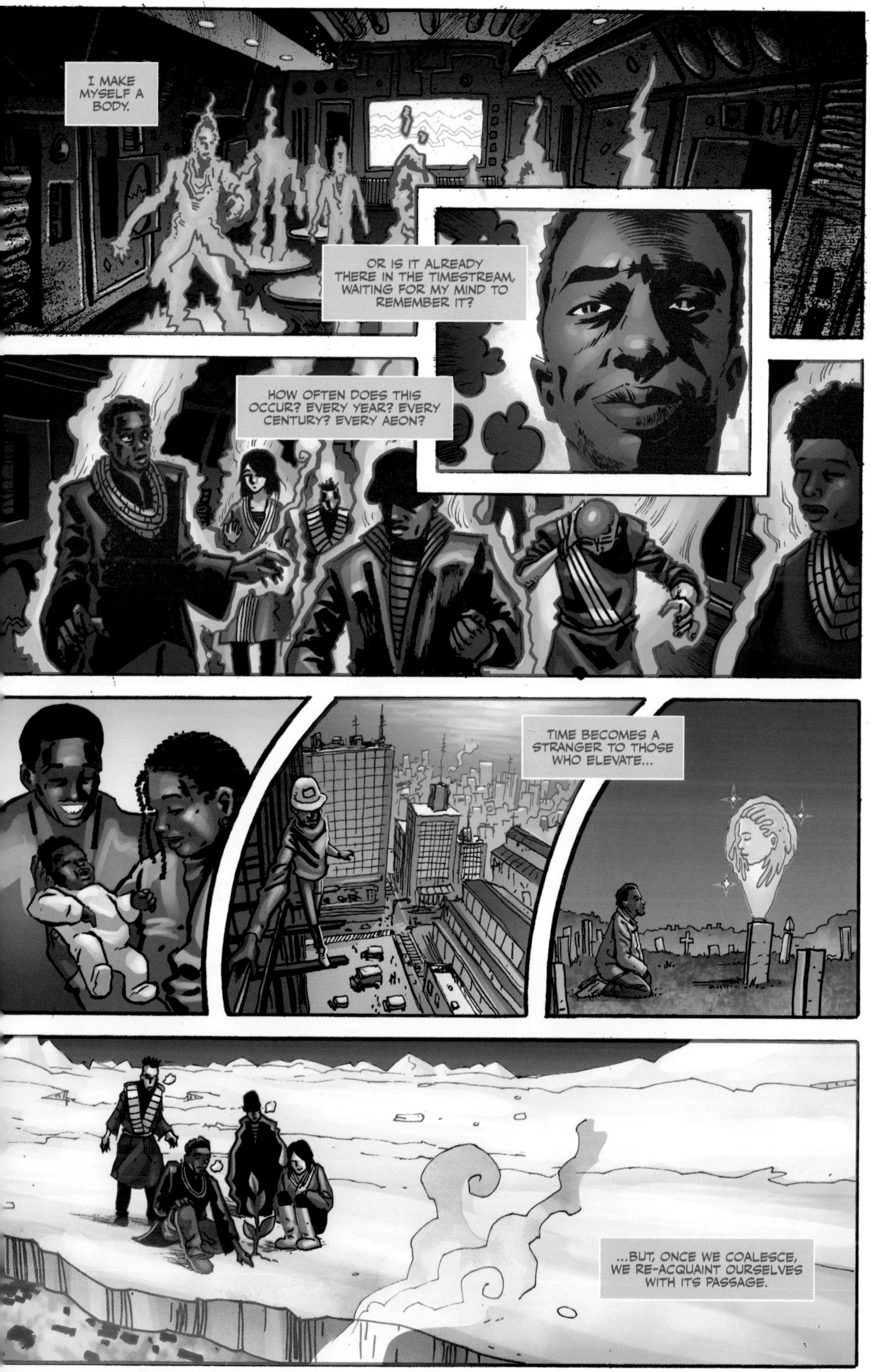
I MAKE MYSELF A BODY.
OR IS IT ALREADY THERE IN THE TIMESTREAM, WAITING FOR MY MIND TO REMEMBER IT?
HOW OFTEN DOES THIS OCCUR? EVERY YEAR? EVERY CENTURY? EVERY AEON?
TIME BECOMES A STRANGER TO THOSE WHO ELEVATE...
...BUT, ONCE WE COALESCE, WE RE-ACQUAINT OURSELVES WITH ITS PASSAGE.

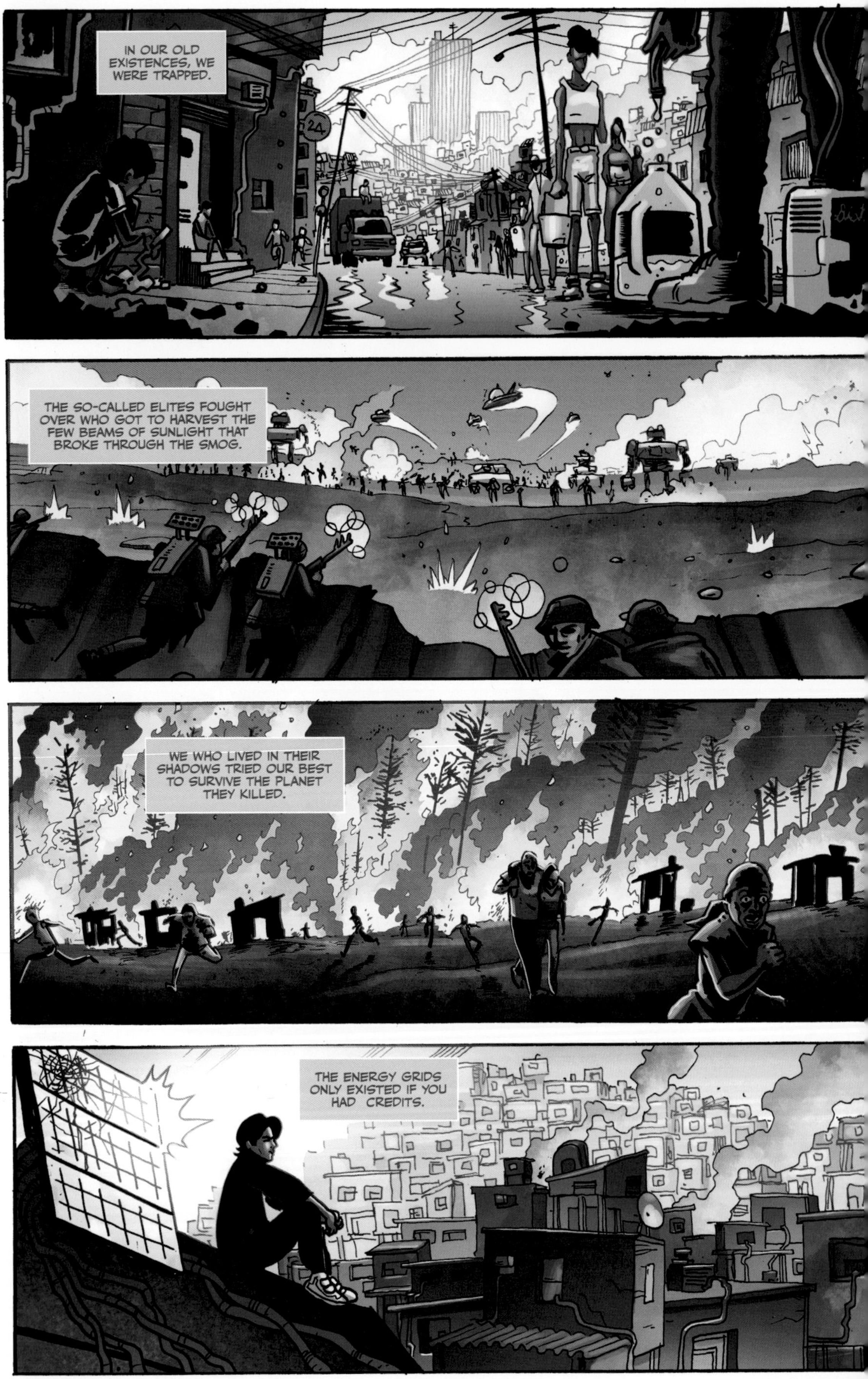
IN OUR OLD EXISTENCES, WE WERE TRAPPED.
24
THE SO-CALLED ELITES FOUGHT OVER WHO GOT TO HARVEST THE FEW BEAMS OF SUNLIGHT THAT BROKE THROUGH THE SMOG.
WE WHO LIVED IN THEIR SHADOWS TRIED OUR BEST TO SURVIVE THE PLANET THEY KILLED.
THE ENERGY GRIDS ONLY EXISTED IF YOU HAD CREDITS.

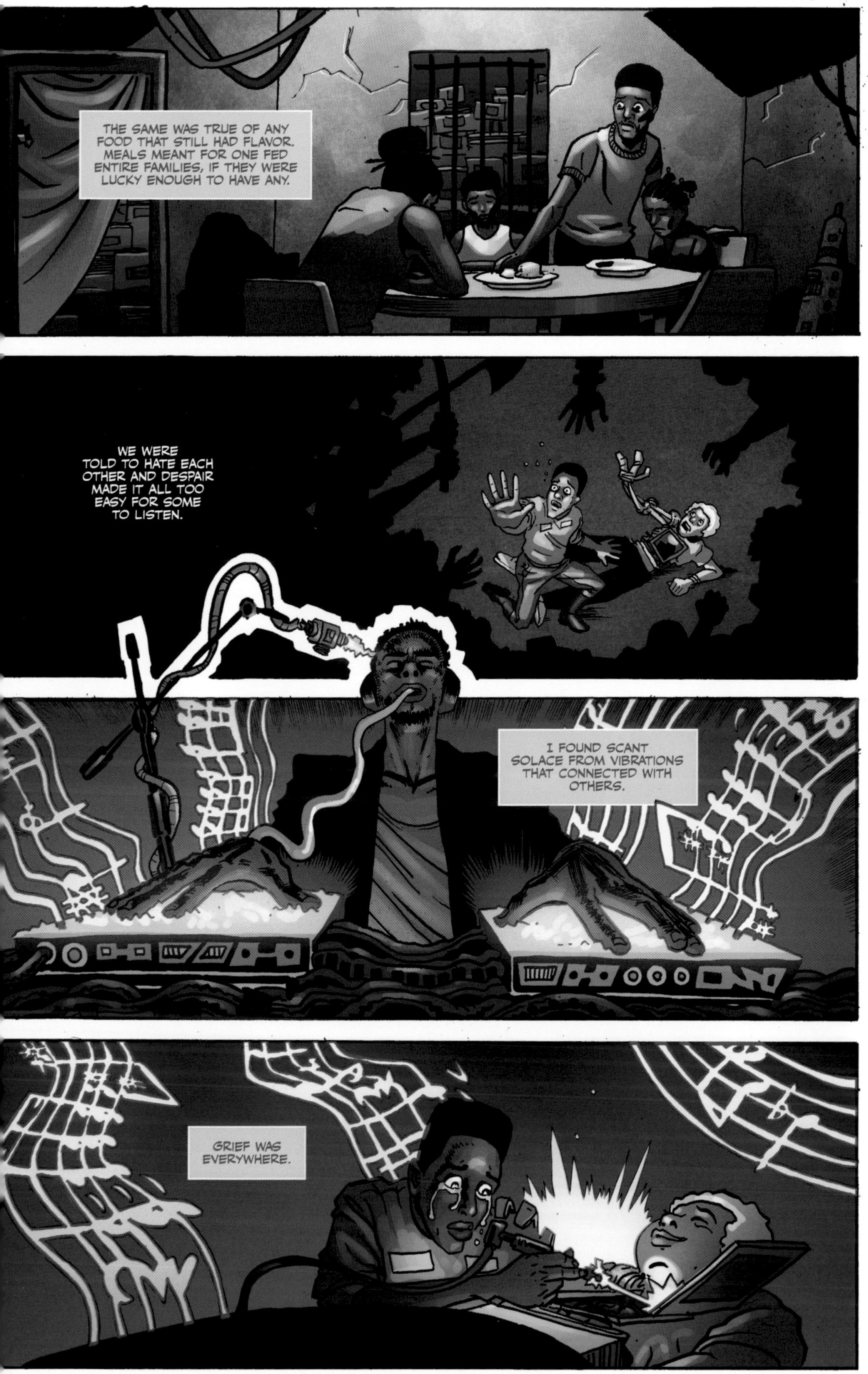
THE SAME WAS TRUE OF ANY FOOD THAT STILL HAD FLAVOR. MEALS MEANT FOR ONE FED ENTIRE FAMILIES, IF THEY WERE LUCKY ENOUGH TO HAVE ANY.
WE WERE TOLD TO HATE EACH OTHER AND DESPAIR MADE IT ALL TOO EASY FOR SOME TO LISTEN.
I FOUND SCANT SOLACE FROM VIBRATIONS THAT CONNECTED WITH OTHERS.
GRIEF WAS EVERYWHERE.

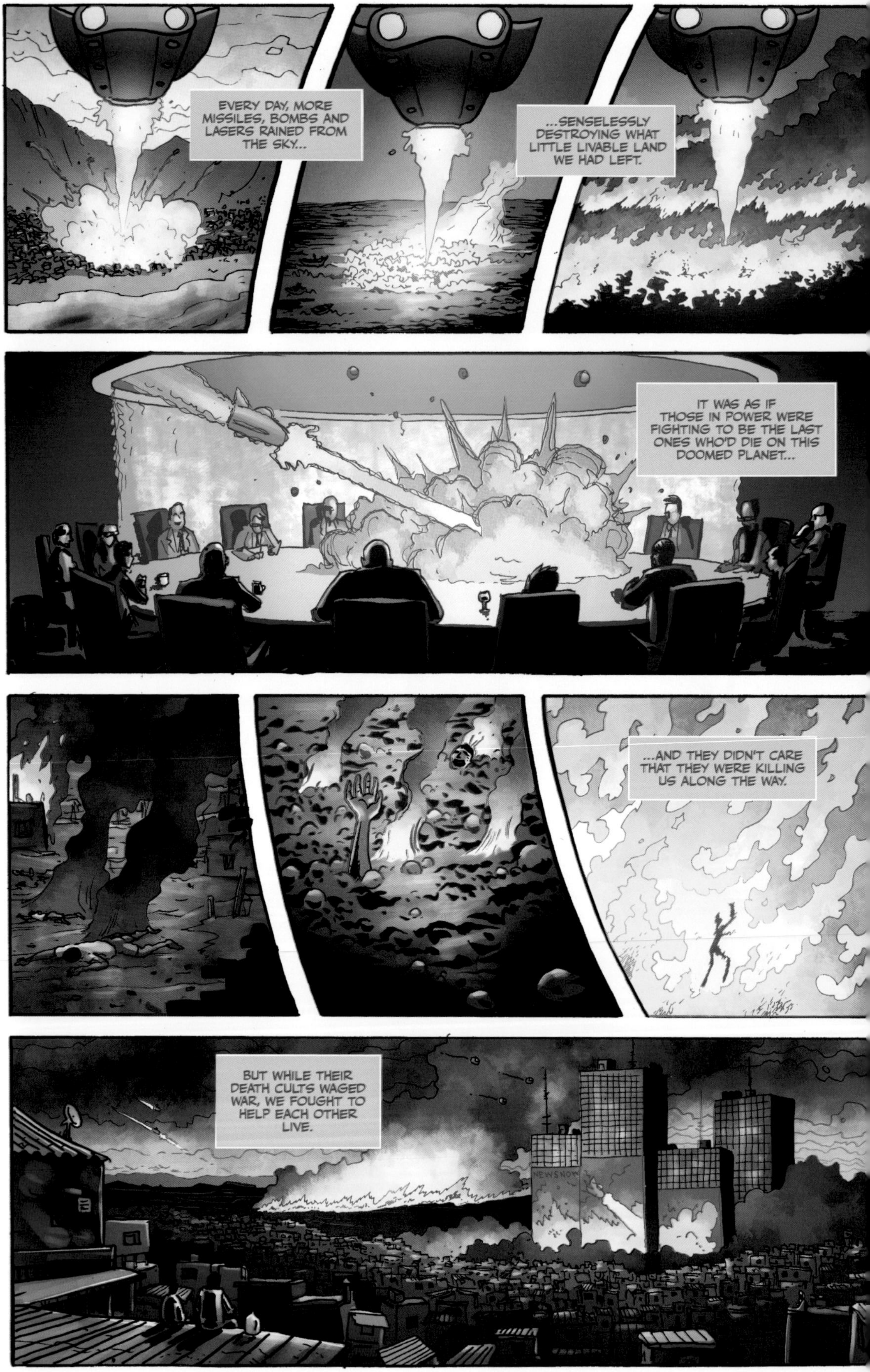
EVERY DAY, MORE MISSILES, BOMBS AND LASERS RAINED FROM THE SKY...
...SENSELESSLY DESTROYING WHAT LITTLE LIVABLE LAND WE HAD LEFT.
IT WAS AS IF THOSE IN POWER WERE FIGHTING TO BE THE LAST ONES WHO'D DIE ON THIS DOOMED PLANET...
...AND THEY DIDN'T CARE THAT THEY WERE KILLING US ALONG THE WAY.
BUT WHILE THEIR DEATH CULTS WAGED WAR, WE FOUGHT TO HELP EACH OTHER LIVE.
NEWSNOW

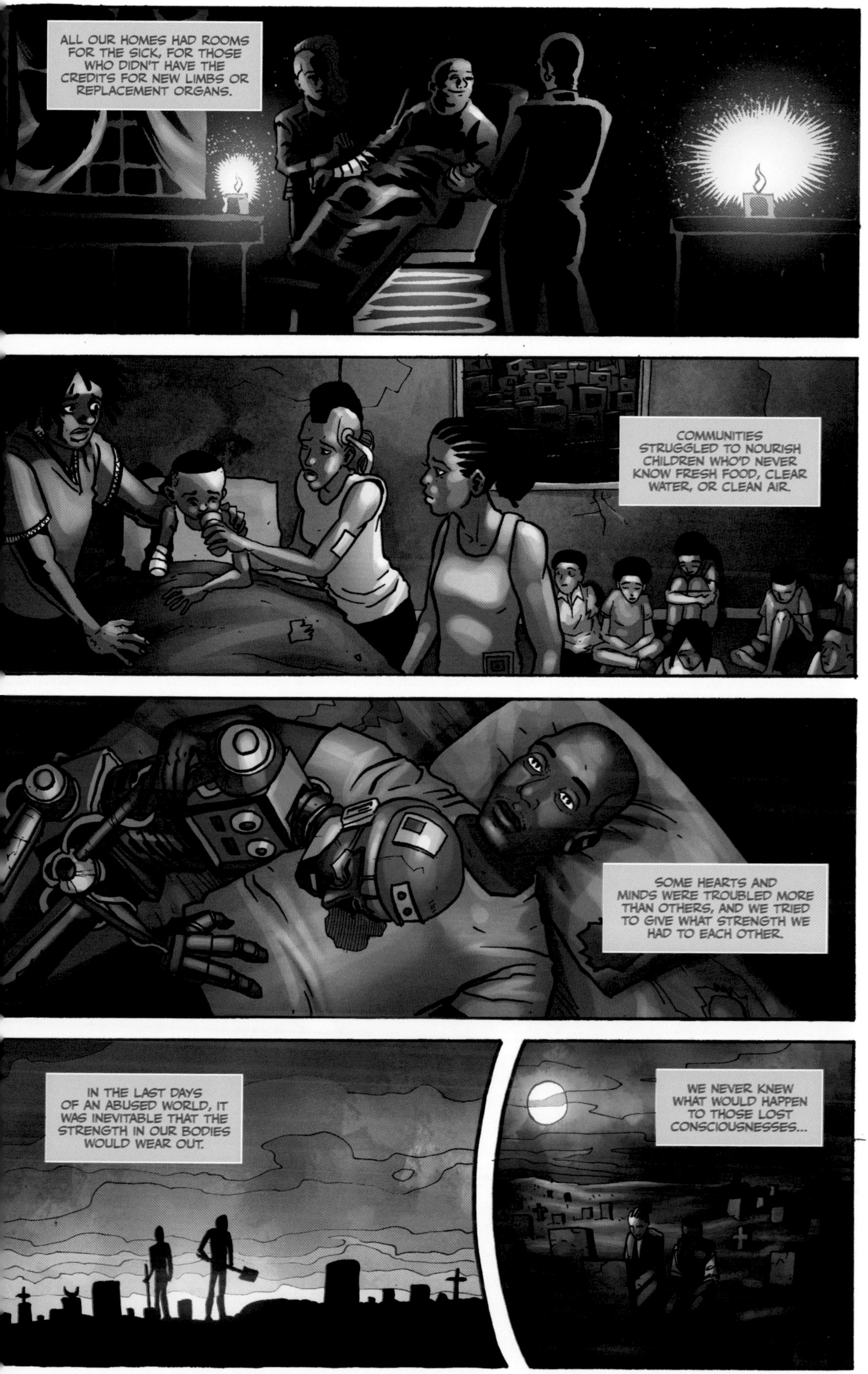
ALL OUR HOMES HAD ROOMS FOR THE SICK, FOR THOSE WHO DIDN'T HAVE THE CREDITS FOR NEW LIMBS OR REPLACEMENT ORGANS.
COMMUNITIES STRUGGLED TO NOURISH CHILDREN WHO'D NEVER KNOW FRESH FOOD, CLEAR WATER, OR CLEAN AIR.
SOME HEARTS AND MINDS WERE TROUBLED MORE THAN OTHERS, AND WE TRIED TO GIVE WHAT STRENGTH WE HAD TO EACH OTHER.
IN THE LAST DAYS OF AN ABUSED WORLD, IT WAS INEVITABLE THAT THE STRENGTH IN OUR BODIES WOULD WEAR OUT.
WE NEVER KNEW WHAT WOULD HAPPEN TO THOSE LOST CONSCIOUSNESSES...

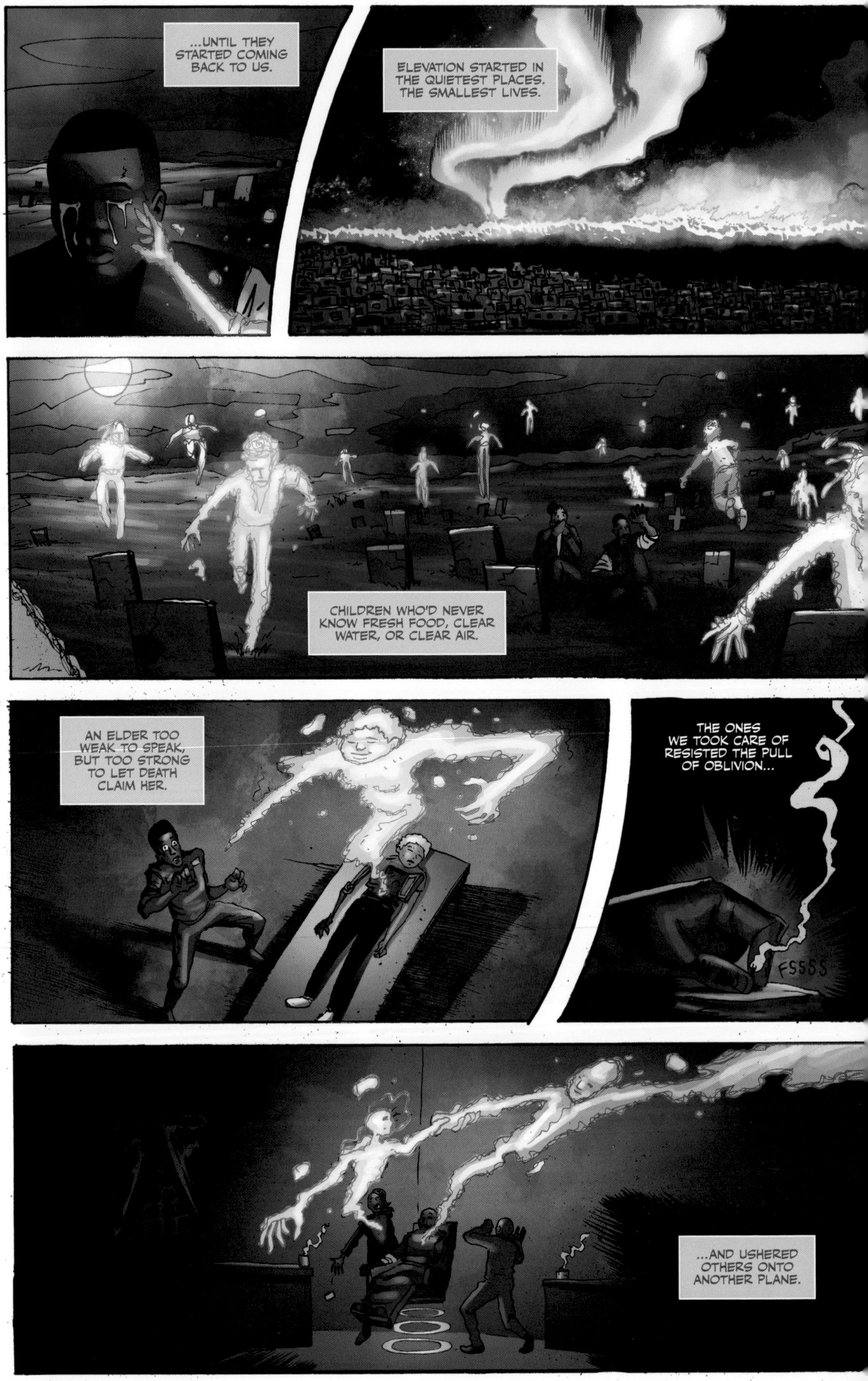
...UNTIL THEY STARTED COMING BACK TO US.
ELEVATION STARTED IN THE QUIETEST PLACES. THE SMALLEST LIVES.
CHILDREN WHO'D NEVER KNOW FRESH FOOD, CLEAR WATER, OR CLEAR AIR.
AN ELDER TOO WEAK TO SPEAK, BUT TOO STRONG TO LET DEATH CLAIM HER.
THE ONES WE TOOK CARE OF RESISTED THE PULL OF OBLIVION...
FSSSS
...AND USHERED OTHERS ONTO ANOTHER PLANE.

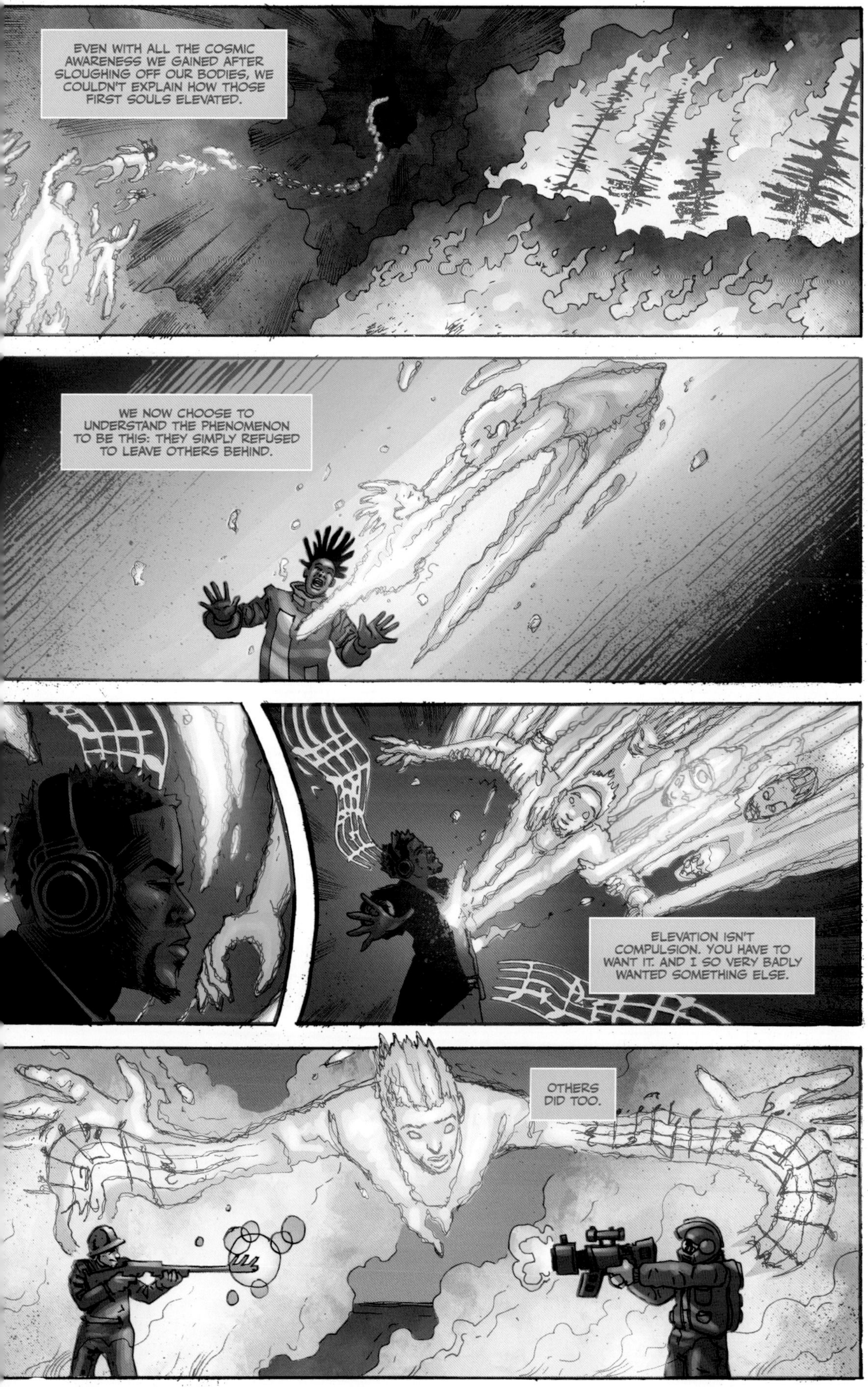

EVEN WITH ALL THE COSMIC AWARENESS WE GAINED AFTER SLOUGHING OFF OUR BODIES, WE COULDN'T EXPLAIN HOW THOSE FIRST SOULS ELEVATED.
WE NOW CHOOSE TO UNDERSTAND THE PHENOMENON TO BE THIS: THEY SIMPLY REFUSED TO LEAVE OTHERS BEHIND.
ELEVATION ISN'T COMPULSION. YOU HAVE TO WANT IT. AND I SO VERY BADLY WANTED SOMETHING ELSE.
OTHERS DID TOO.

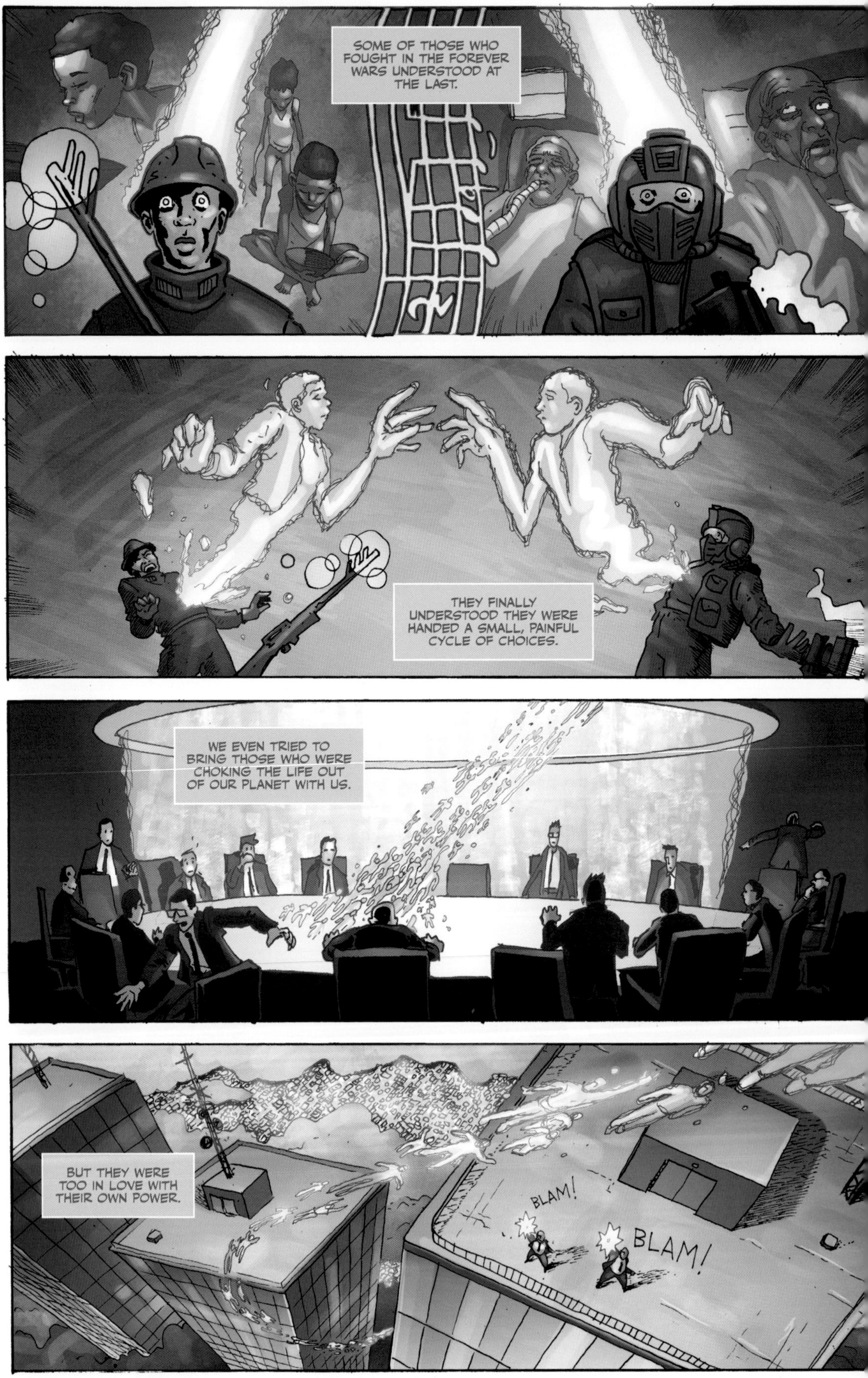
SOME OF THOSE WHO FOUGHT IN THE FOREVER WARS UNDERSTOOD AT THE LAST.
THEY FINALLY UNDERSTOOD THEY WERE HANDED A SMALL, PAINFUL CYCLE OF CHOICES.
WE EVEN TRIED TO BRING THOSE WHO WERE CHOKING THE LIFE OUT OF OUR PLANET WITH US.
BUT THEY WERE TOO IN LOVE WITH THEIR OWN POWER.
BLAM!
BLAM!

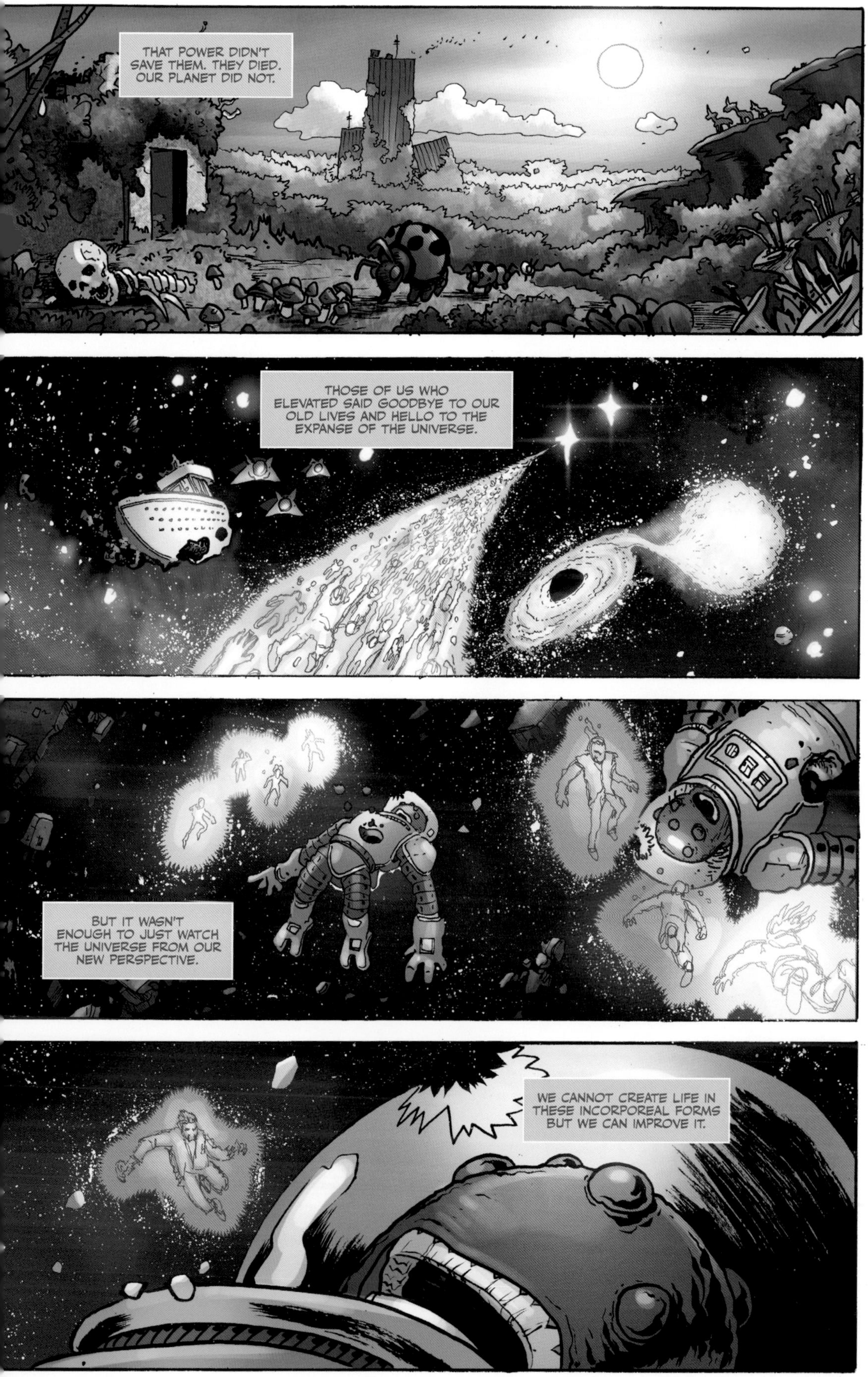
THAT POWER DIDN'T SAVE THEM. THEY DIED. OUR PLANET DID NOT.
THOSE OF US WHO ELEVATED SAID GOODBYE TO OUR OLD LIVES AND HELLO TO THE EXPANSE OF THE UNIVERSE.
BUT IT WASN'T ENOUGH TO JUST WATCH THE UNIVERSE FROM OUR NEW PERSPECTIVE.
WE CANNOT CREATE LIFE IN THESE INCORPOREAL FORMS BUT WE CAN IMPROVE IT.

WITH WHAT WE'D BEEN THROUGH, WE KNEW WE HAD TO BE A FORCE FOR JUSTICE IN THE UNIVERSE.

WE HAD TO HELP.

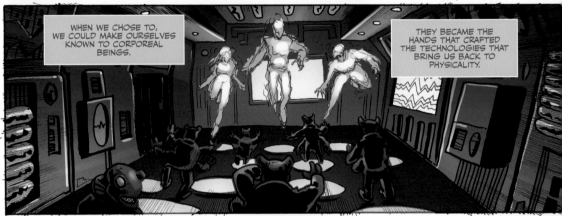

WHEN WE CHOSE TO, WE COULD MAKE OURSELVES KNOWN TO CORPOREAL BEINGS.

THEY BECAME THE HANDS THAT CRAFTED THE TECHNOLOGIES THAT BRING US BACK TO PHYSICALITY.

ONCE, WE BELIEVED THE FUTURE HELD NOTHING ELSE BUT CONFRONTATION. BUT WE GAVE UP CONFRONTATION AND FOUND A FUTURE THAT HELD POSSIBILITIES.

AND SO CAME COALESCENCE.

WE COALESCE TO REMEMBER WHERE WE CAME FROM, TO HONOR THOSE STILL STRUGGLE THROUGH AN INDIFFERENT COSMOS.

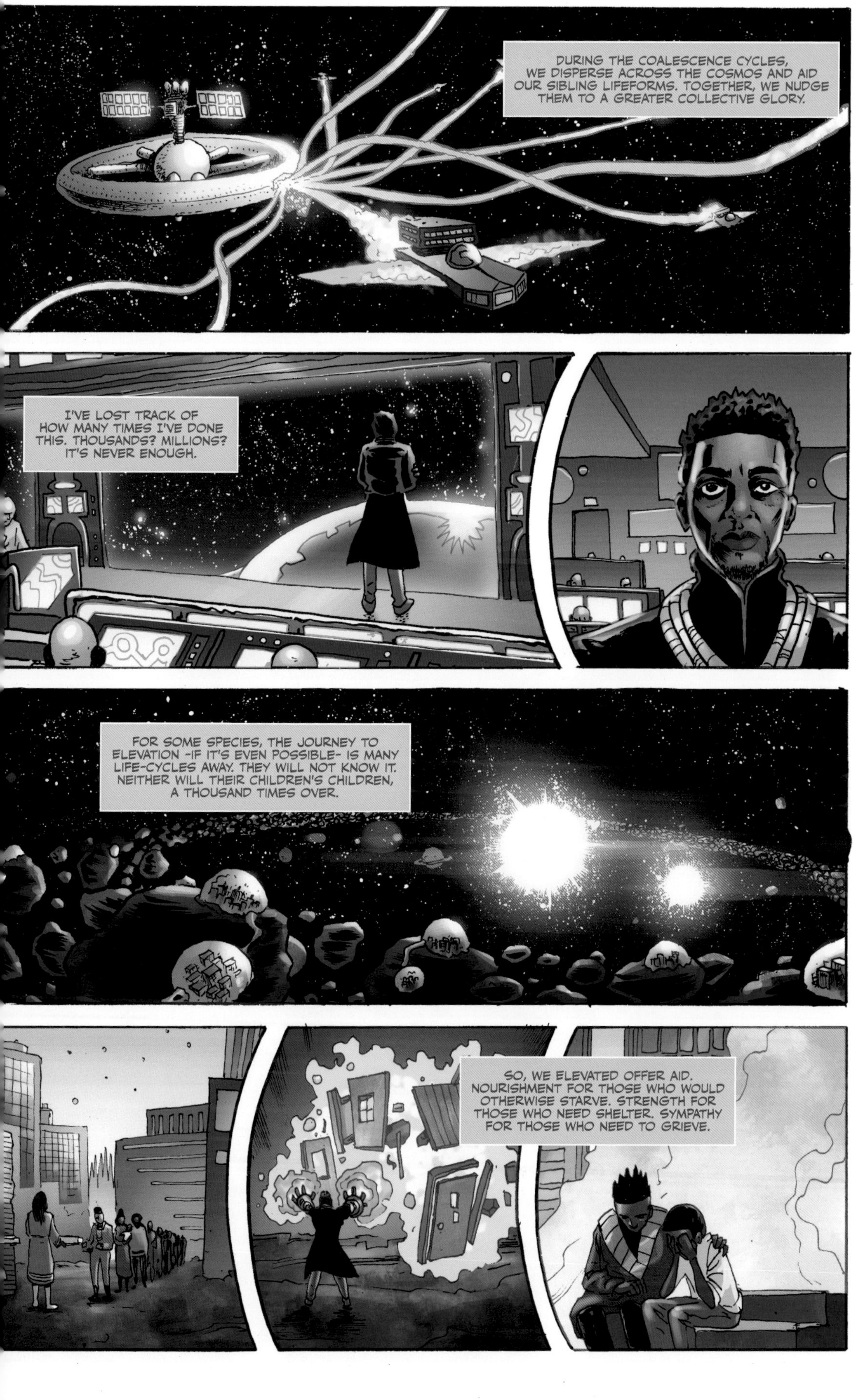
DURING THE COALESCENCE CYCLES, WE DISPERSE ACROSS THE COSMOS AND AID OUR SIBLING LIFEFORMS. TOGETHER, WE NUDGE THEM TO A GREATER COLLECTIVE GLORY.
I'VE LOST TRACK OF HOW MANY TIMES I'VE DONE THIS. THOUSANDS? MILLIONS? IT'S NEVER ENOUGH.
FOR SOME SPECIES, THE JOURNEY TO ELEVATION -IF IT'S EVEN POSSIBLE- IS MANY LIFE-CYCLES AWAY. THEY WILL NOT KNOW IT. NEITHER WILL THEIR CHILDREN'S CHILDREN, A THOUSAND TIMES OVER.
SO, WE ELEVATED OFFER AID. NOURISHMENT FOR THOSE WHO WOULD OTHERWISE STARVE. STRENGTH FOR THOSE WHO NEED SHELTER. SYMPATHY FOR THOSE WHO NEED TO GRIEVE.

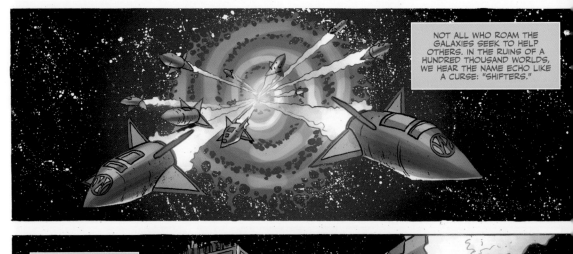

NOT ALL WHO ROAM THE GALAXIES SEEK TO HELP OTHERS. IN THE RUINS OF A HUNDRED THOUSAND WORLDS, WE HEAR THE NAME ECHO LIKE A CURSE: "SHIFTERS."

WE'VE SEEN THEM CREEP FROM SOLAR SYSTEM TO SOLAR SYSTEM, PLUNDERING AS THEY PLEASE.

THEY MAKE FIRST CONTACT WITH OVERTURES OF AID.

THEN THEY INTERVENE IN THE AFFAIRS OF OTHER CIVILIZATIONS...

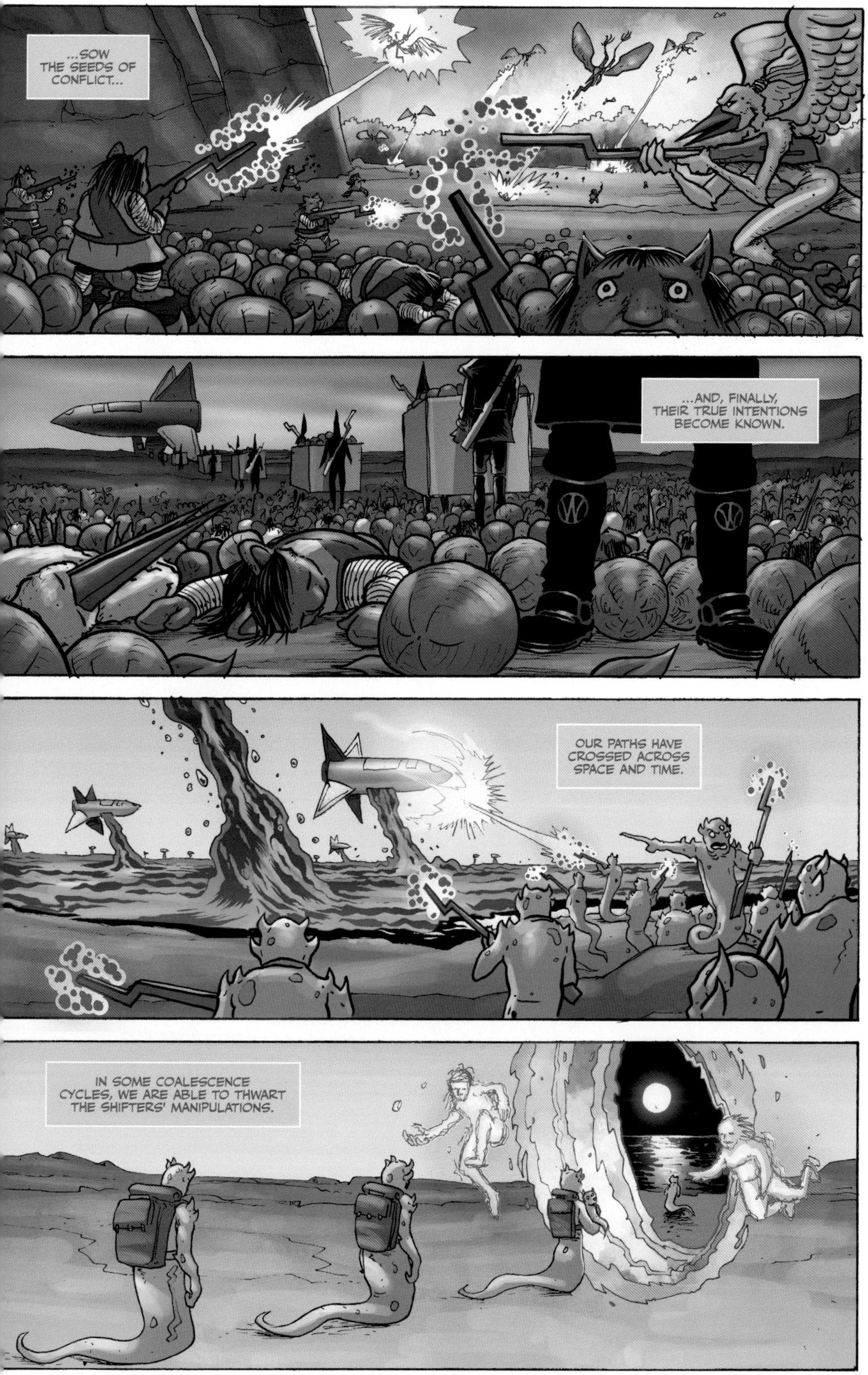
...SOW THE SEEDS OF CONFLICT...
...AND, FINALLY, THEIR TRUE INTENTIONS BECOME KNOWN.
OUR PATHS HAVE CROSSED ACROSS SPACE AND TIME.
IN SOME COALESCENCE CYCLES, WE ARE ABLE TO THWART THE SHIFTERS' MANIPULATIONS.

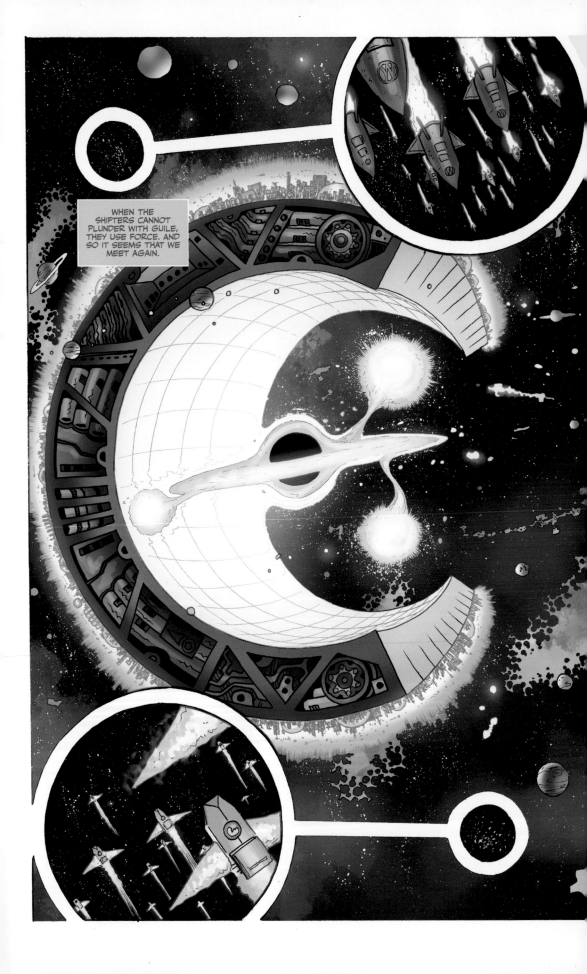

WHEN THE SHIFTERS CANNOT PLUNDER WITH GUILE, THEY USE FORCE. AND SO IT SEEMS THAT WE MEET AGAIN.

TO A MARAUDING COLLECTIVE LIKE THE SHIFTERS, THE CELESTIAL NECKLACE GALAXY PRESENTS A PRIZE LIKE NO OTHER.

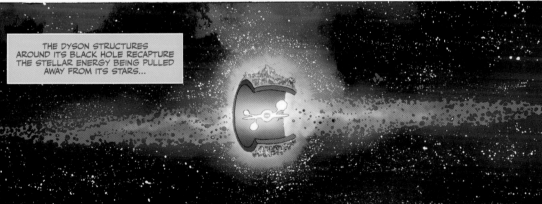

THE DYSON STRUCTURES AROUND ITS BLACK HOLE RECAPTURE THE STELLAR ENERGY BEING PULLED AWAY FROM ITS STARS...

...AND BOUNCE IT BACK TO A STELLAR RELAY NETWORK THAT PROVIDES HEAT AND LIGHT FOR THE PLANETS IN THE SYSTEM.

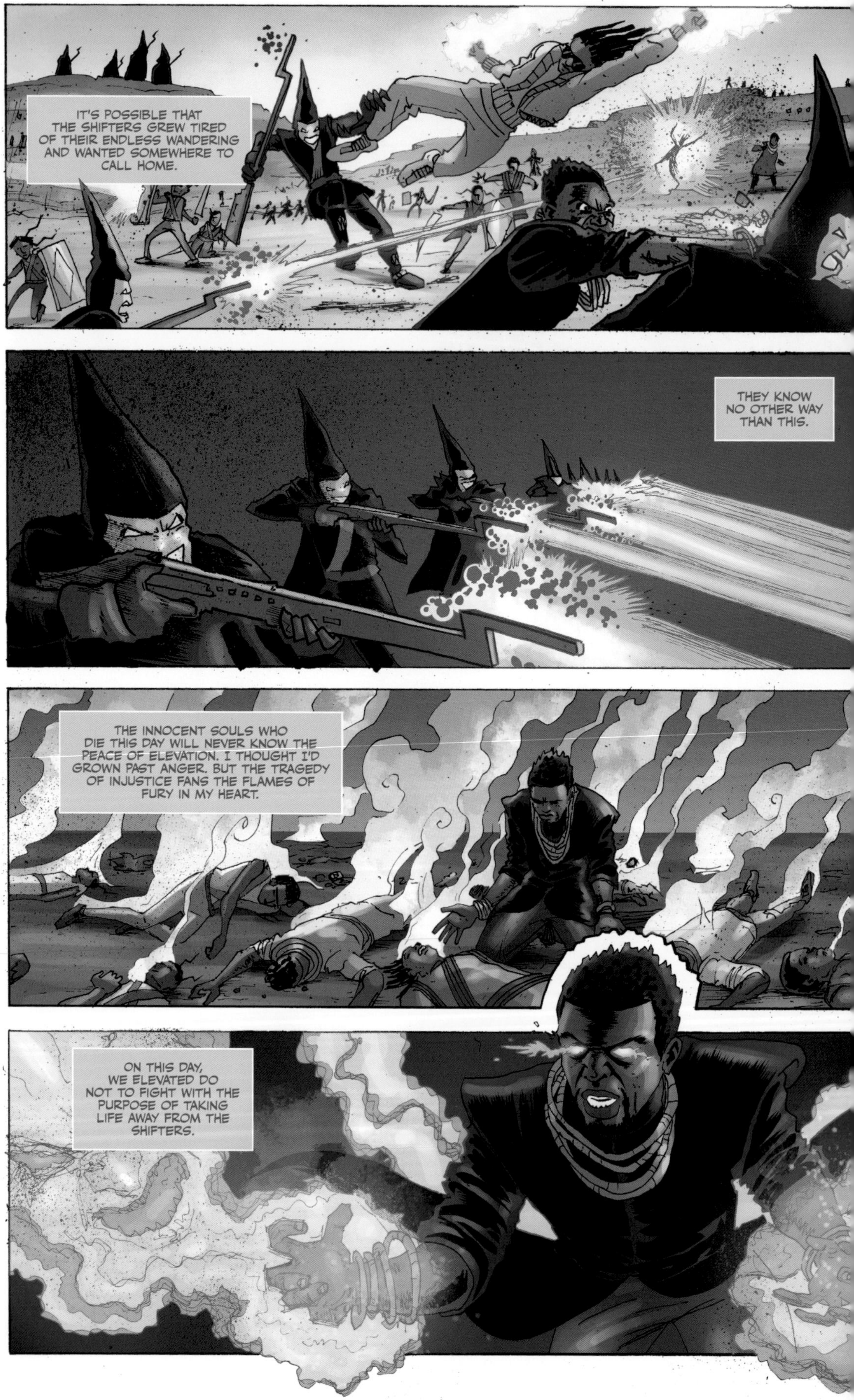
IT'S POSSIBLE THAT THE SHIFTERS GREW TIRED OF THEIR ENDLESS WANDERING AND WANTED SOMEWHERE TO CALL HOME.
THEY KNOW NO OTHER WAY THAN THIS.
THE INNOCENT SOULS WHO DIE THIS DAY WILL NEVER KNOW THE PEACE OF ELEVATION. I THOUGHT I'D GROWN PAST ANGER. BUT THE TRAGEDY OF INJUSTICE FANS THE FLAMES OF FURY IN MY HEART.
ON THIS DAY, WE ELEVATED DO NOT TO FIGHT WITH THE PURPOSE OF TAKING LIFE AWAY FROM THE SHIFTERS.

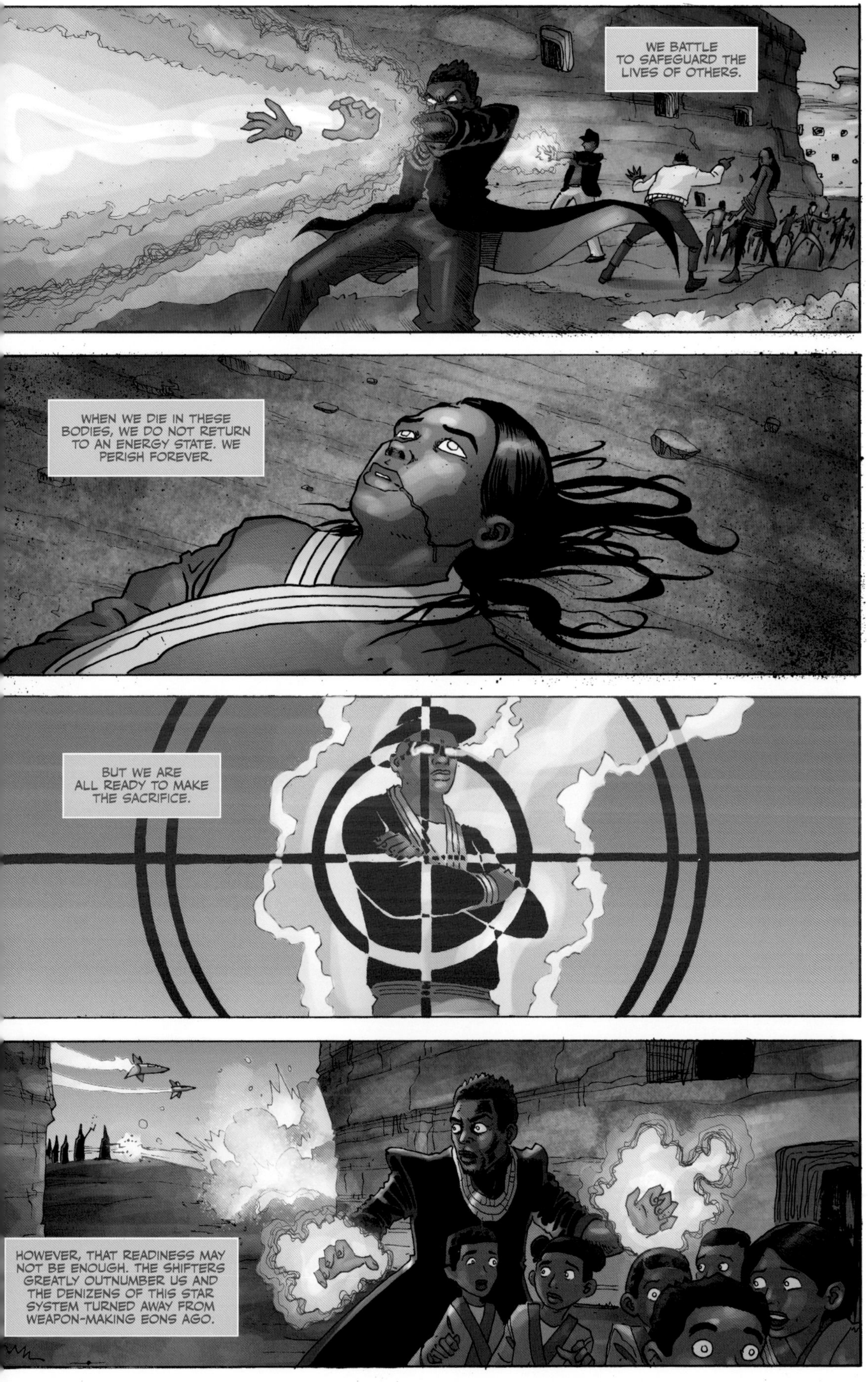

WE BATTLE TO SAFEGUARD THE LIVES OF OTHERS.
WHEN WE DIE IN THESE BODIES, WE DO NOT RETURN TO AN ENERGY STATE. WE PERISH FOREVER.
BUT WE ARE ALL READY TO MAKE THE SACRIFICE.
HOWEVER, THAT READINESS MAY NOT BE ENOUGH. THE SHIFTERS GREATLY OUTNUMBER US AND THE DENIZENS OF THIS STAR SYSTEM TURNED AWAY FROM WEAPON-MAKING EONS AGO.

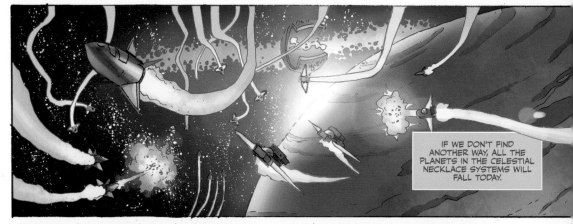

IF WE DON'T FIND ANOTHER WAY, ALL THE PLANETS IN THE CELESTIAL NECKLACE SYSTEMS WILL FALL TODAY.

WE HAVE LIVED AS FLESH. LIVED AS ENERGY. LIVED LONG ENOUGH TO SEE STARS BURST INTO EXISTENCE AND FADE INTO DEATH WITH FLICKERS.

WE'VE ACQUIRED MORE KNOWLEDGE THAN MOST SENTIENT BEINGS CAN EVEN IMAGINE. PLAYED WITH INVISIBLE ENERGIES THAT THEY'LL NEVER SEE.

AND THEN, I REALIZE, IT IS THAT KNOWLEDGE THAT HOLDS THE ANSWER.

IN THOSE SECOND LIVES, WE *LEARNED* HOW TO SPEAK TO QUARKS, SUPERNOVAE, AND PULSARS.

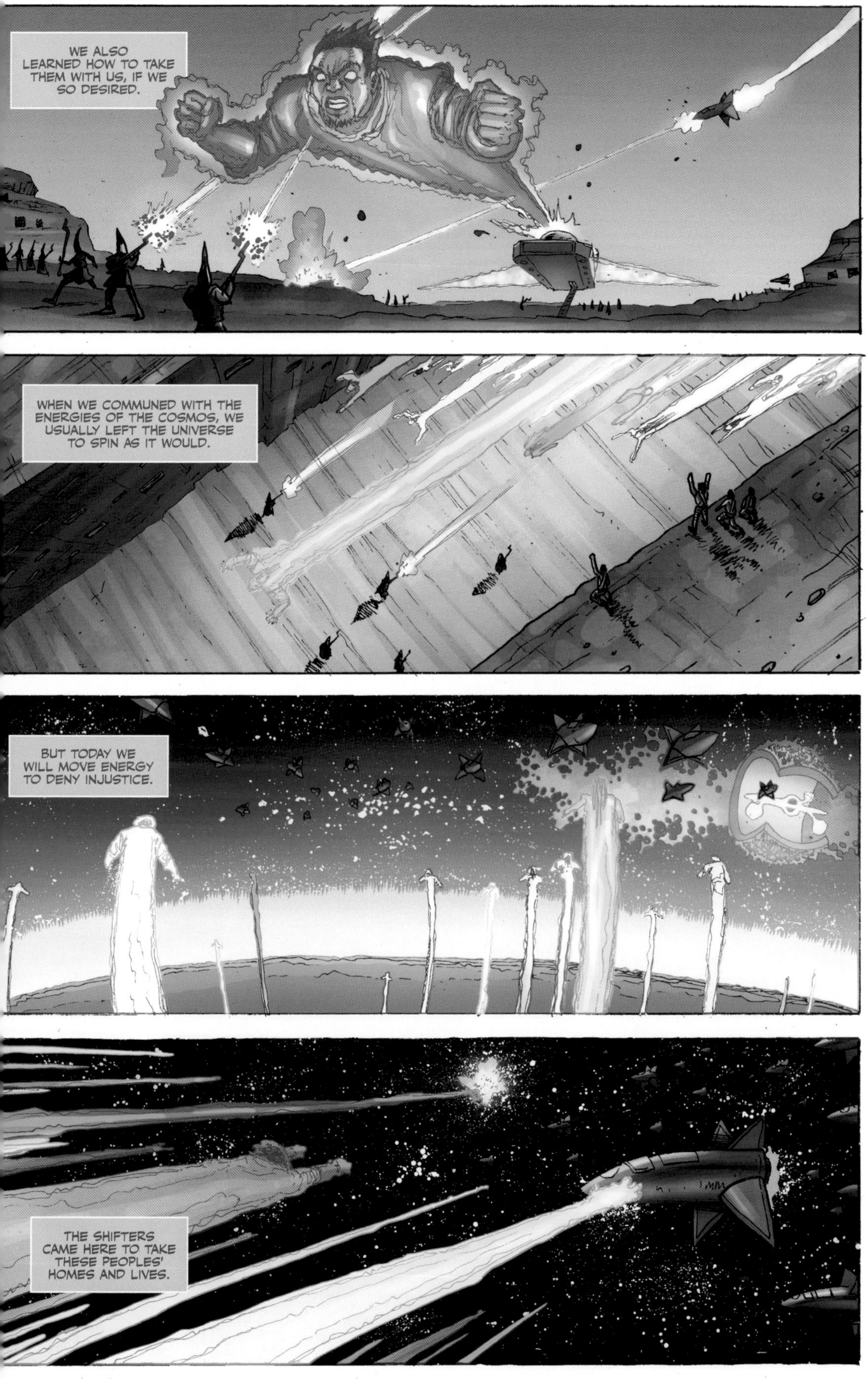
WE ALSO LEARNED HOW TO TAKE THEM WITH US, IF WE SO DESIRED.
WHEN WE COMMUNED WITH THE ENERGIES OF THE COSMOS, WE USUALLY LEFT THE UNIVERSE TO SPIN AS IT WOULD.
BUT TODAY WE WILL MOVE ENERGY TO DENY INJUSTICE.
THE SHIFTERS CAME HERE TO TAKE THESE PEOPLES' HOMES AND LIVES.

INSTEAD, WE DRAIN THEIR SHIPS OF THE POWER THEY NEED TO MAKE WAR.

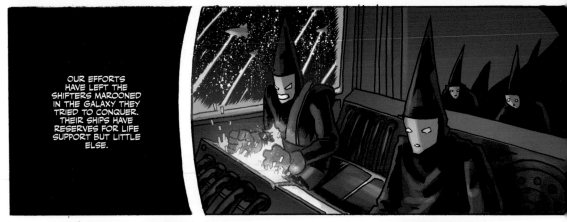

OUR EFFORTS HAVE LEFT THE SHIFTERS MAROONED IN THE GALAXY THEY TRIED TO CONQUER. THEIR SHIPS HAVE RESERVES FOR LIFE SUPPORT BUT LITTLE ELSE.

WHAT HAPPENS NEXT IS UP TO THE PEOPLE OF THE CELESTIAL NECKLACE.

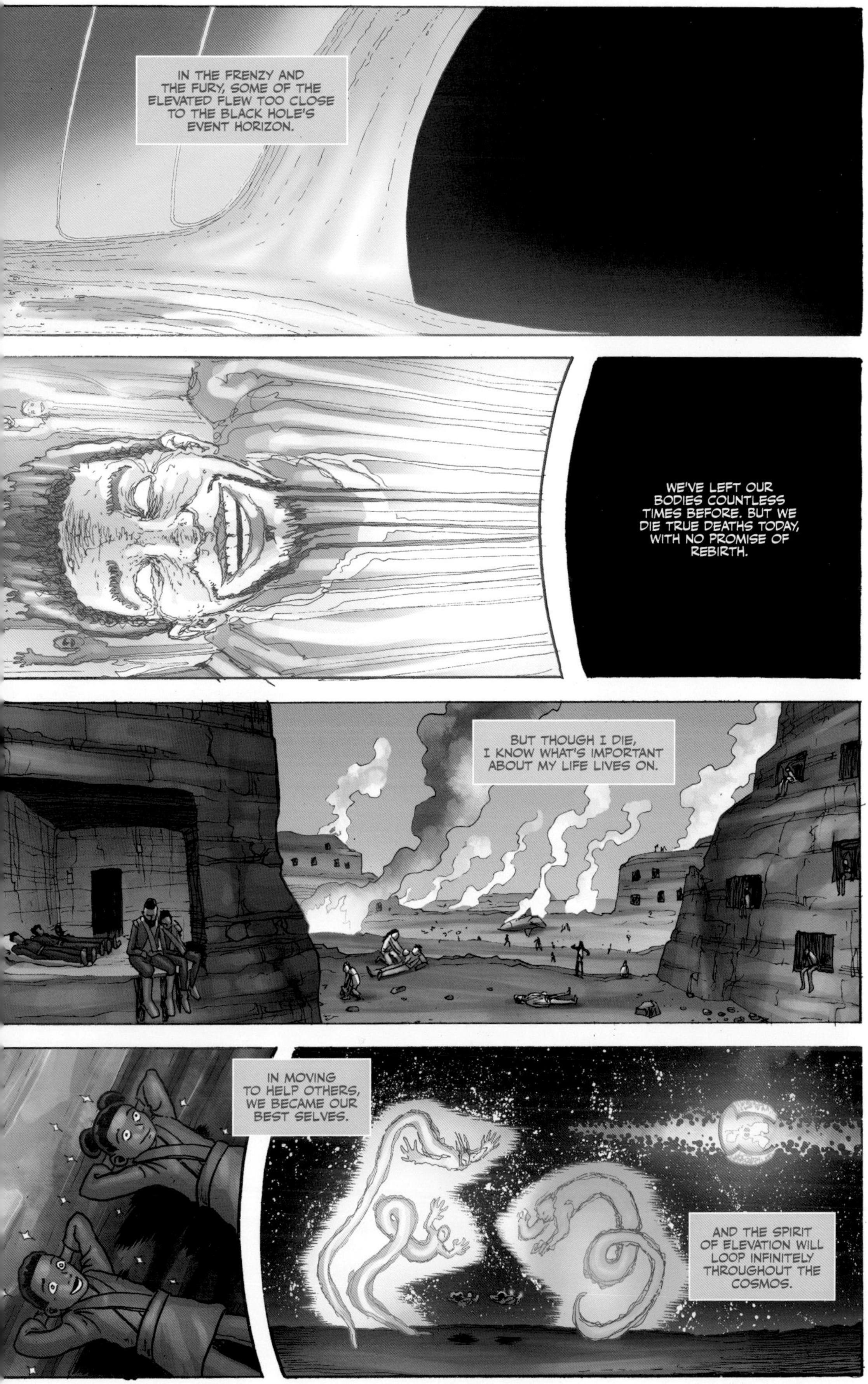
IN THE FRENZY AND THE FURY, SOME OF THE ELEVATED FLEW TOO CLOSE TO THE BLACK HOLE'S EVENT HORIZON.
WE'VE LEFT OUR BODIES COUNTLESS TIMES BEFORE. BUT WE DIE TRUE DEATHS TODAY, WITH NO PROMISE OF REBIRTH.
BUT THOUGH I DIE, I KNOW WHAT'S IMPORTANT ABOUT MY LIFE LIVES ON.
IN MOVING TO HELP OTHERS, WE BECAME OUR BEST SELVES.
AND THE SPIRIT OF ELEVATION WILL LOOP INFINITELY THROUGHOUT THE COSMOS.

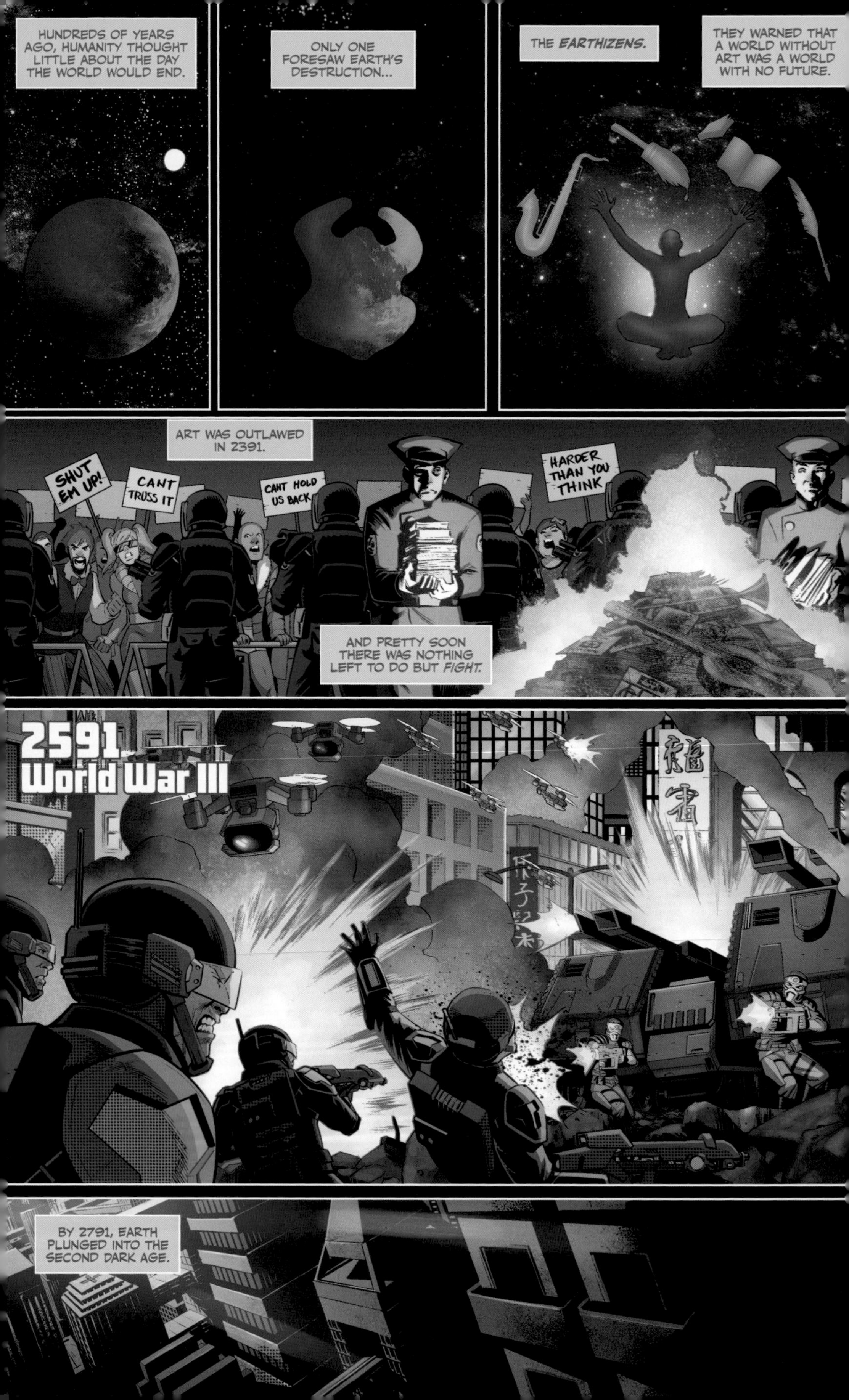

HUNDREDS OF YEARS AGO, HUMANITY THOUGHT LITTLE ABOUT THE DAY THE WORLD WOULD END.
ONLY ONE FORESAW EARTH'S DESTRUCTION...
THE *EARTHIZENS.*
THEY WARNED THAT A WORLD WITHOUT ART WAS A WORLD WITH NO FUTURE.
ART WAS OUTLAWED IN 2391.
SHUT EM UP!
CANT TRUSS IT
CANT HOLD US BACK
HARDER THAN YOU THINK
AND PRETTY SOON THERE WAS NOTHING LEFT TO DO BUT *FIGHT.*
2591.
World War III
BY 2791, EARTH PLUNGED INTO THE SECOND DARK AGE.

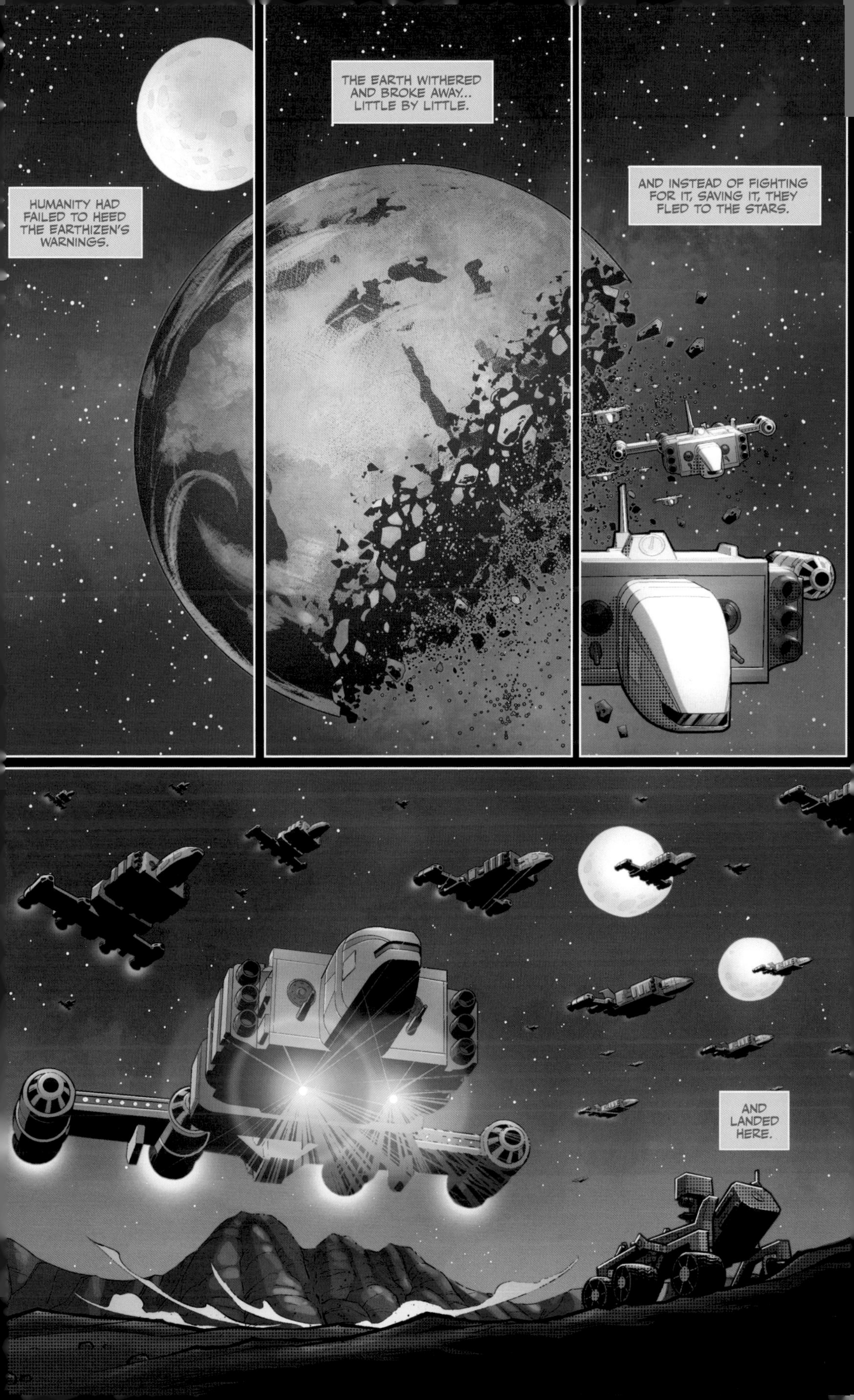
HUMANITY HAD FAILED TO HEED THE EARTHIZEN'S WARNINGS.
THE EARTH WITHERED AND BROKE AWAY... LITTLE BY LITTLE.
AND INSTEAD OF FIGHTING FOR IT, SAVING IT, THEY FLED TO THE STARS.
AND LANDED HERE.

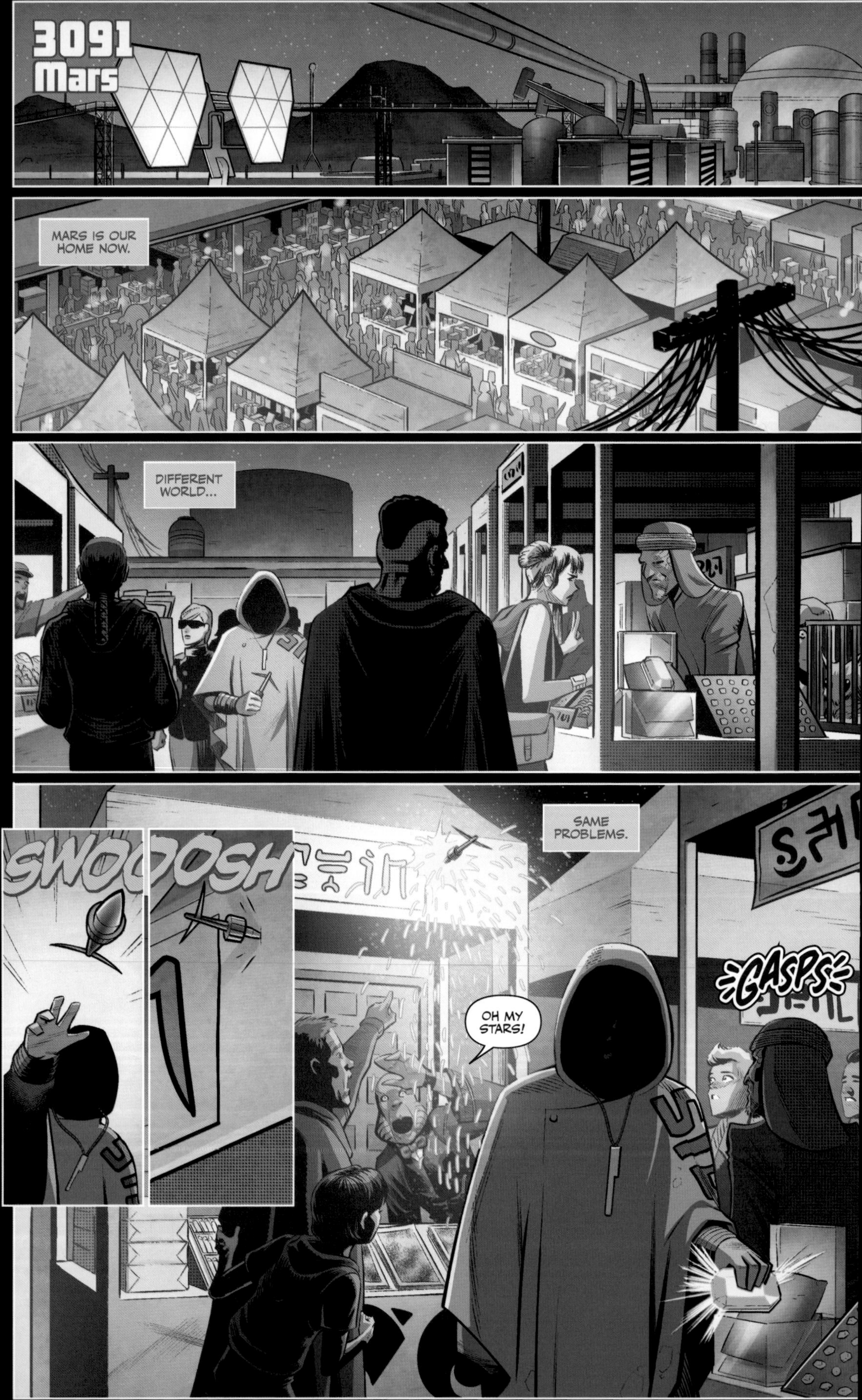
3091
Mars
MARS IS OUR HOME NOW.
DIFFERENT WORLD...
SAME PROBLEMS.
SWOOOSH
OH MY STARS!
GASPS

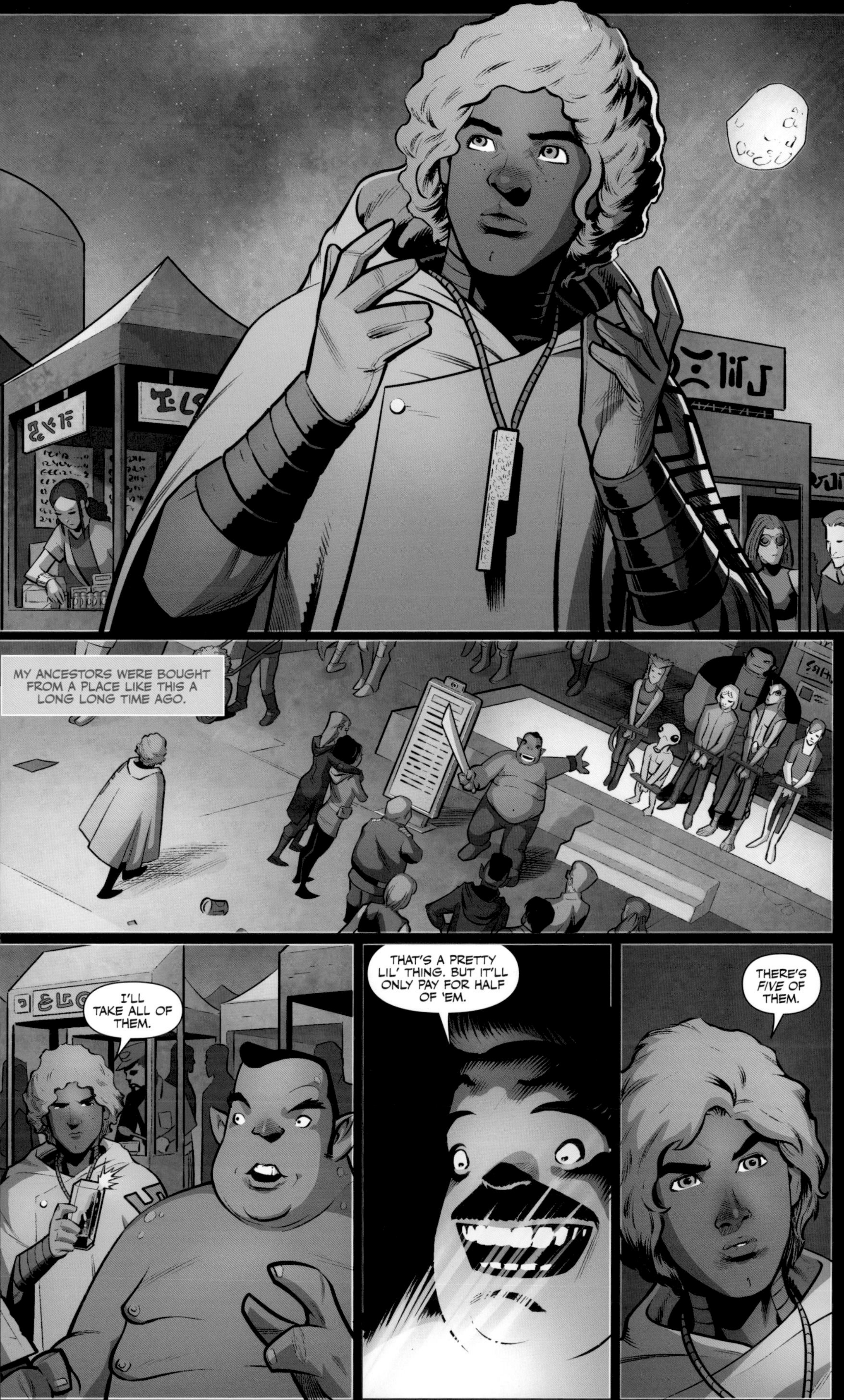
MY ANCESTORS WERE BOUGHT FROM A PLACE LIKE THIS A LONG LONG TIME AGO.
I'LL TAKE ALL OF THEM.
THAT'S A PRETTY LIL' THING. BUT IT'LL ONLY PAY FOR HALF OF 'EM.
THERE'S *FIVE* OF THEM.

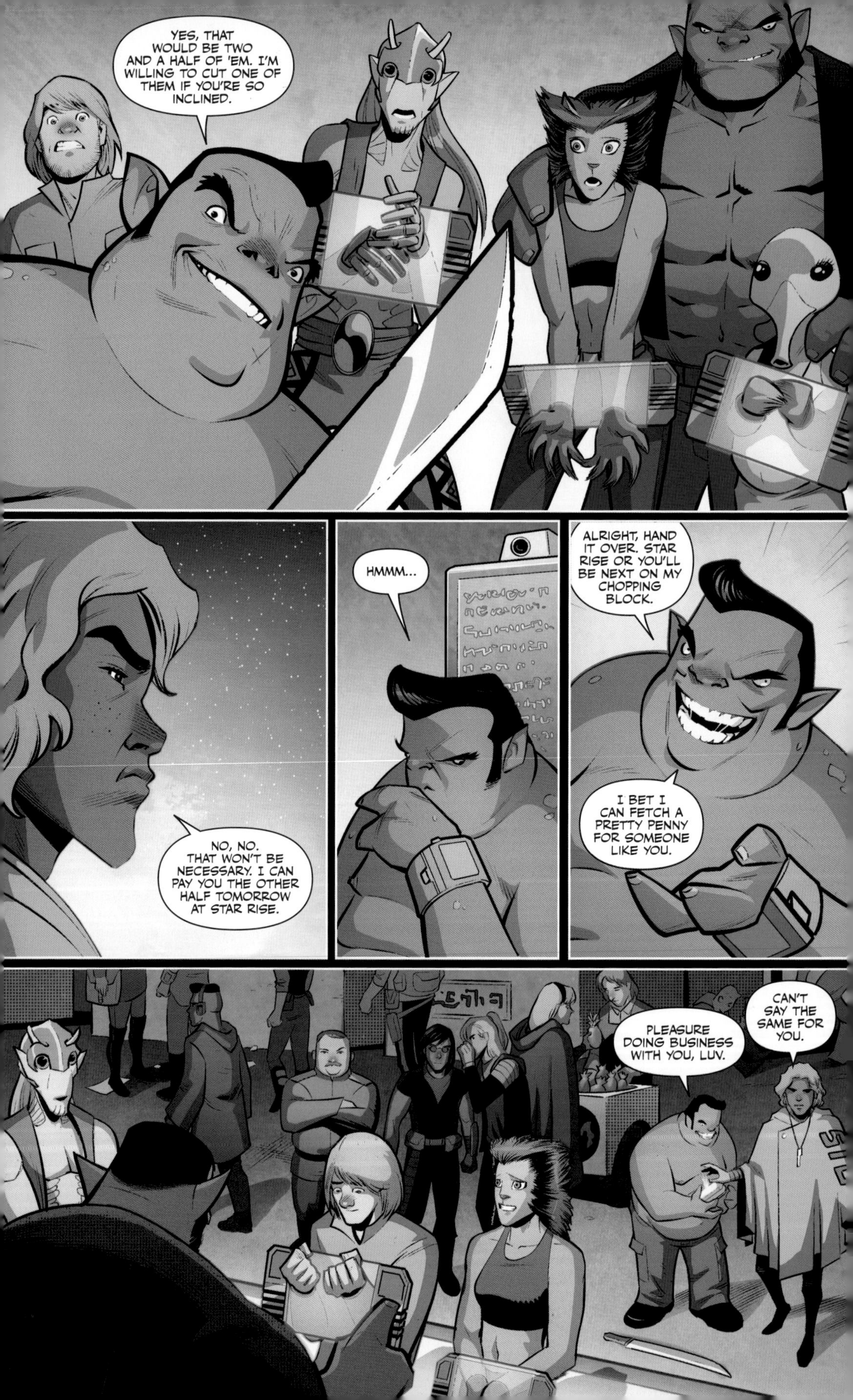
YES, THAT WOULD BE TWO AND A HALF OF 'EM. I'M WILLING TO CUT ONE OF THEM IF YOU'RE SO INCLINED.
NO, NO. THAT WON'T BE NECESSARY. I CAN PAY YOU THE OTHER HALF TOMORROW AT STAR RISE.
HMMM...
ALRIGHT, HAND IT OVER. STAR RISE OR YOU'LL BE NEXT ON MY CHOPPING BLOCK.
I BET I CAN FETCH A PRETTY PENNY FOR SOMEONE LIKE YOU.
PLEASURE DOING BUSINESS WITH YOU, LUV.
CAN'T SAY THE SAME FOR YOU.

I GUESS I CAN CALL IT A DAY THEN. SEE YOU TOMORROW SWEETNESS.

YOU'RE ALL FREE TO GO. I'M NO *MASTER*, JUST A HUMANITARIAN.

HEY, WAIT UP!

WHAT DO YA WANT?

ᛕᛟᛞᛟᛃ ᛏᚾ ᛖ ᛃᛒᚻᛞᛟᛞᛟᚷ ᛏᚻᛖᚷᛃ'ᛏ ᛏᚻᛖᚷᚷ'ᛏ ᛚᚾᛒ ᛚᛘᛒᛃ ᛏᚷᚷ ᚷᛒᛞᚾᛃᛏᚷ ᛟᚾᚷᛒᚷᛏᛃᛏ

HUH?

SORRY, I JUST WANTED TO SAY I THANK MY LUCKY STARS THAT YOU CAME TODAY OF ALL DAYS.

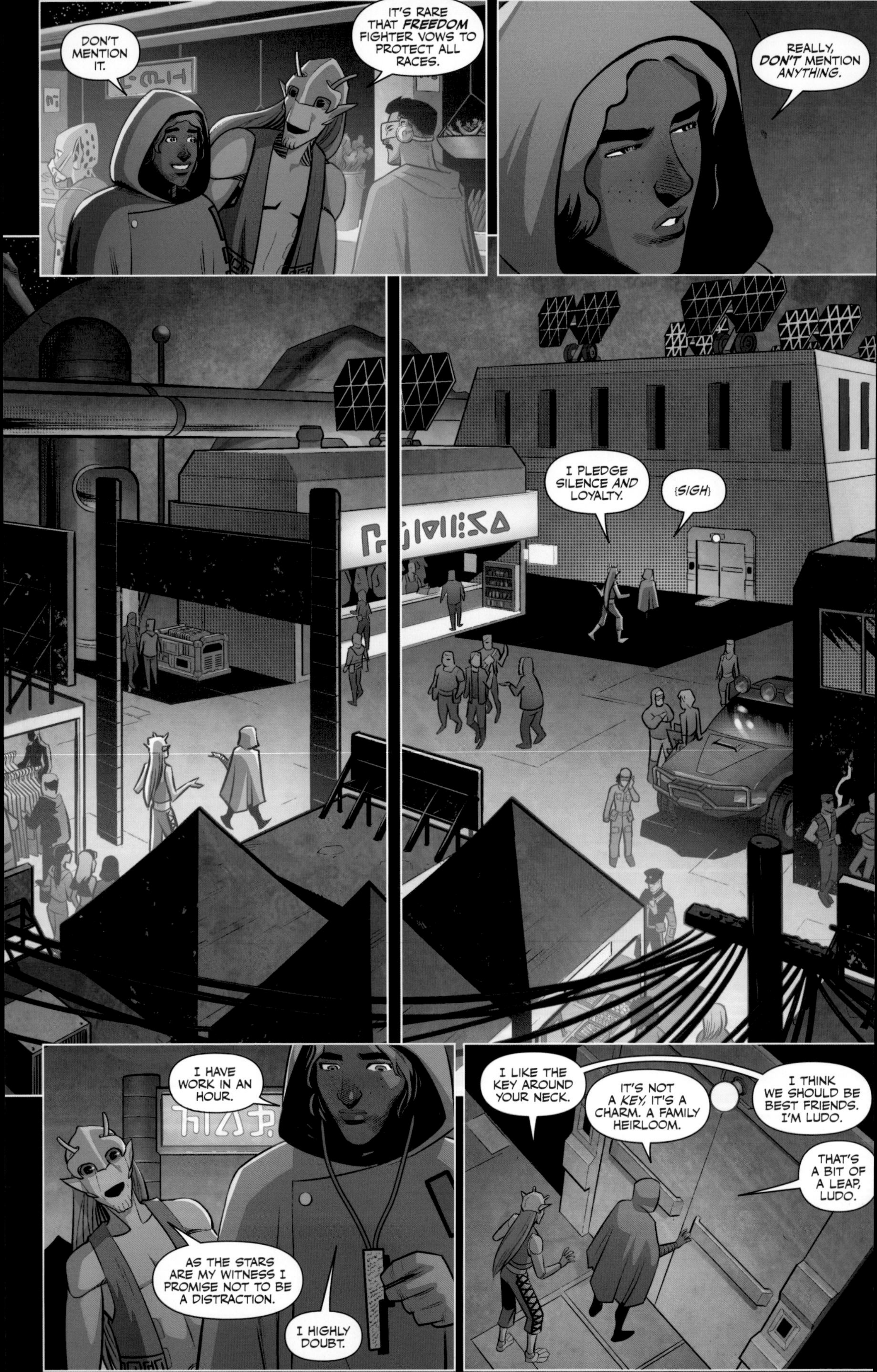
DON'T MENTION IT.
IT'S RARE THAT *FREEDOM* FIGHTER VOWS TO PROTECT ALL RACES.
REALLY, *DON'T* MENTION *ANYTHING*.
I PLEDGE SILENCE *AND* LOYALTY.
{*SIGH*}
I HAVE WORK IN AN HOUR.
AS THE STARS ARE MY WITNESS I PROMISE NOT TO BE A DISTRACTION.
I HIGHLY DOUBT.
I LIKE THE KEY AROUND YOUR NECK.
IT'S NOT A *KEY*, IT'S A CHARM. A FAMILY HEIRLOOM.
I THINK WE SHOULD BE BEST FRIENDS. I'M LUDO.
THAT'S A BIT OF A LEAP, LUDO.

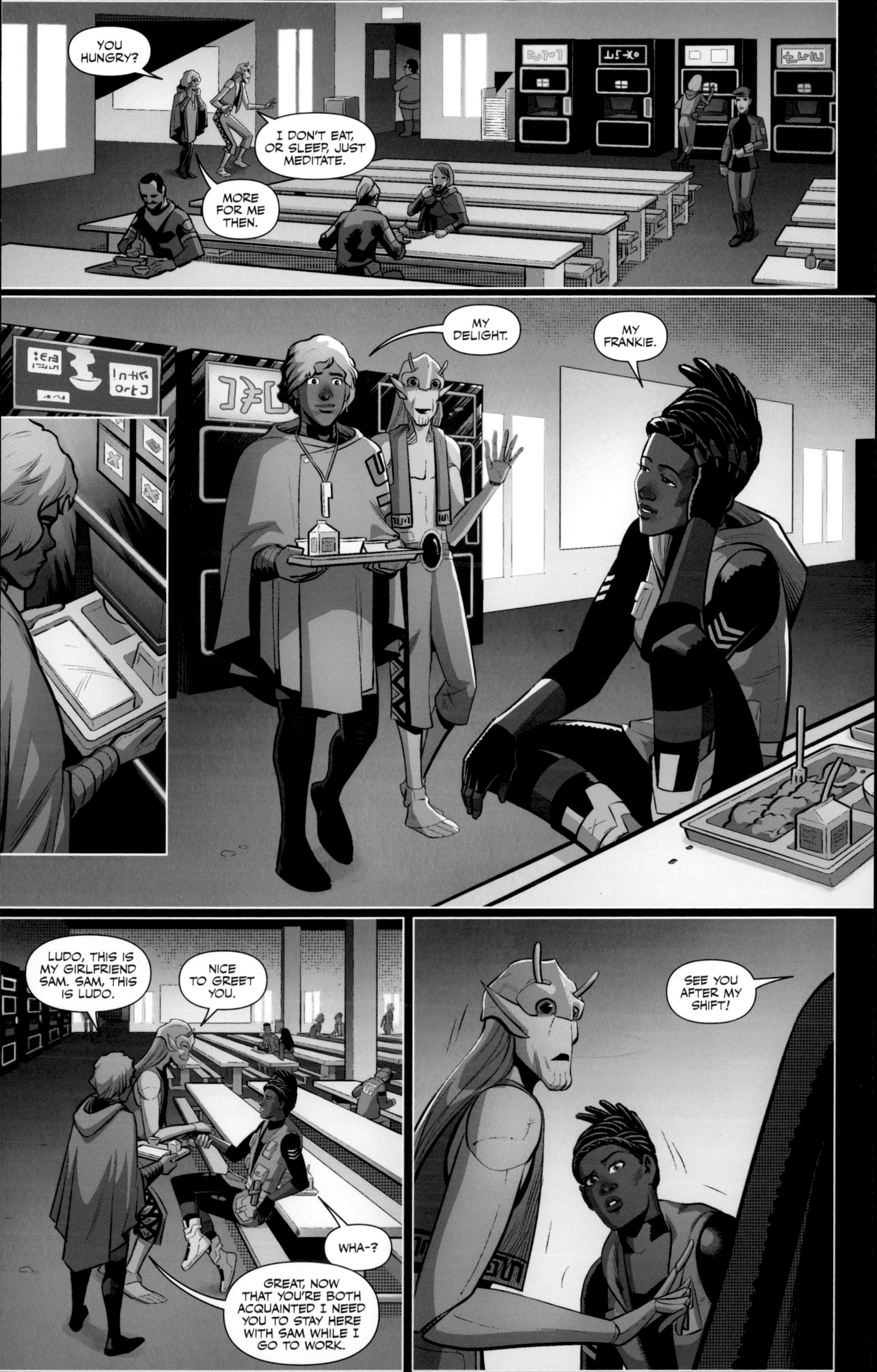
YOU HUNGRY?
I DON'T EAT, OR SLEEP, JUST MEDITATE.
MORE FOR ME THEN.
MY DELIGHT.
MY FRANKIE.
LUDO, THIS IS MY GIRLFRIEND SAM. SAM, THIS IS LUDO.
NICE TO GREET YOU.
WHA-?
GREAT, NOW THAT YOU'RE BOTH ACQUAINTED I NEED YOU TO STAY HERE WITH SAM WHILE I GO TO WORK.
SEE YOU AFTER MY SHIFT!

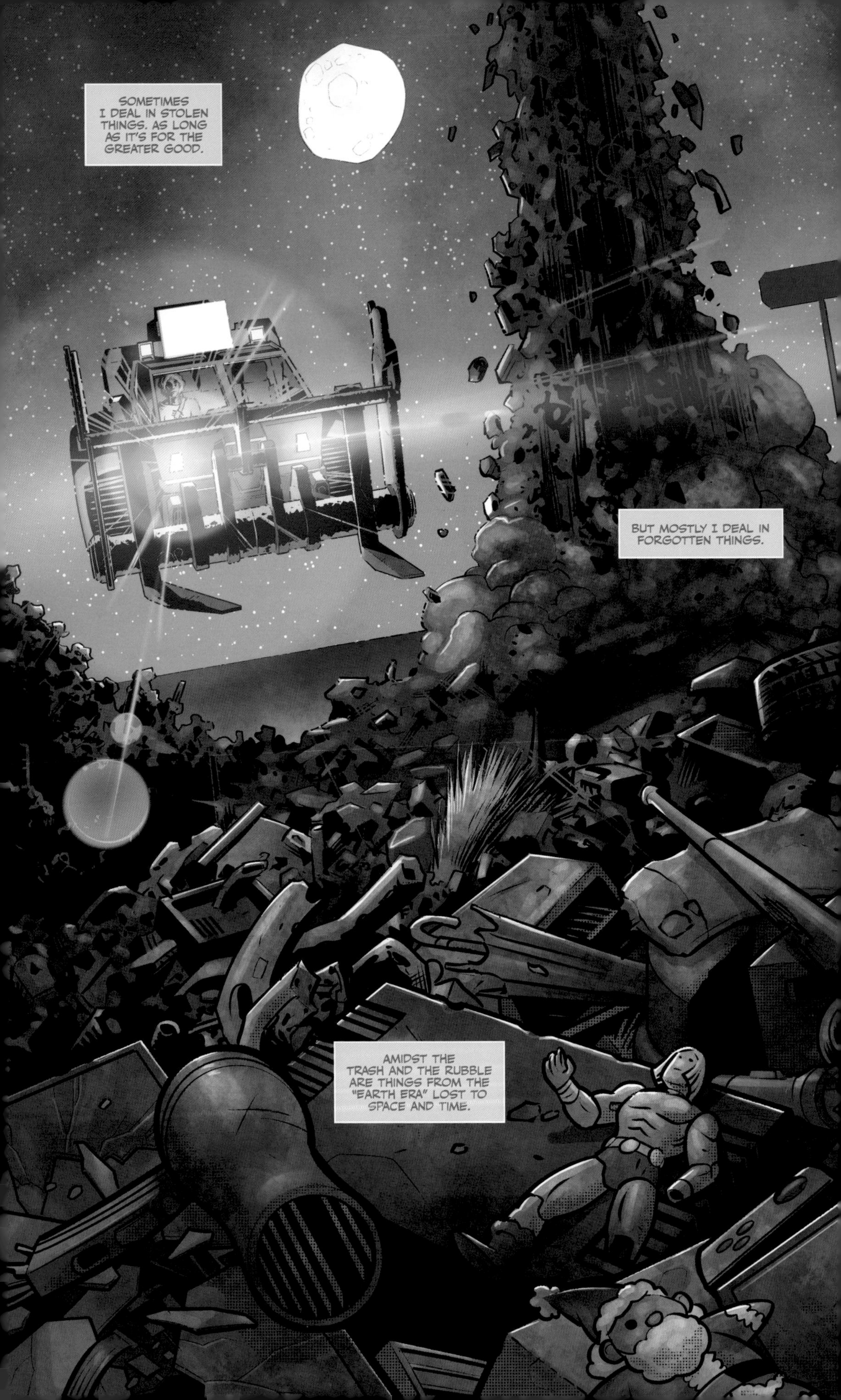
SOMETIMES I DEAL IN STOLEN THINGS. AS LONG AS IT'S FOR THE GREATER GOOD.
BUT MOSTLY I DEAL IN FORGOTTEN THINGS.
AMIDST THE TRASH AND THE RUBBLE ARE THINGS FROM THE "EARTH ERA" LOST TO SPACE AND TIME.

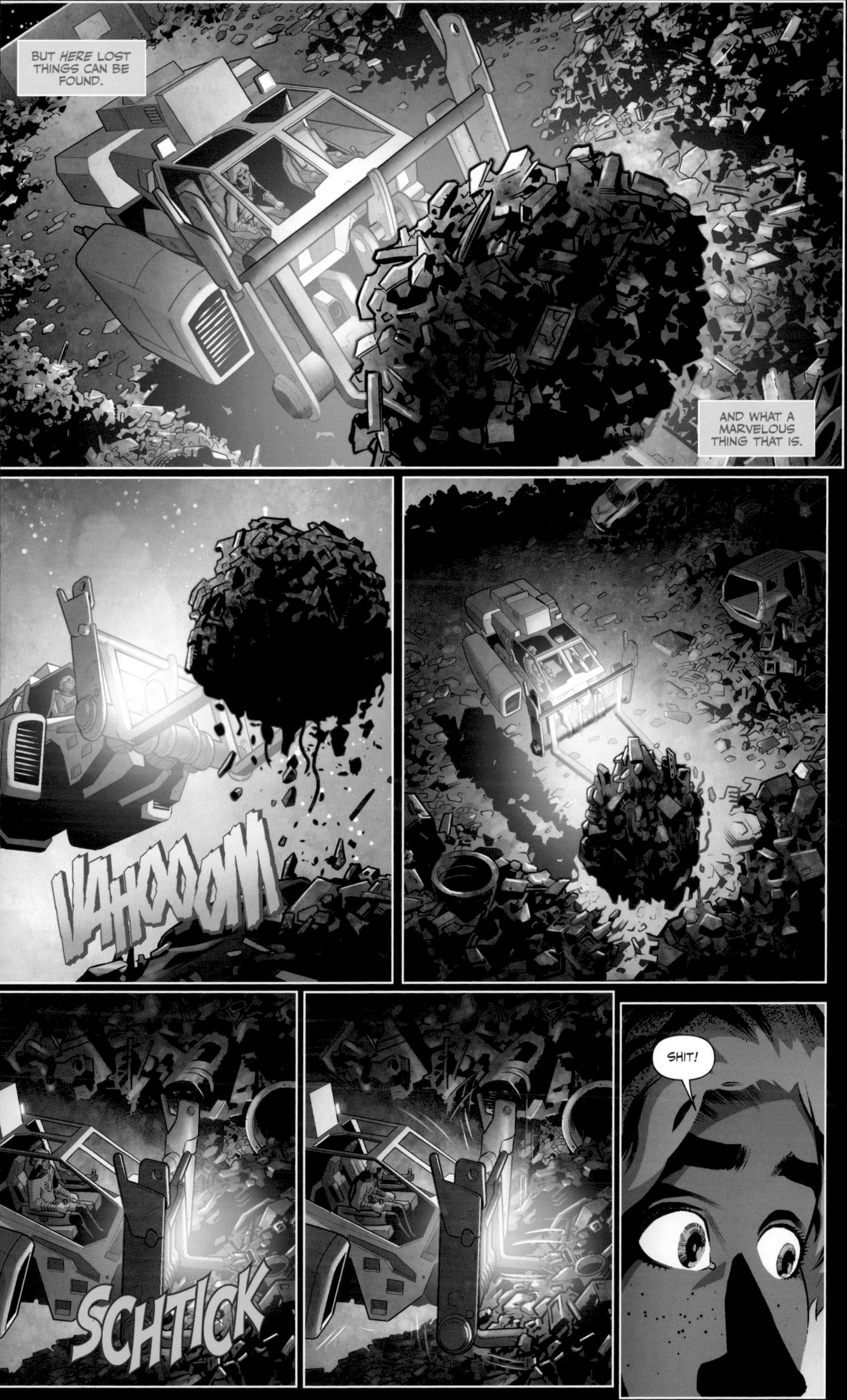

BUT *HERE* LOST THINGS CAN BE FOUND.
AND WHAT A MARVELOUS THING THAT IS.
VAHOOOM
SCHTICK
SHIT!

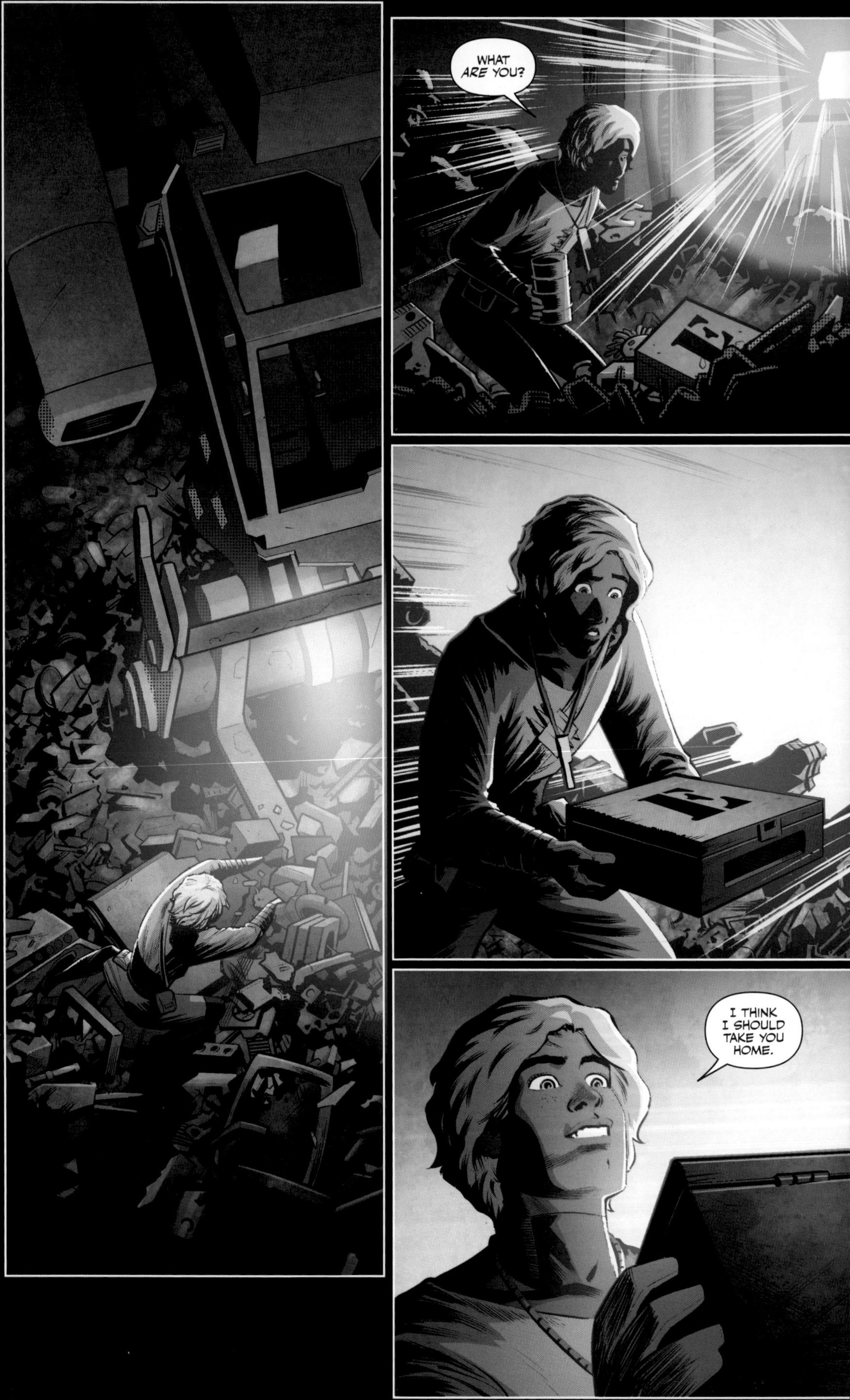
WHAT ARE YOU?
I THINK I SHOULD TAKE YOU HOME.

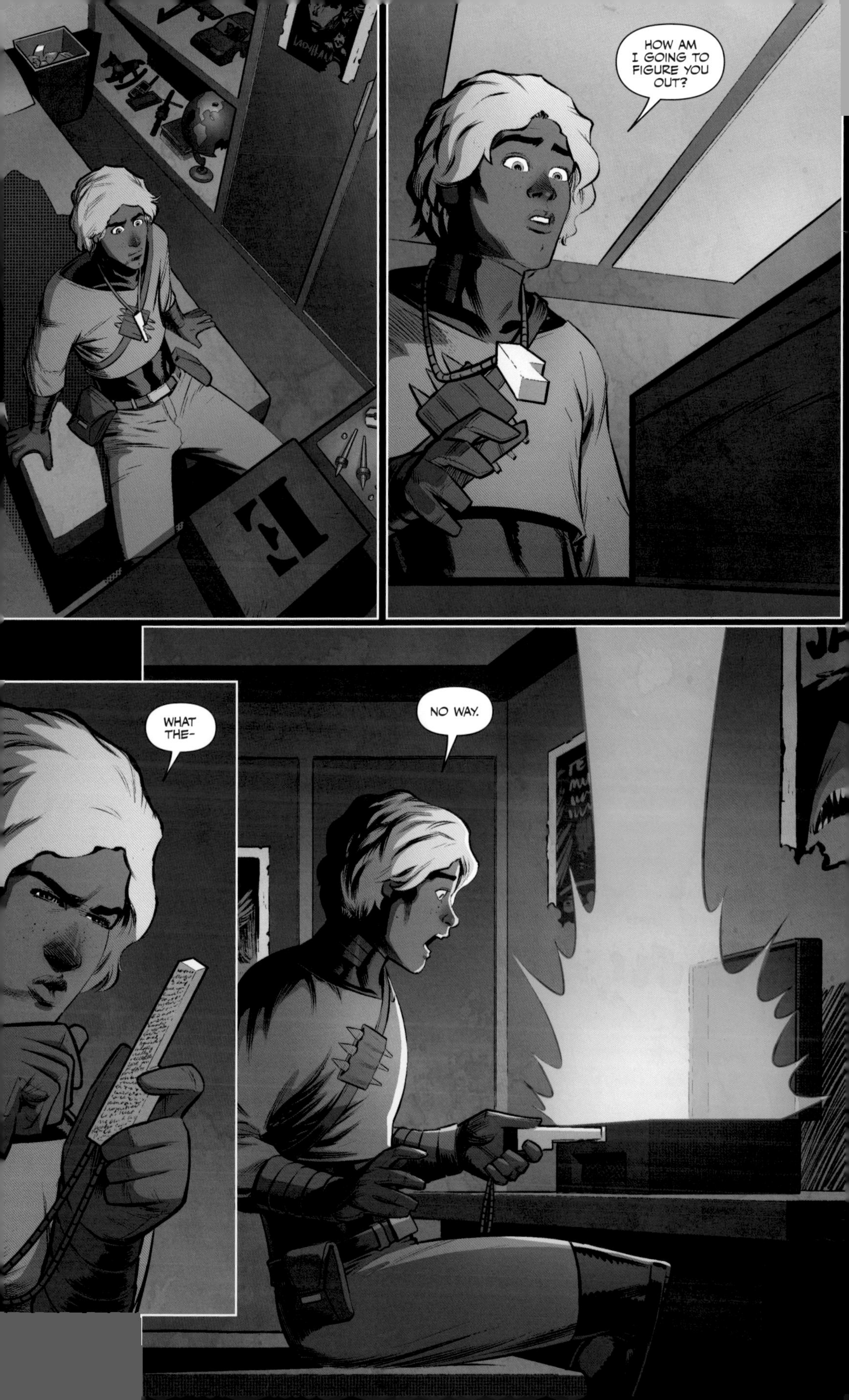
HOW AM I GOING TO FIGURE YOU OUT?
WHAT THE-
NO WAY.

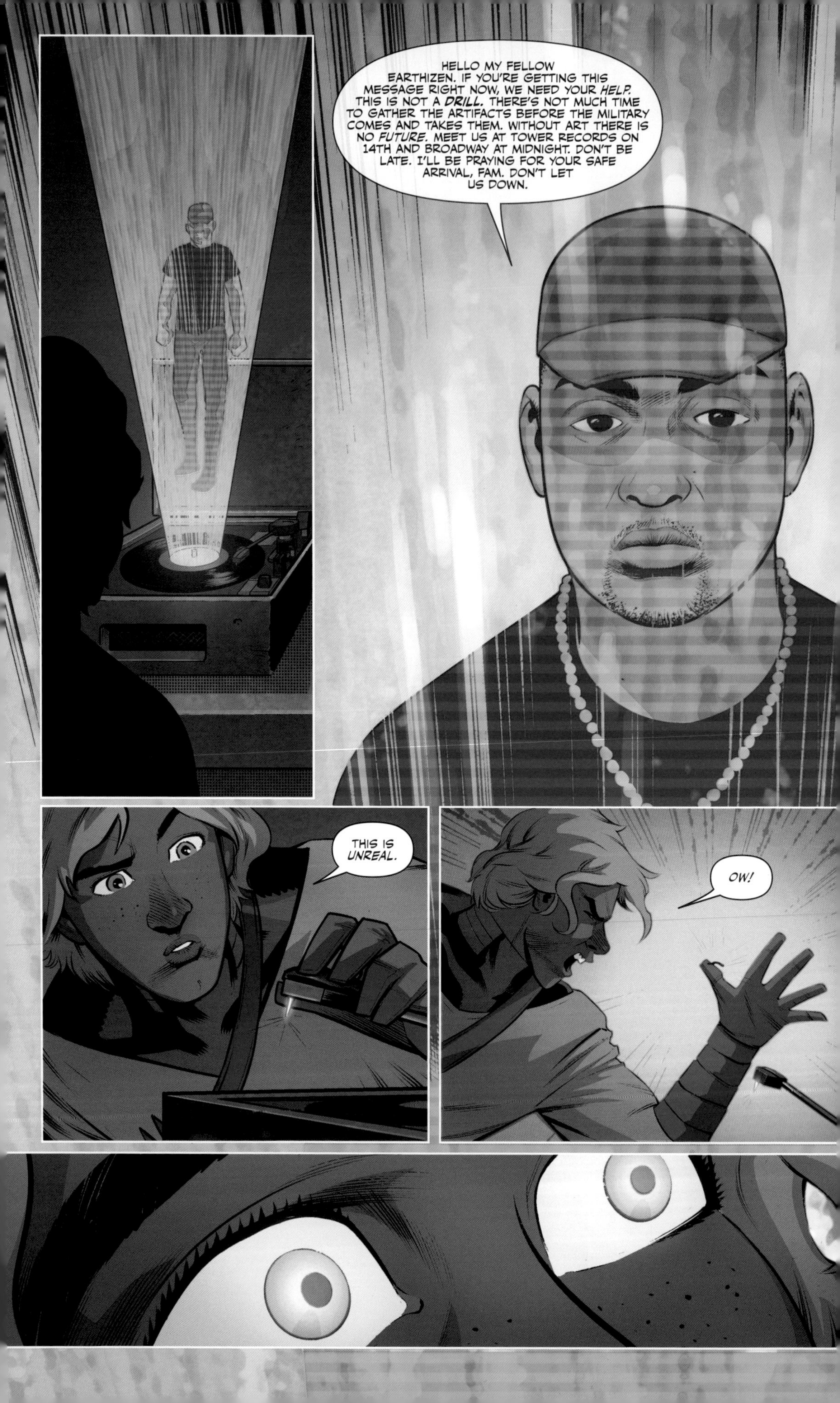
HELLO MY FELLOW EARTHIZEN. IF YOU'RE GETTING THIS MESSAGE RIGHT NOW, WE NEED YOUR *HELP.* THIS IS NOT A ***DRILL.*** THERE'S NOT MUCH TIME TO GATHER THE ARTIFACTS BEFORE THE MILITARY COMES AND TAKES THEM. WITHOUT ART THERE IS NO *FUTURE.* MEET US AT TOWER RECORDS ON 14TH AND BROADWAY AT MIDNIGHT. DON'T BE LATE. I'LL BE PRAYING FOR YOUR SAFE ARRIVAL, FAM. DON'T LET US DOWN.
THIS IS *UNREAL.*
OW!

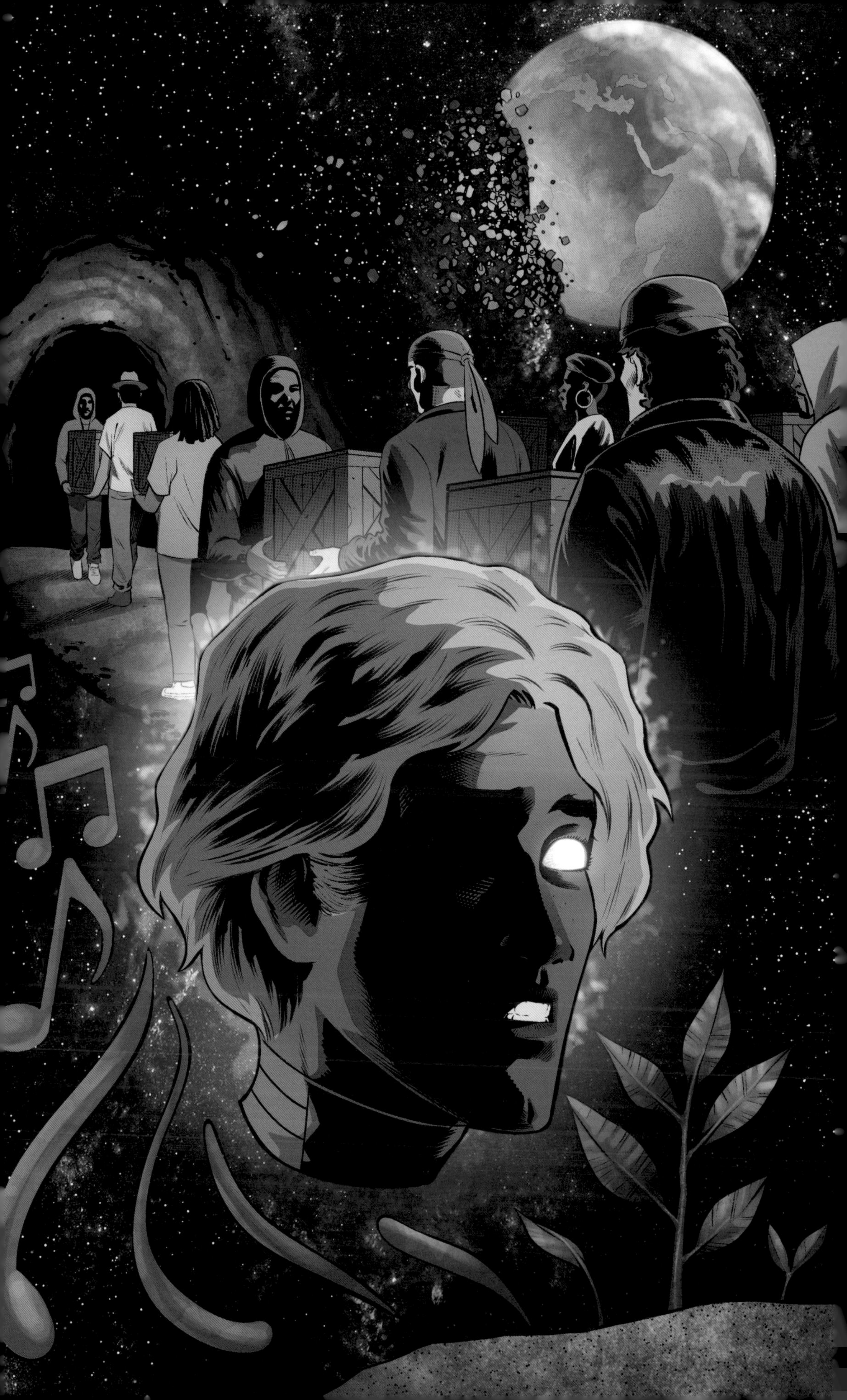

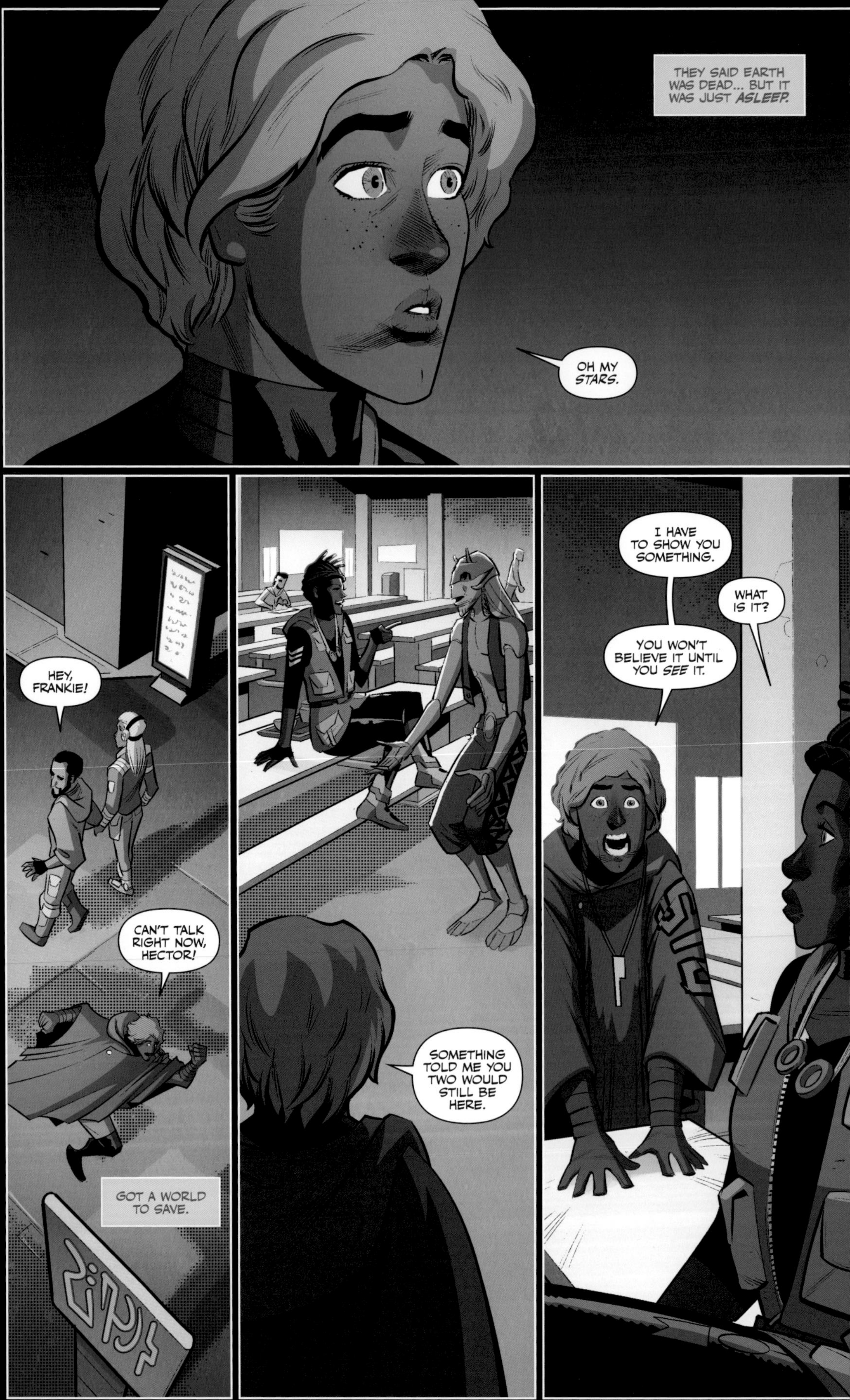
THEY SAID EARTH WAS DEAD... BUT IT WAS JUST *ASLEEP.*
OH MY *STARS.*
HEY, FRANKIE!
CAN'T TALK RIGHT NOW, HECTOR!
GOT A WORLD TO SAVE.
SOMETHING TOLD ME YOU TWO WOULD STILL BE HERE.
I HAVE TO SHOW YOU SOMETHING.
WHAT IS IT?
YOU WON'T BELIEVE IT UNTIL YOU *SEE* IT.

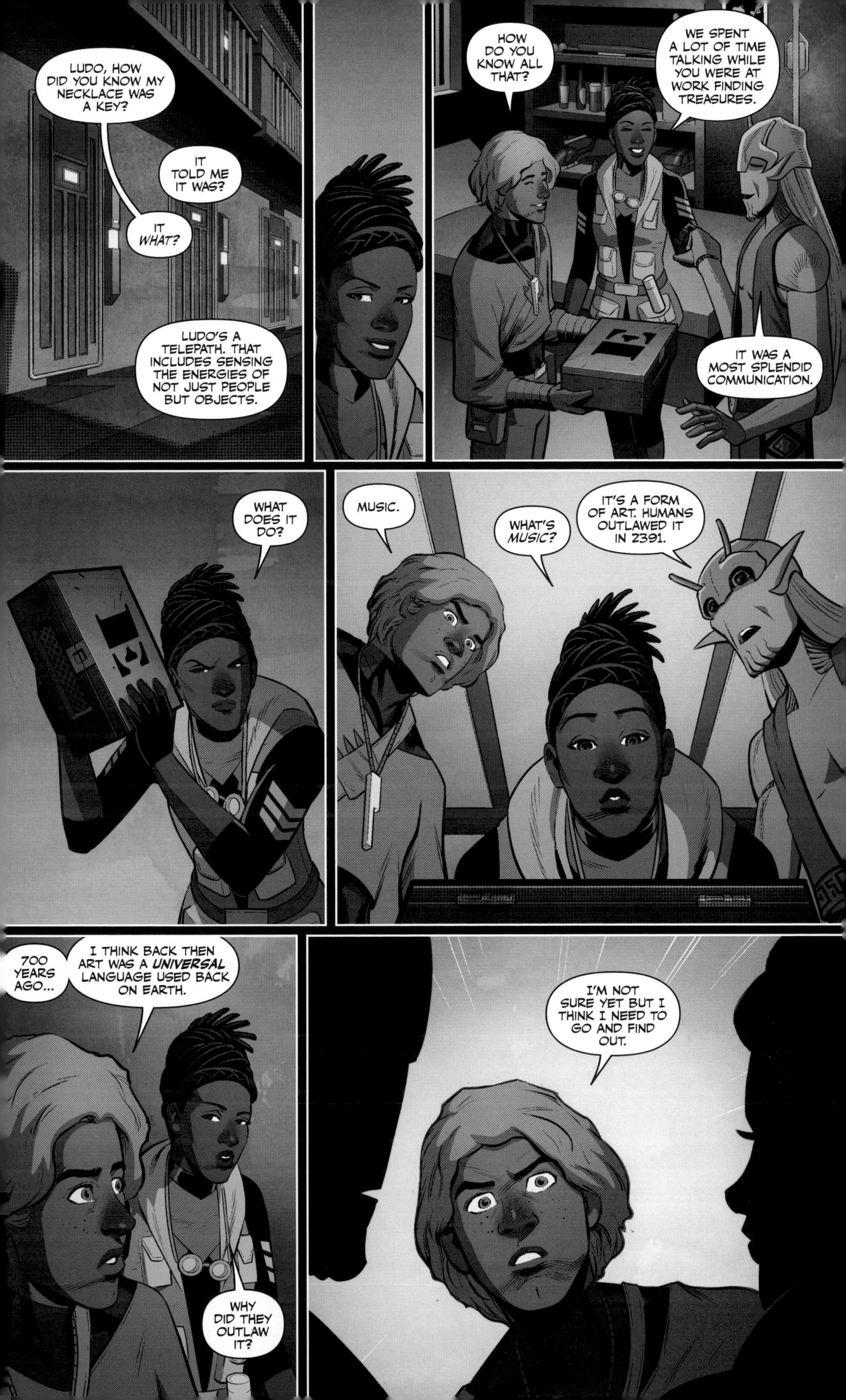
LUDO, HOW DID YOU KNOW MY NECKLACE WAS A KEY?
IT TOLD ME IT WAS?
IT *WHAT?*
LUDO'S A TELEPATH. THAT INCLUDES SENSING THE ENERGIES OF NOT JUST PEOPLE BUT OBJECTS.
HOW DO YOU KNOW ALL THAT?
WE SPENT A LOT OF TIME TALKING WHILE YOU WERE AT WORK FINDING TREASURES.
IT WAS A MOST SPLENDID COMMUNICATION.
WHAT DOES IT DO?
MUSIC.
WHAT'S *MUSIC?*
IT'S A FORM OF ART. HUMANS OUTLAWED IT IN 2391.
700 YEARS AGO...
I THINK BACK THEN ART WAS A *UNIVERSAL* LANGUAGE USED BACK ON EARTH.
WHY DID THEY OUTLAW IT?
I'M NOT SURE YET BUT I THINK I NEED TO GO AND FIND OUT.

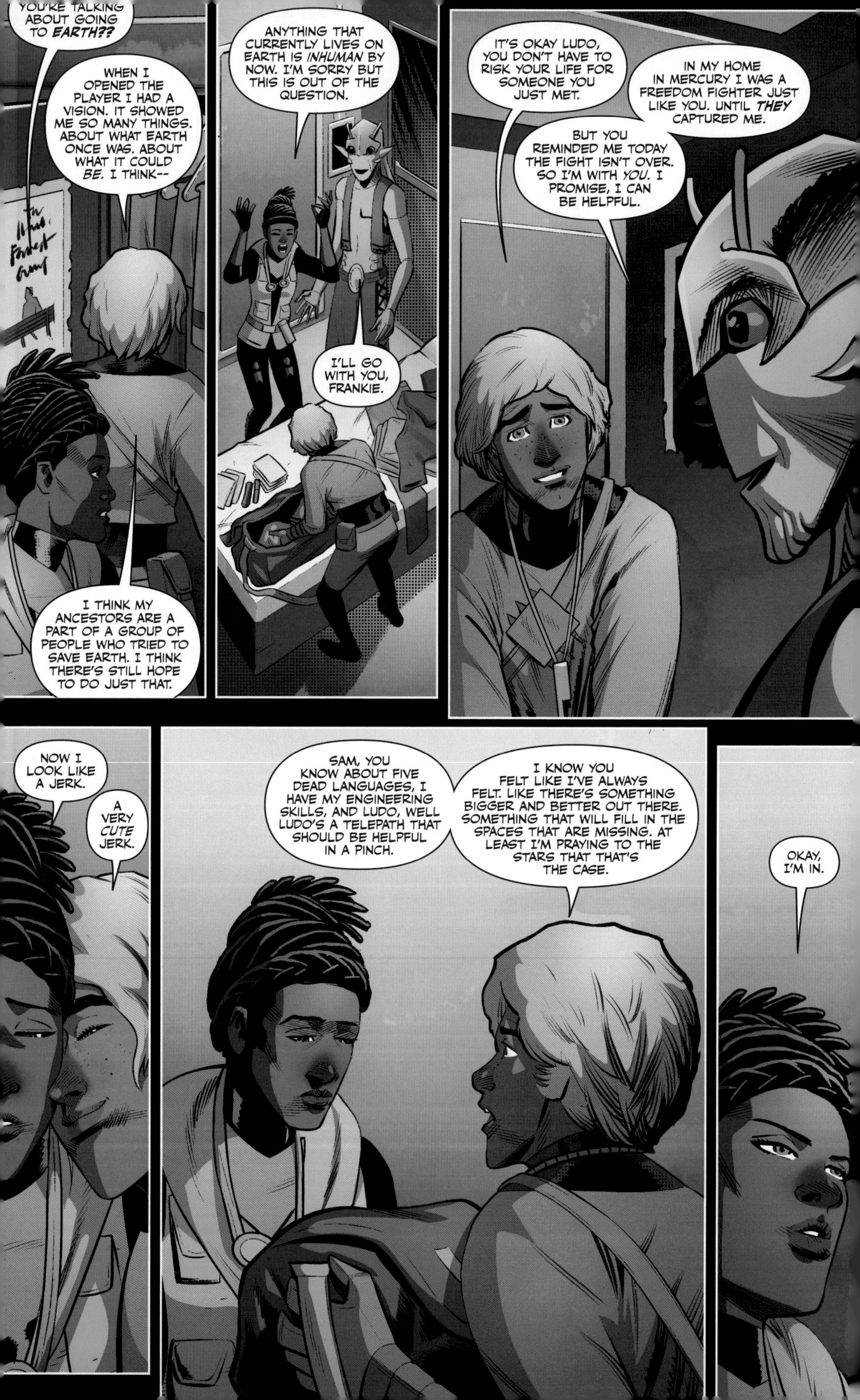
YOU'RE TALKING ABOUT GOING TO EARTH??
WHEN I OPENED THE PLAYER I HAD A VISION. IT SHOWED ME SO MANY THINGS. ABOUT WHAT EARTH ONCE WAS. ABOUT WHAT IT COULD BE. I THINK--
I THINK MY ANCESTORS ARE A PART OF A GROUP OF PEOPLE WHO TRIED TO SAVE EARTH. I THINK THERE'S STILL HOPE TO DO JUST THAT.
ANYTHING THAT CURRENTLY LIVES ON EARTH IS INHUMAN BY NOW. I'M SORRY BUT THIS IS OUT OF THE QUESTION.
I'LL GO WITH YOU, FRANKIE.
IT'S OKAY LUDO, YOU DON'T HAVE TO RISK YOUR LIFE FOR SOMEONE YOU JUST MET.
IN MY HOME IN MERCURY I WAS A FREEDOM FIGHTER JUST LIKE YOU. UNTIL THEY CAPTURED ME.
BUT YOU REMINDED ME TODAY THE FIGHT ISN'T OVER. SO I'M WITH YOU. I PROMISE, I CAN BE HELPFUL.
NOW I LOOK LIKE A JERK.
A VERY CUTE JERK.
SAM, YOU KNOW ABOUT FIVE DEAD LANGUAGES, I HAVE MY ENGINEERING SKILLS, AND LUDO, WELL LUDO'S A TELEPATH THAT SHOULD BE HELPFUL IN A PINCH.
I KNOW YOU FELT LIKE I'VE ALWAYS FELT. LIKE THERE'S SOMETHING BIGGER AND BETTER OUT THERE. SOMETHING THAT WILL FILL IN THE SPACES THAT ARE MISSING. AT LEAST I'M PRAYING TO THE STARS THAT THAT'S THE CASE.
OKAY, I'M IN.

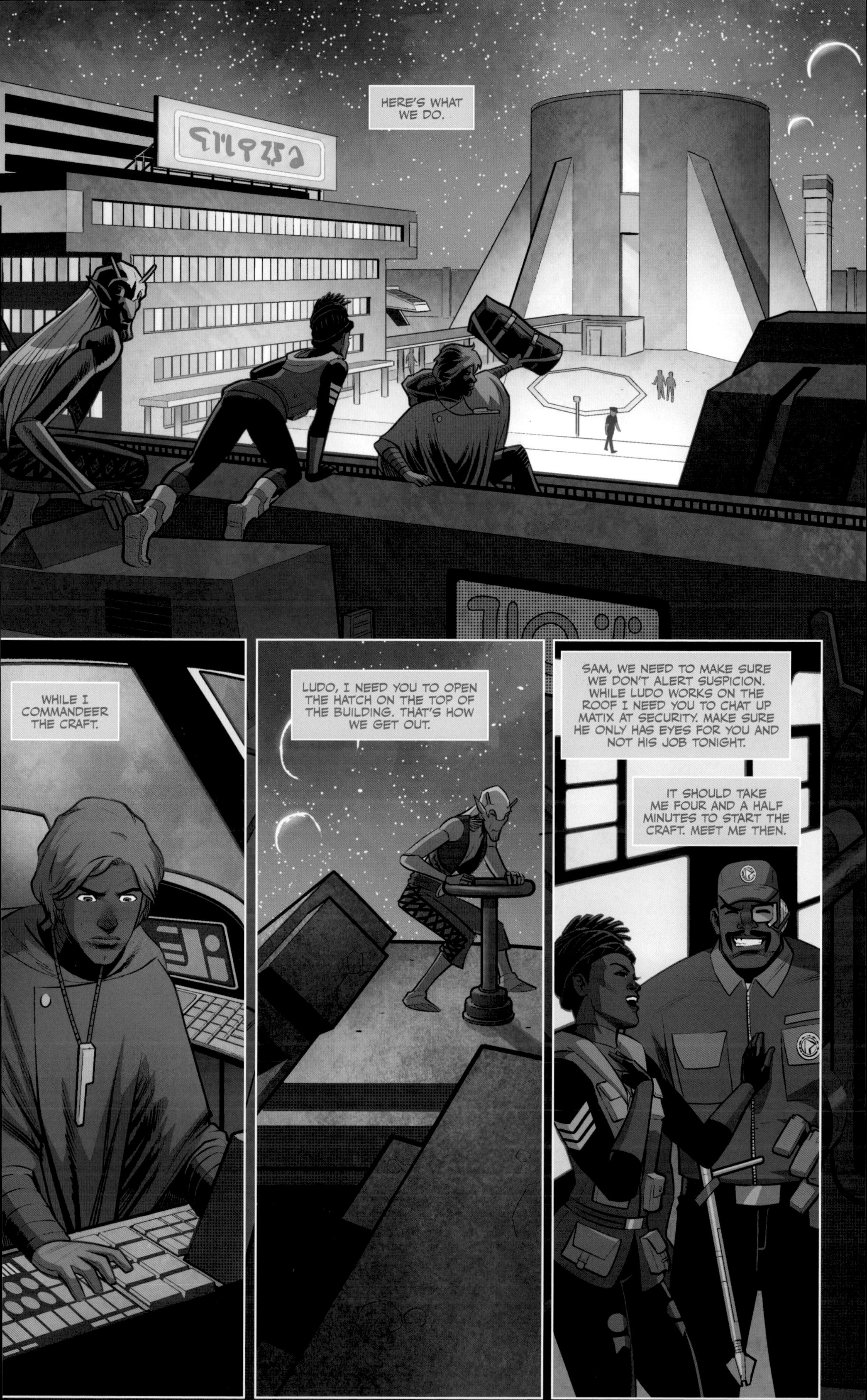
HERE'S WHAT WE DO.
WHILE I COMMANDEER THE CRAFT.
LUDO, I NEED YOU TO OPEN THE HATCH ON THE TOP OF THE BUILDING. THAT'S HOW WE GET OUT.
SAM, WE NEED TO MAKE SURE WE DON'T ALERT SUSPICION. WHILE LUDO WORKS ON THE ROOF I NEED YOU TO CHAT UP MATIX AT SECURITY. MAKE SURE HE ONLY HAS EYES FOR YOU AND NOT HIS JOB TONIGHT.
IT SHOULD TAKE ME FOUR AND A HALF MINUTES TO START THE CRAFT. MEET ME THEN.

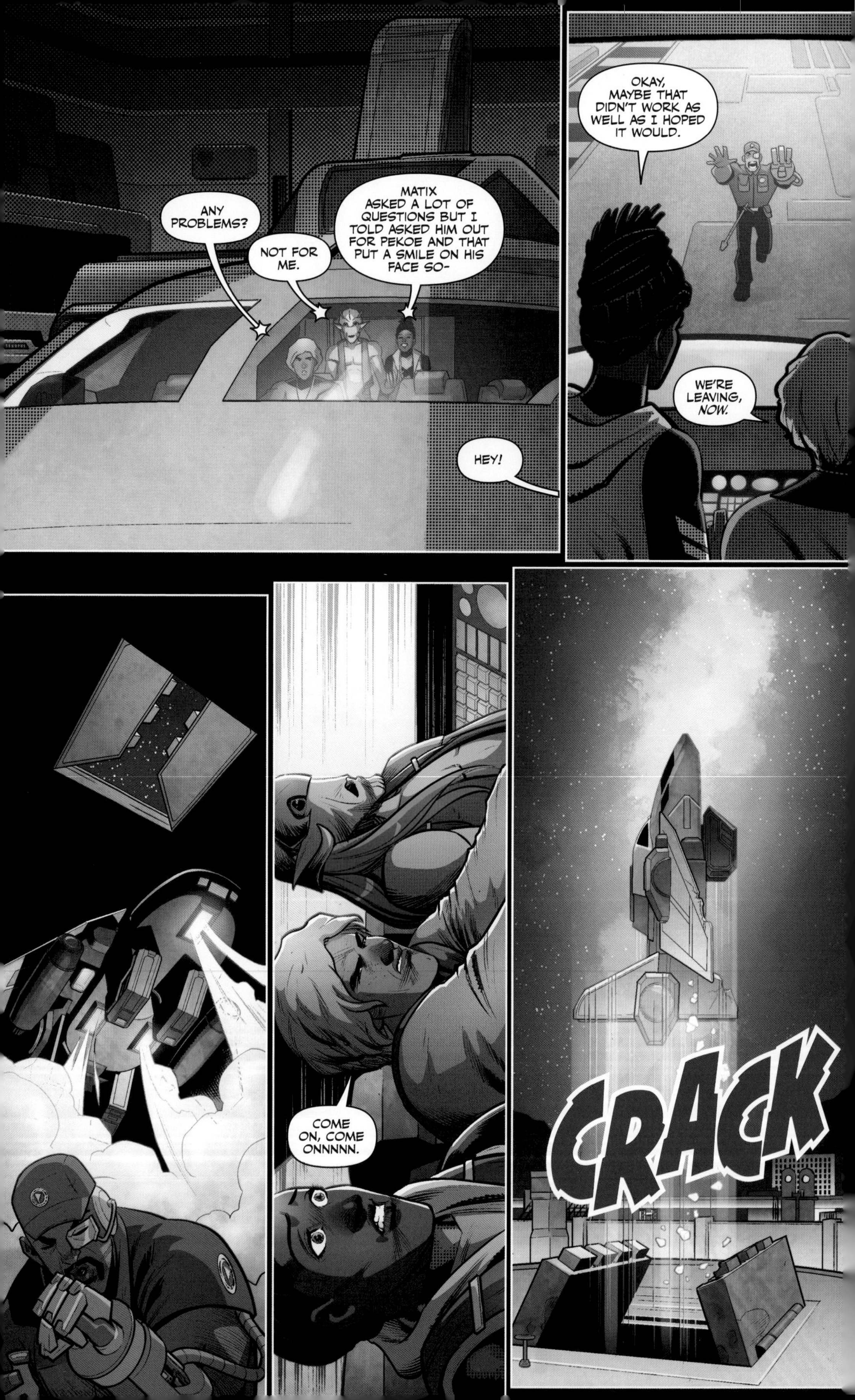
ANY PROBLEMS?
NOT FOR ME.
MATIX ASKED A LOT OF QUESTIONS BUT I TOLD ASKED HIM OUT FOR PEKOE AND THAT PUT A SMILE ON HIS FACE SO-
HEY!
OKAY, MAYBE THAT DIDN'T WORK AS WELL AS I HOPED IT WOULD.
WE'RE LEAVING, *NOW.*
COME ON, COME ONNNNN.
CRACK

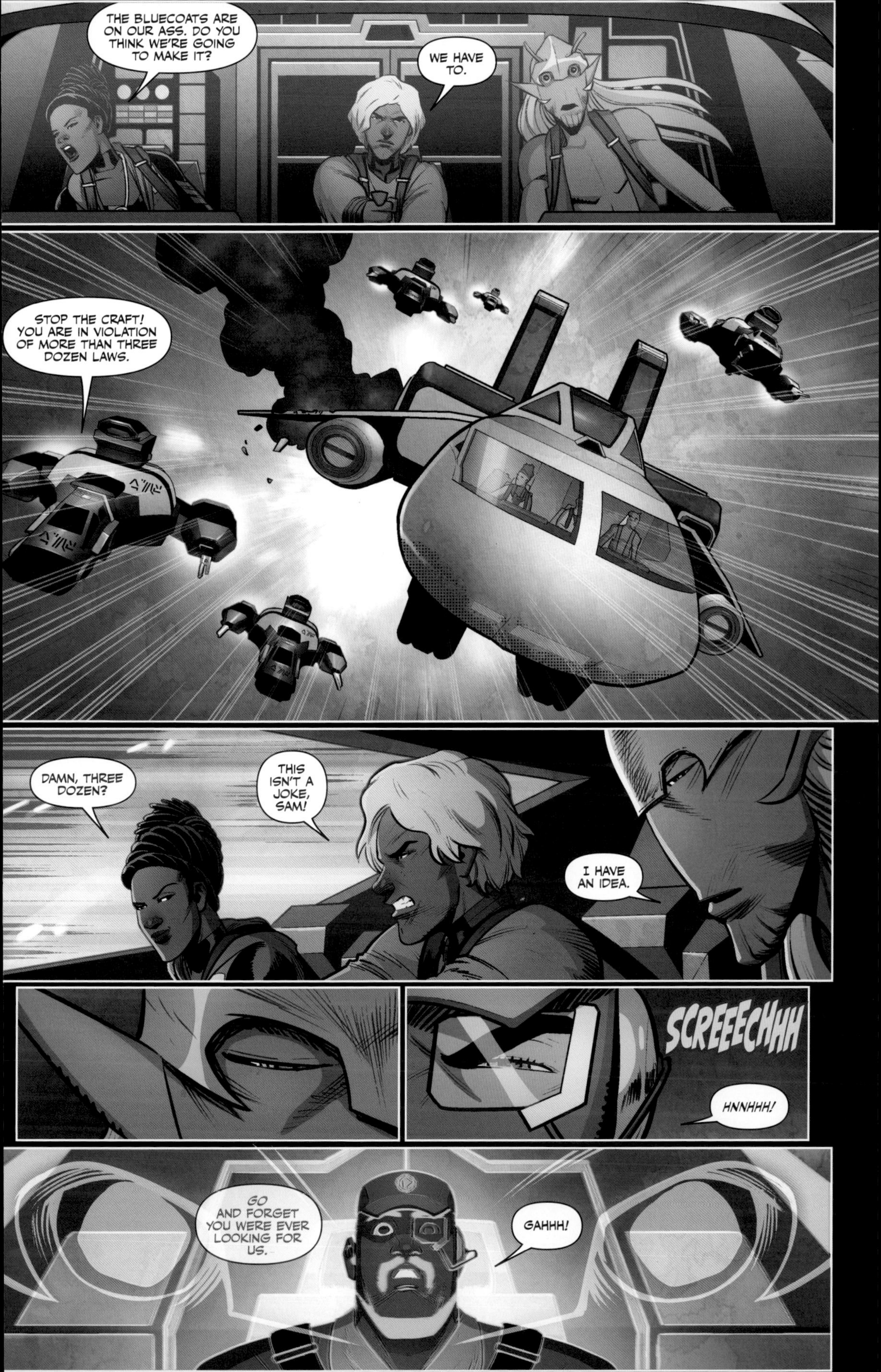

THE BLUECOATS ARE ON OUR ASS. DO YOU THINK WE'RE GOING TO MAKE IT?
WE HAVE TO.
STOP THE CRAFT! YOU ARE IN VIOLATION OF MORE THAN THREE DOZEN LAWS.
DAMN, THREE DOZEN?
THIS ISN'T A JOKE, SAM!
I HAVE AN IDEA.
SCREEECHHH
HNNHHH!
GO AND FORGET YOU WERE EVER LOOKING FOR US.
GAHHH!

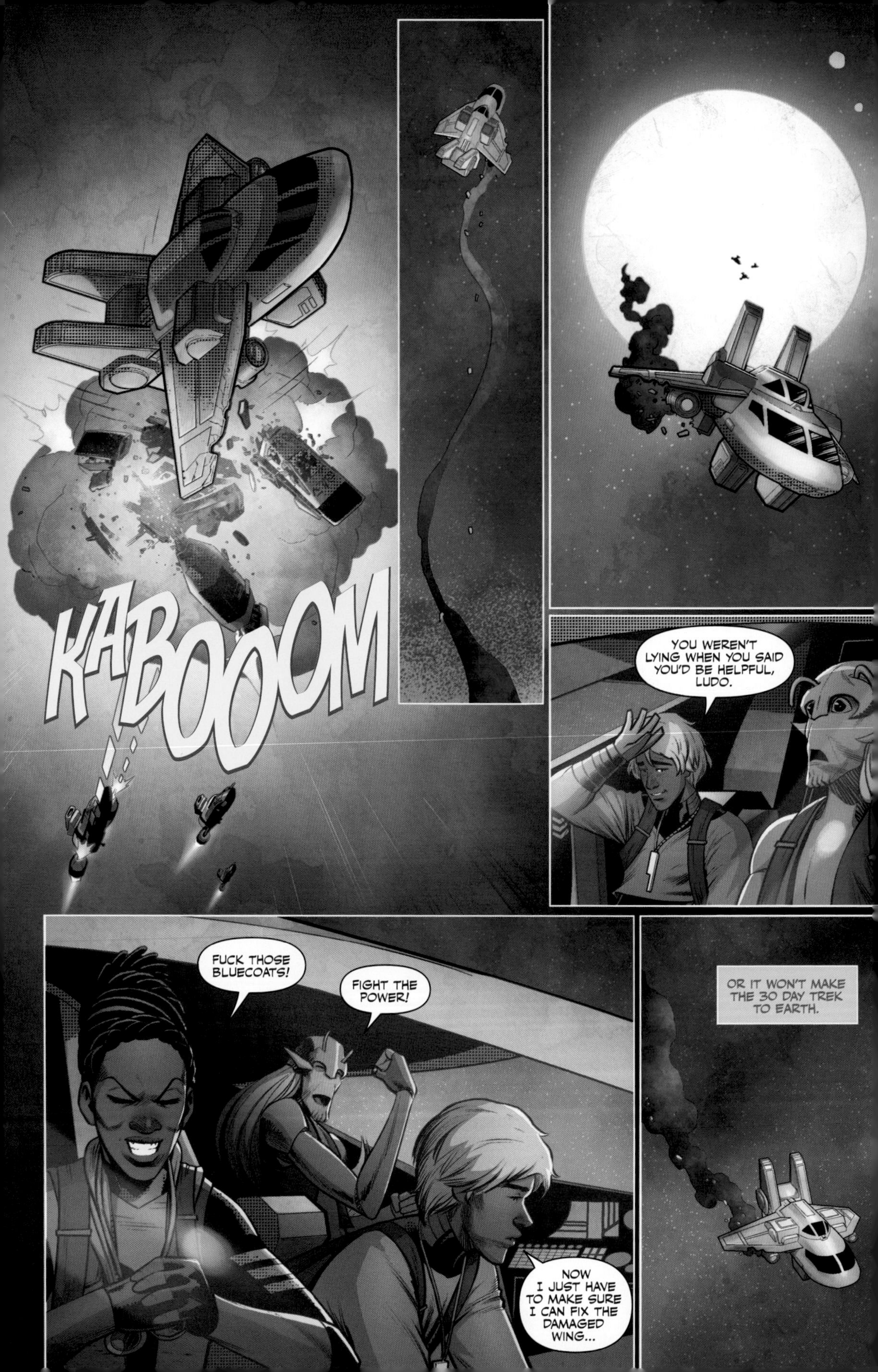
KABOOOM
YOU WEREN'T LYING WHEN YOU SAID YOU'D BE HELPFUL, LUDO.
FUCK THOSE BLUECOATS!
FIGHT THE POWER!
NOW I JUST HAVE TO MAKE SURE I CAN FIX THE DAMAGED WING...
OR IT WON'T MAKE THE 30 DAY TREK TO EARTH.

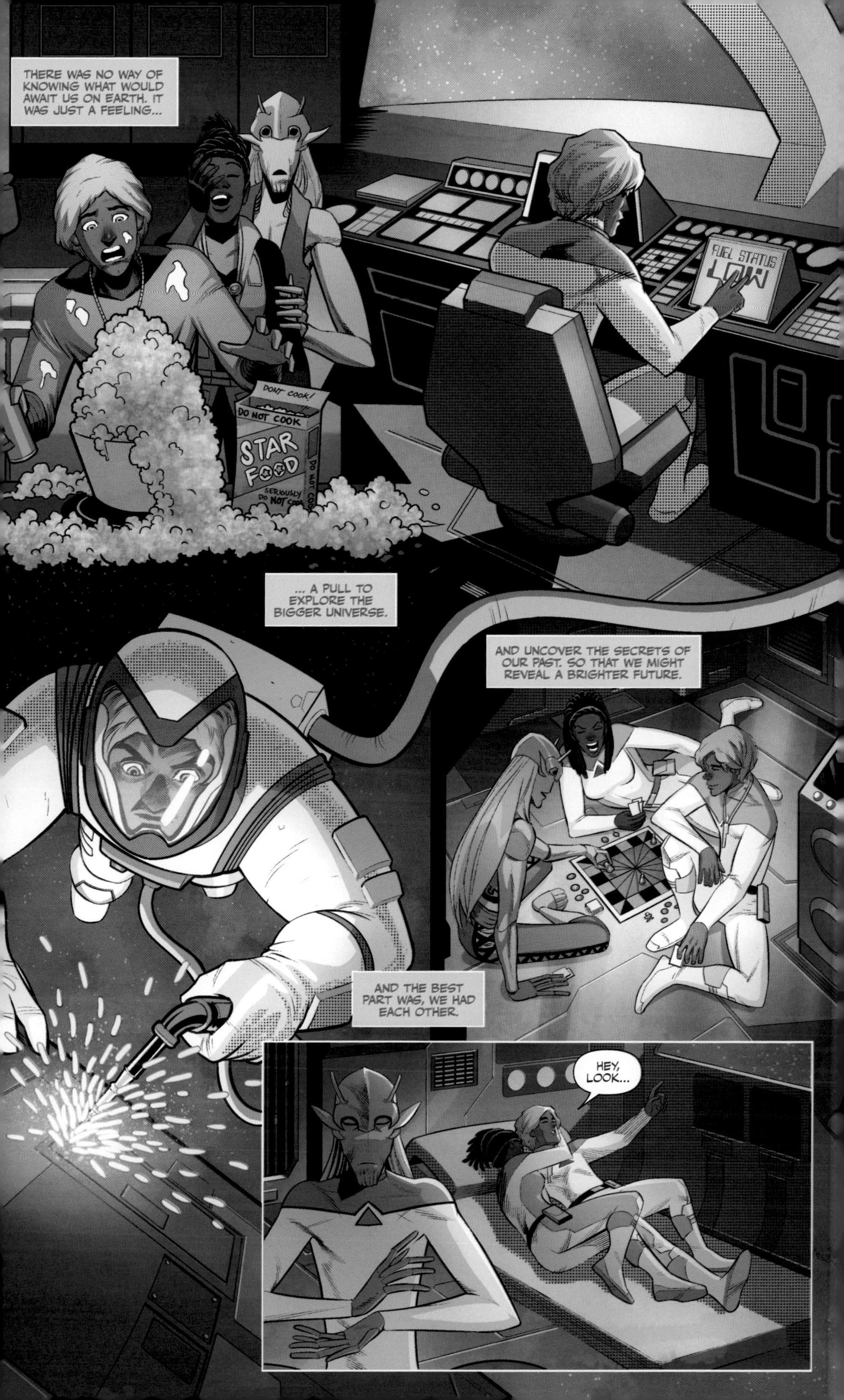
THERE WAS NO WAY OF KNOWING WHAT WOULD AWAIT US ON EARTH. IT WAS JUST A FEELING...
DONT COOK!
DO NOT COOK
STAR FOOD
SERIOUSLY DO NOT COOK
DO NOT COOK
FUEL STATUS
LOW
... A PULL TO EXPLORE THE BIGGER UNIVERSE.
AND UNCOVER THE SECRETS OF OUR PAST. SO THAT WE MIGHT REVEAL A BRIGHTER FUTURE.
AND THE BEST PART WAS, WE HAD EACH OTHER.
HEY, LOOK...

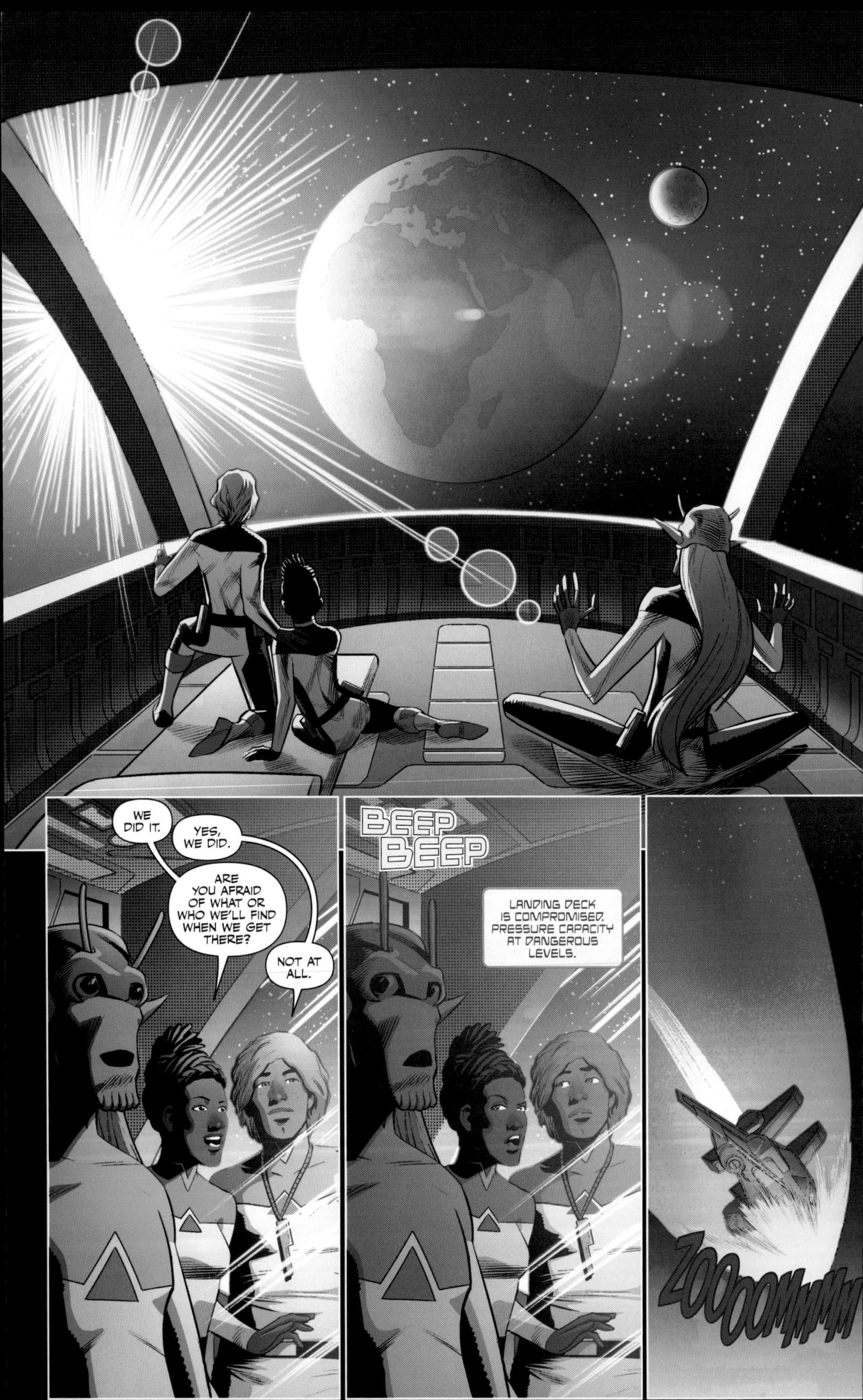
WE DID IT.
YES, WE DID.
ARE YOU AFRAID OF WHAT OR WHO WE'LL FIND WHEN WE GET THERE?
NOT AT ALL.
BEEP BEEP
LANDING DECK IS COMPROMISED. PRESSURE CAPACITY AT DANGEROUS LEVELS.
ZOOOOOMMMMM

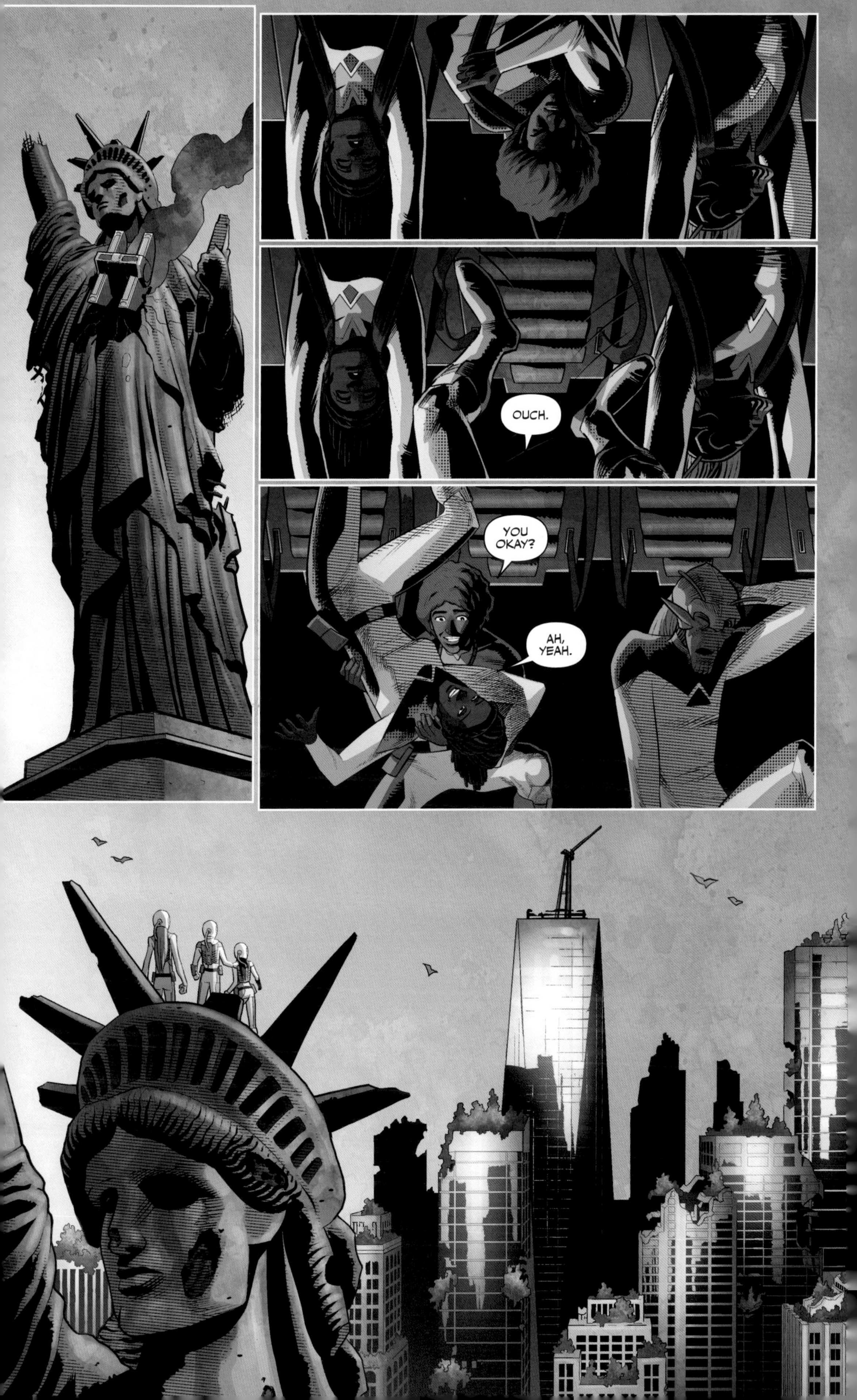
OUCH.
YOU OKAY?
AH, YEAH.

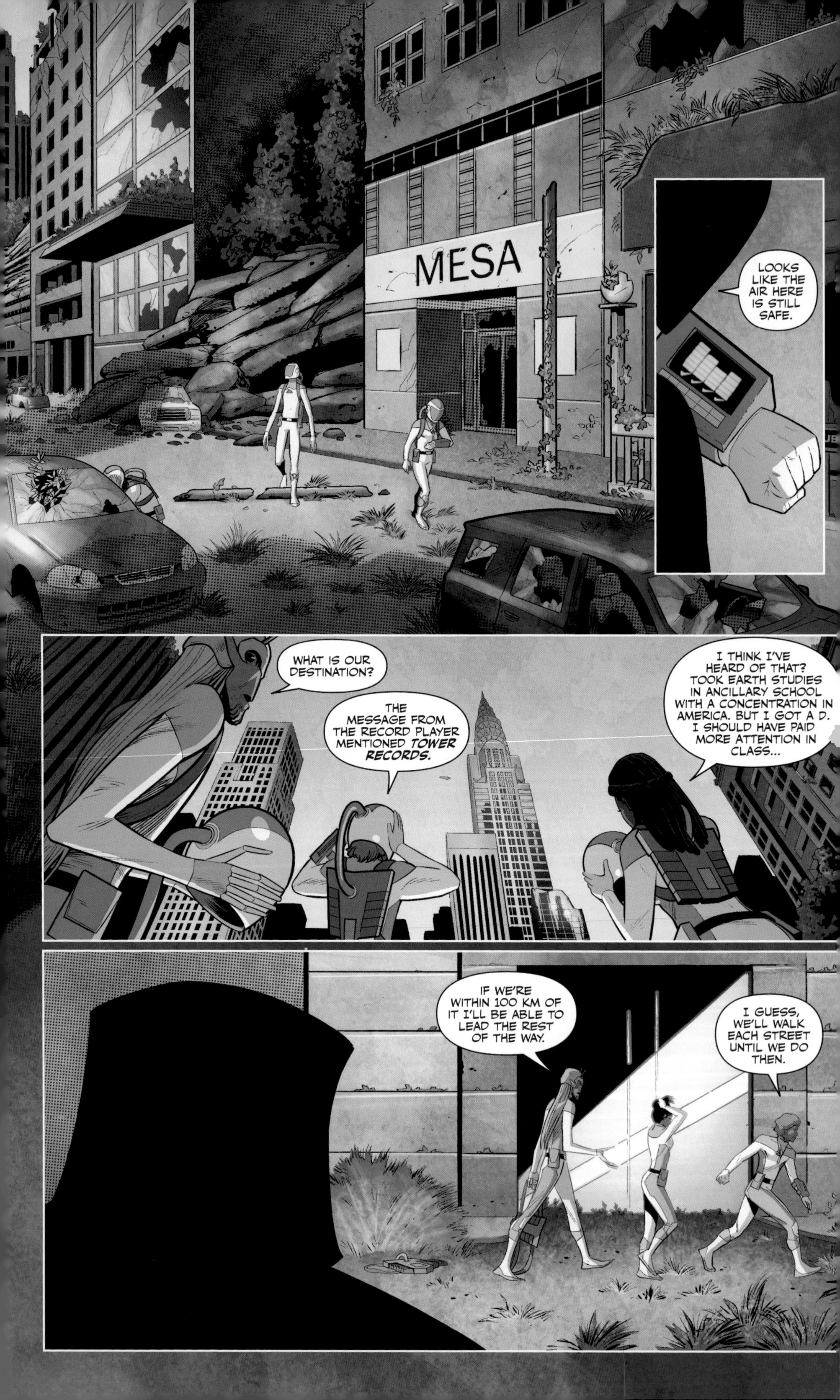

MESA
LOOKS LIKE THE AIR HERE IS STILL SAFE.
WHAT IS OUR DESTINATION?
THE MESSAGE FROM THE RECORD PLAYER MENTIONED TOWER RECORDS.
I THINK I'VE HEARD OF THAT? TOOK EARTH STUDIES IN ANCILLARY SCHOOL WITH A CONCENTRATION IN AMERICA. BUT I GOT A D. I SHOULD HAVE PAID MORE ATTENTION IN CLASS...
IF WE'RE WITHIN 100 KM OF IT I'LL BE ABLE TO LEAD THE REST OF THE WAY.
I GUESS, WE'LL WALK EACH STREET UNTIL WE DO THEN.

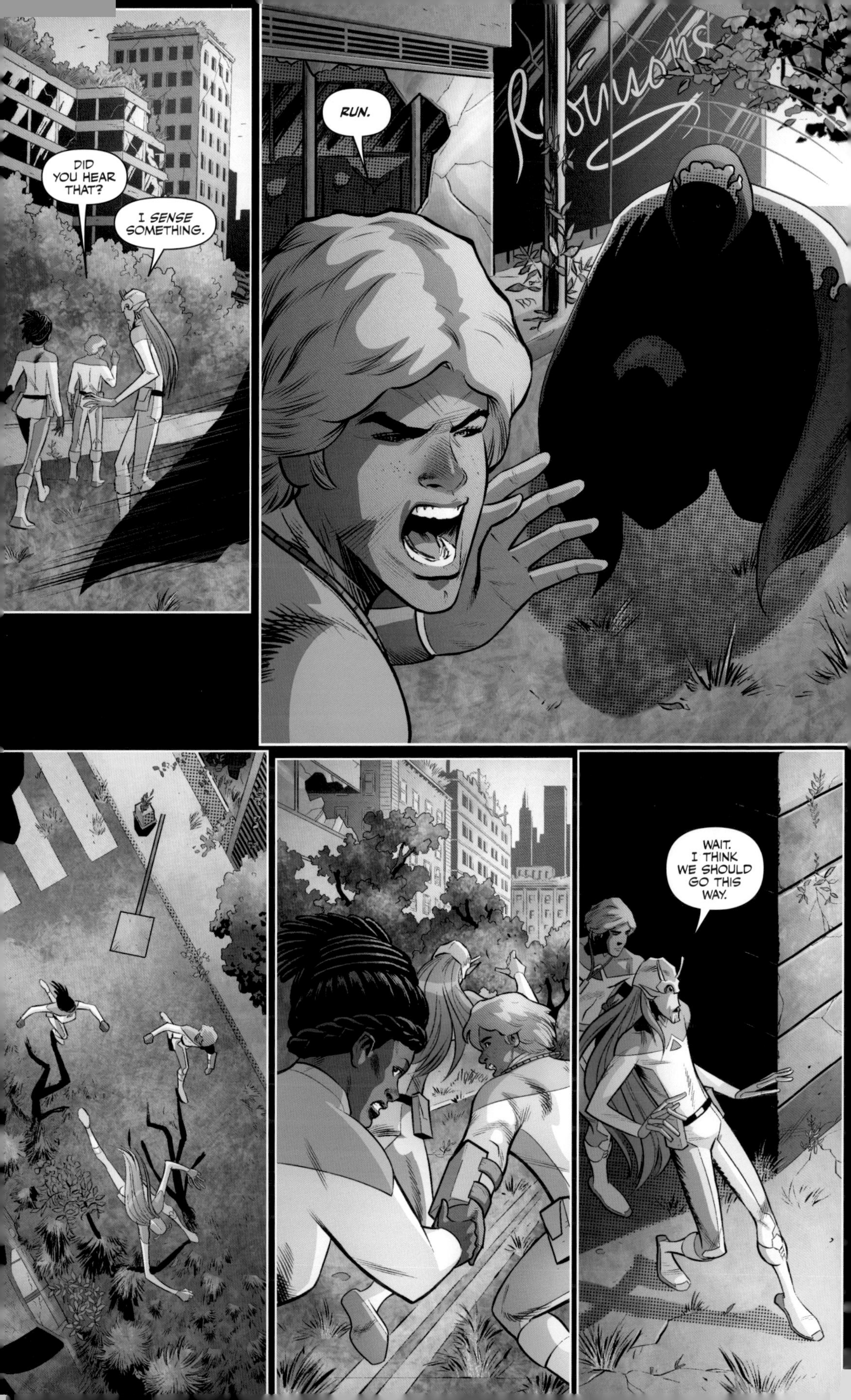
DID YOU HEAR THAT?
I SENSE SOMETHING.
RUN.
Robinson's
WAIT. I THINK WE SHOULD GO THIS WAY.

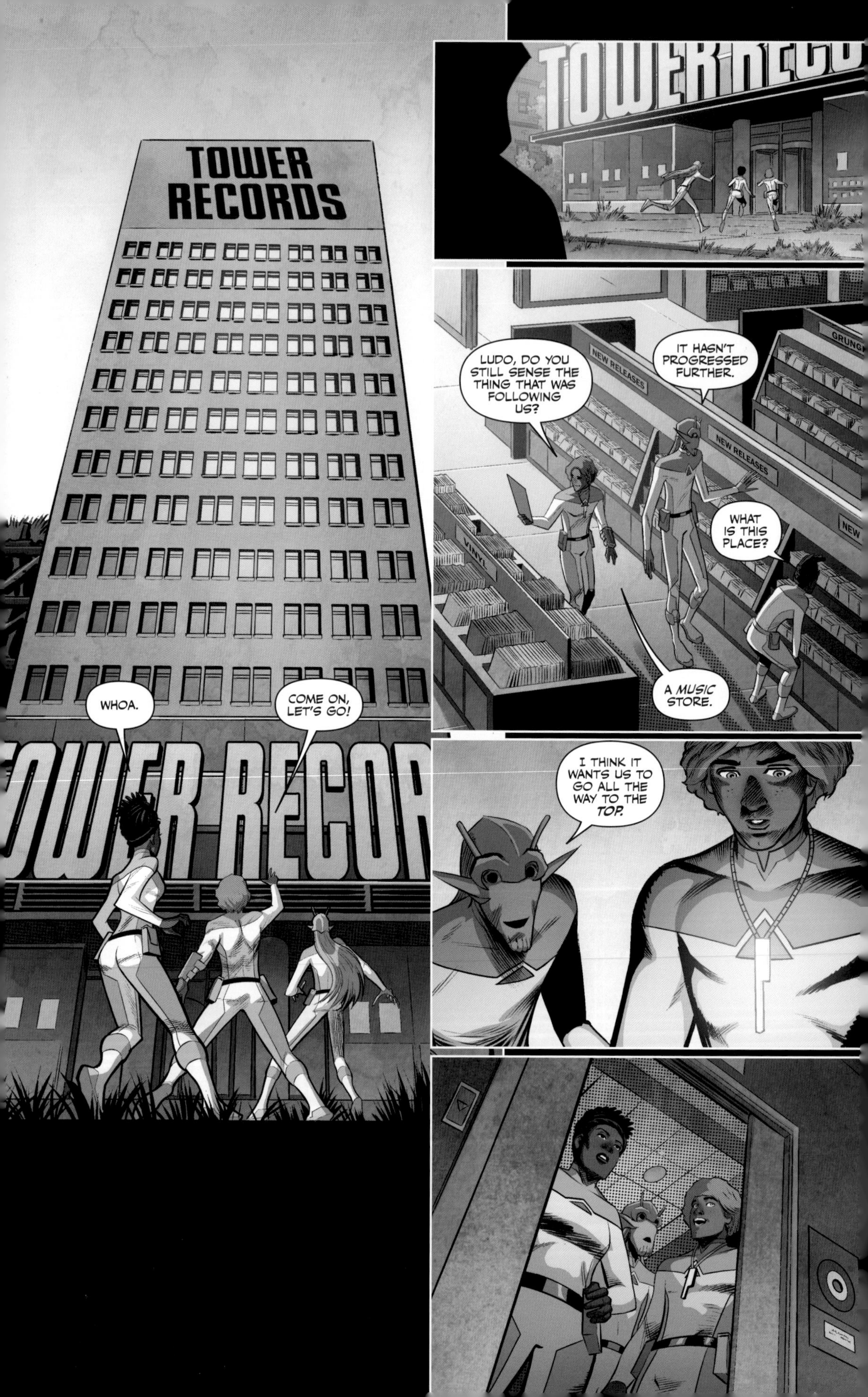
TOWER RECORDS
WHOA.
COME ON, LET'S GO!
LUDO, DO YOU STILL SENSE THE THING THAT WAS FOLLOWING US?
IT HASN'T PROGRESSED FURTHER.
NEW RELEASES
VINYL
WHAT IS THIS PLACE?
A *MUSIC* STORE.
I THINK IT WANTS US TO GO ALL THE WAY TO THE *TOP*.

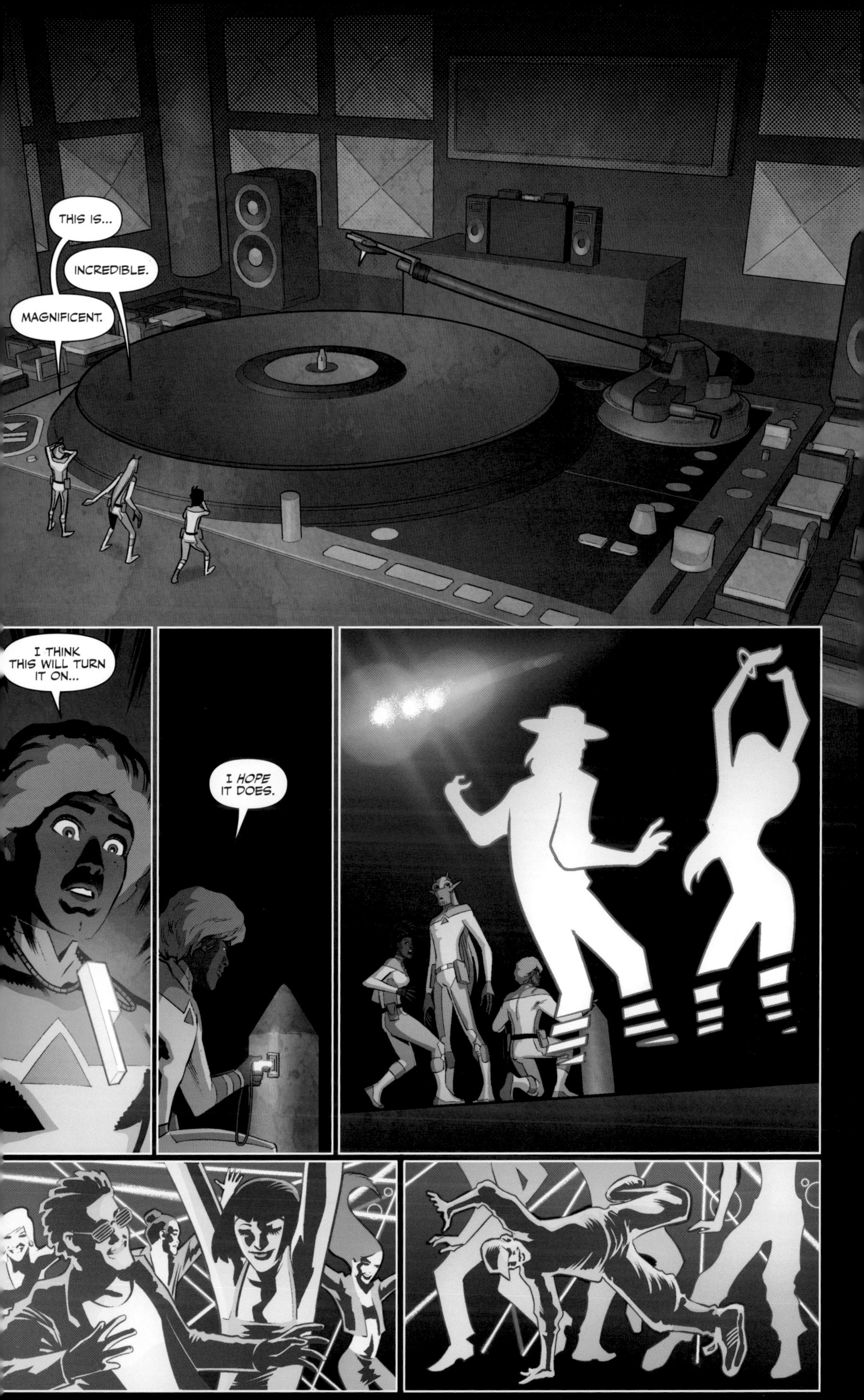
THIS IS...
INCREDIBLE.
MAGNIFICENT.
I THINK THIS WILL TURN IT ON...
I HOPE IT DOES.

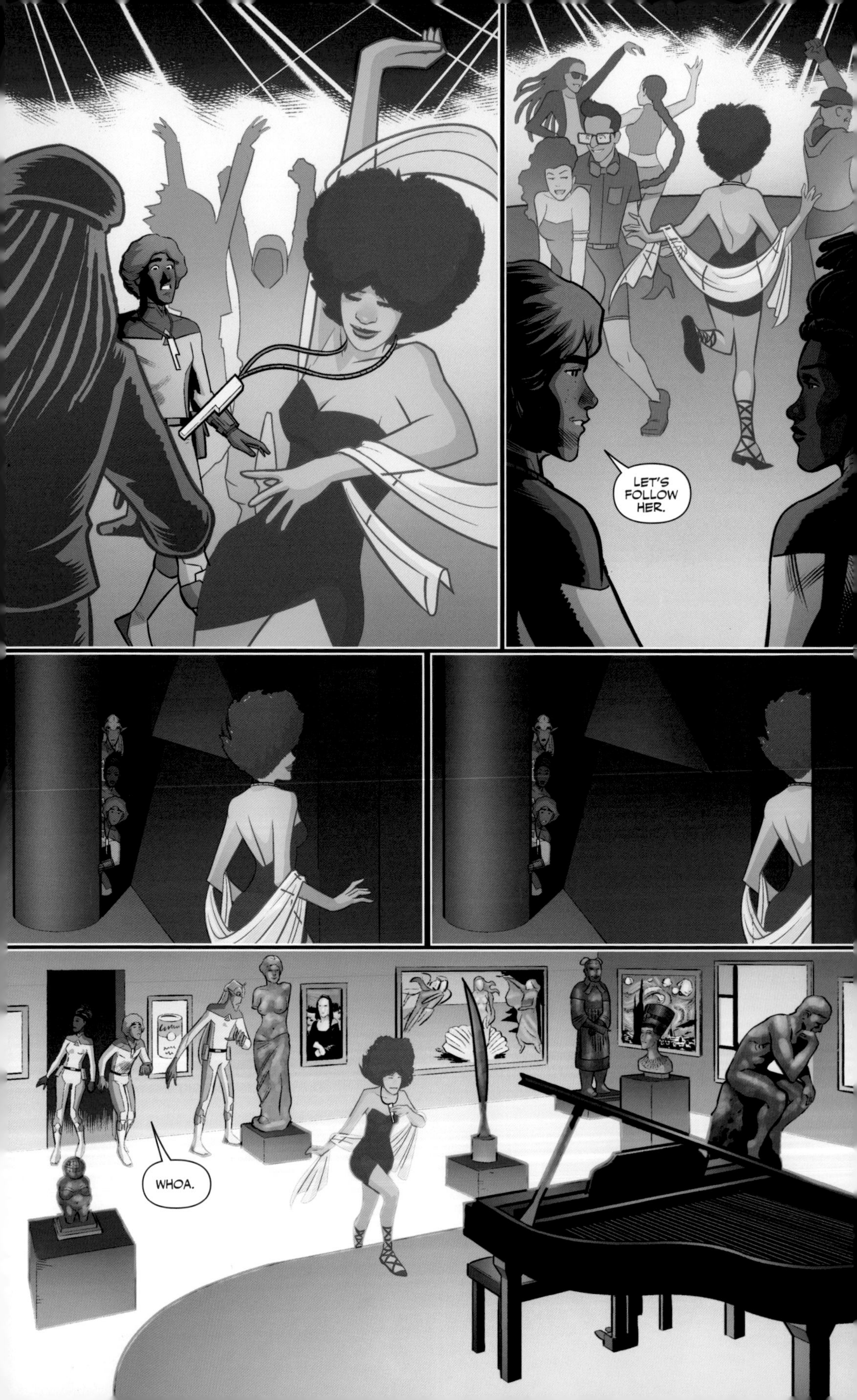
LET'S FOLLOW HER.
WHOA.

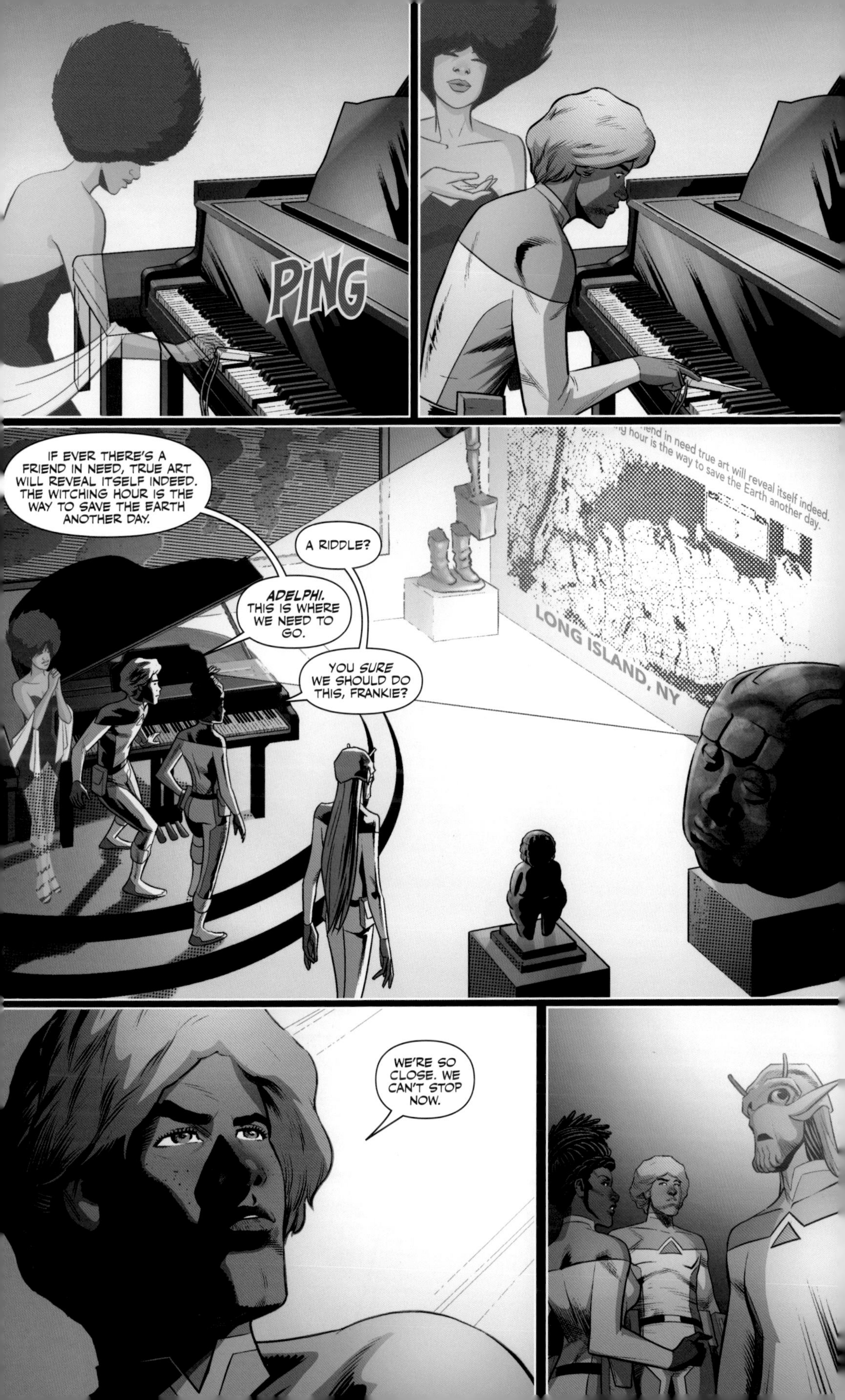
PING
IF EVER THERE'S A FRIEND IN NEED, TRUE ART WILL REVEAL ITSELF INDEED. THE WITCHING HOUR IS THE WAY TO SAVE THE EARTH ANOTHER DAY.
A RIDDLE?
ADELPHI. THIS IS WHERE WE NEED TO GO.
YOU SURE WE SHOULD DO THIS, FRANKIE?
in need true art will reveal itself indeed.
hour is the way to save the Earth another day.
LONG ISLAND, NY
WE'RE SO CLOSE. WE CAN'T STOP NOW.

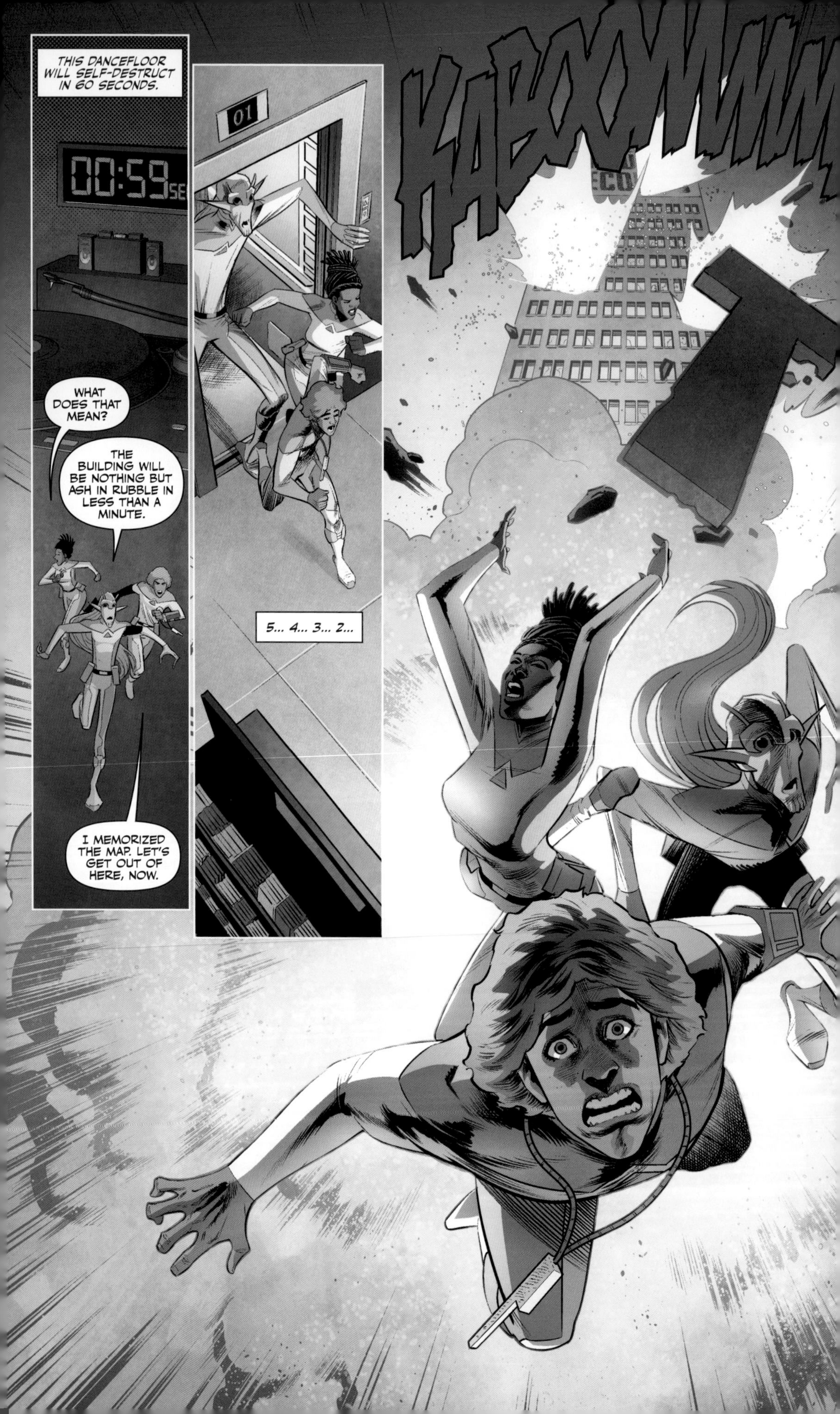
THIS DANCEFLOOR WILL SELF-DESTRUCT IN 60 SECONDS.
00:59 SEC
WHAT DOES THAT MEAN?
THE BUILDING WILL BE NOTHING BUT ASH IN RUBBLE IN LESS THAN A MINUTE.
I MEMORIZED THE MAP. LET'S GET OUT OF HERE, NOW.
01
5... 4... 3... 2...
KABOOMMM

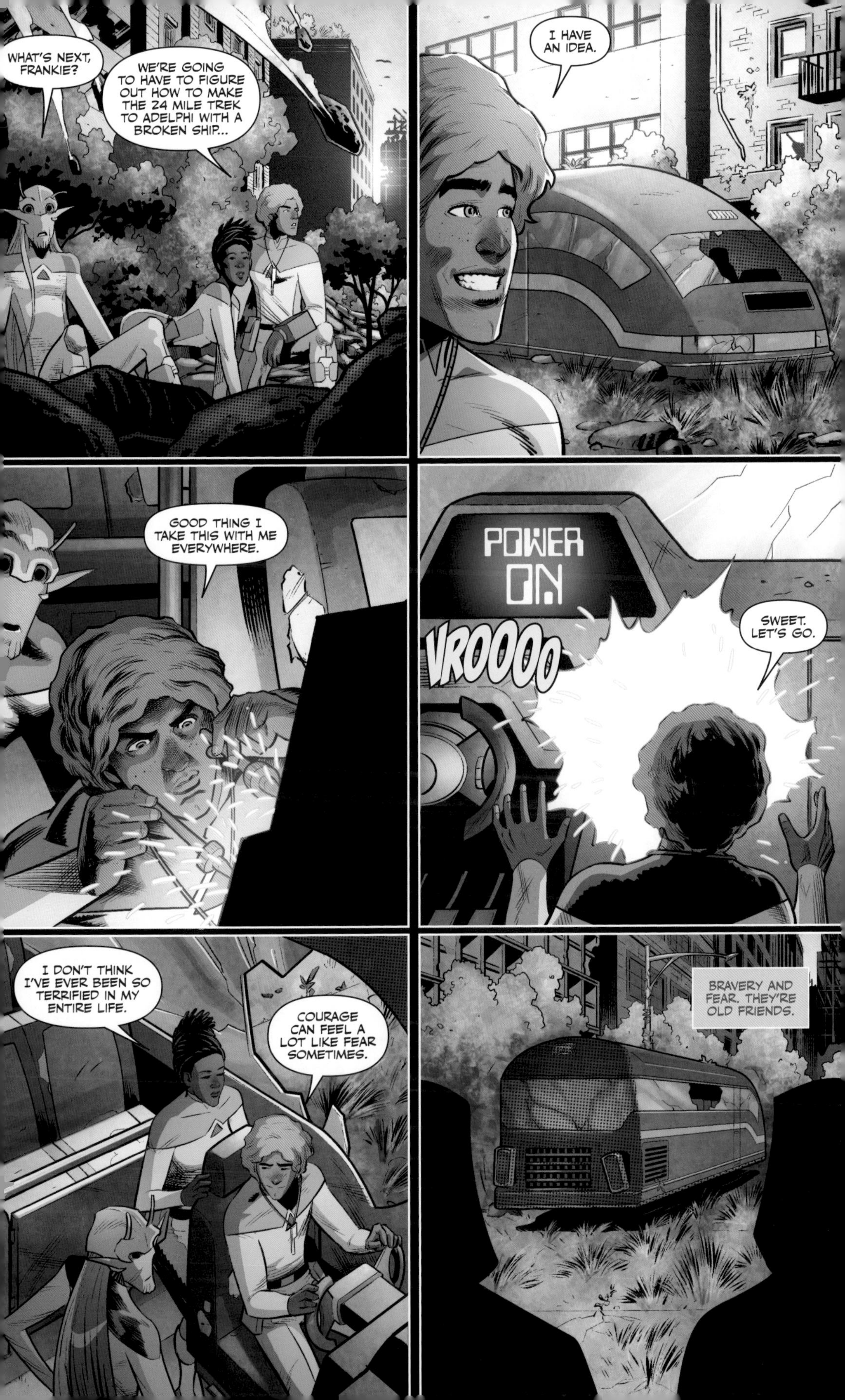
WHAT'S NEXT, FRANKIE?
WE'RE GOING TO HAVE TO FIGURE OUT HOW TO MAKE THE 24 MILE TREK TO ADELPHI WITH A BROKEN SHIP...
I HAVE AN IDEA.
GOOD THING I TAKE THIS WITH ME EVERYWHERE.
POWER ON
VROOOO
SWEET. LET'S GO.
I DON'T THINK I'VE EVER BEEN SO TERRIFIED IN MY ENTIRE LIFE.
COURAGE CAN FEEL A LOT LIKE FEAR SOMETIMES.
BRAVERY AND FEAR. THEY'RE OLD FRIENDS.

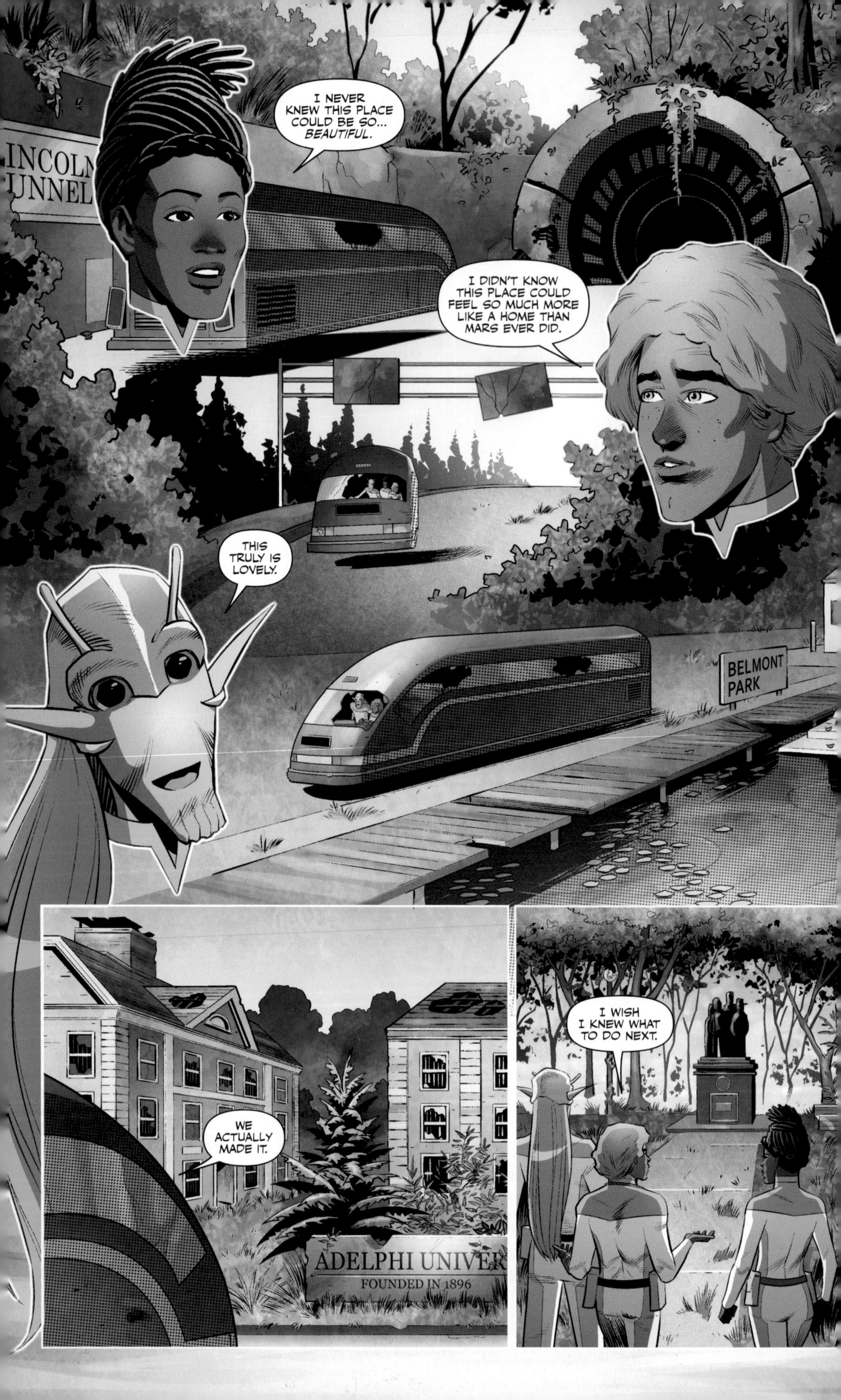
LINCOLN TUNNEL
I NEVER KNEW THIS PLACE COULD BE SO... *BEAUTIFUL*.
I DIDN'T KNOW THIS PLACE COULD FEEL SO MUCH MORE LIKE A HOME THAN MARS EVER DID.
THIS TRULY IS LOVELY.
BELMONT PARK
WE ACTUALLY MADE IT.
ADELPHI UNIVER
FOUNDED IN 1896
I WISH I KNEW WHAT TO DO NEXT.

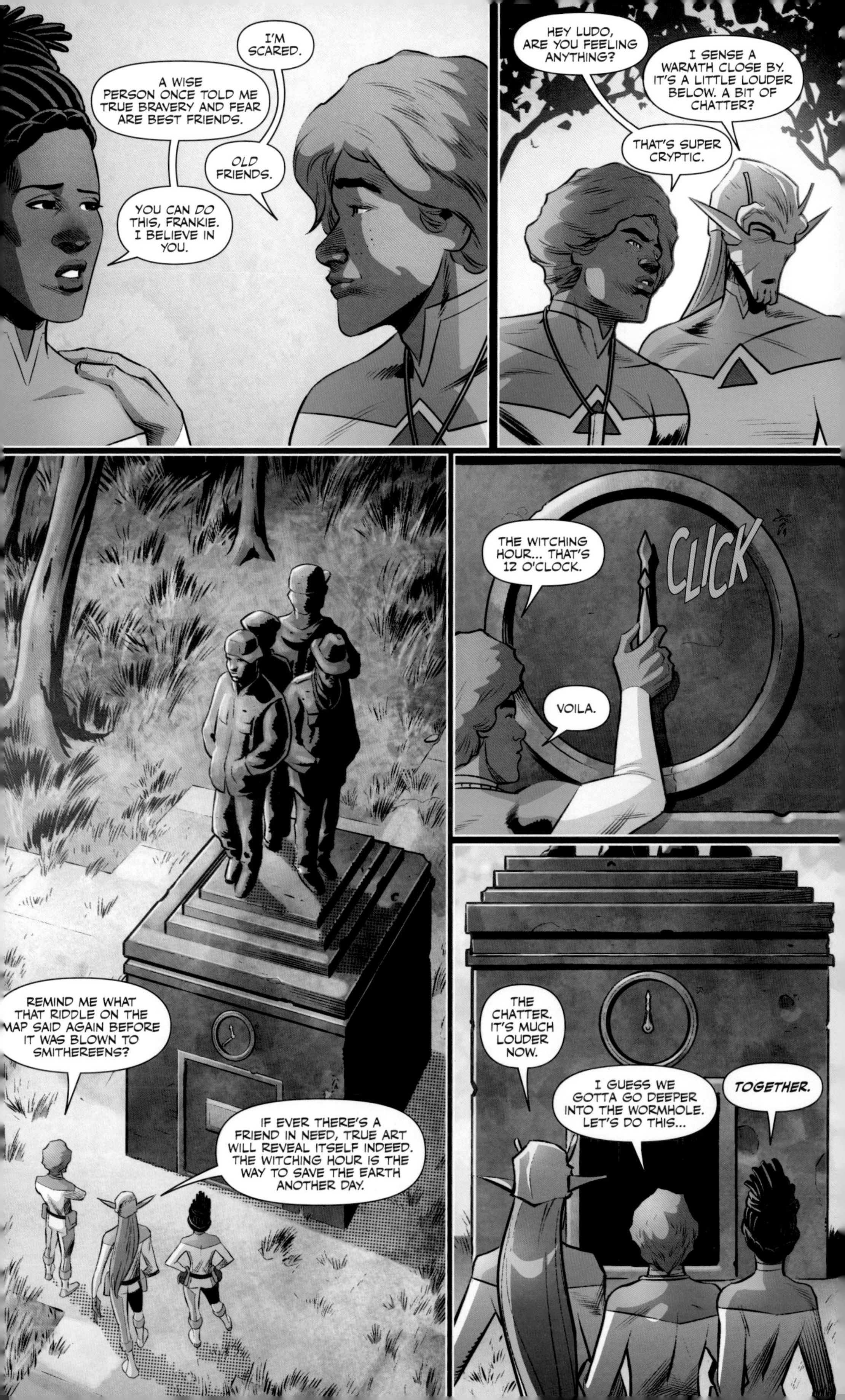
I'M SCARED.
A WISE PERSON ONCE TOLD ME TRUE BRAVERY AND FEAR ARE BEST FRIENDS.
OLD FRIENDS.
YOU CAN *DO* THIS, FRANKIE. I BELIEVE IN YOU.
HEY LUDO, ARE YOU FEELING ANYTHING?
I SENSE A WARMTH CLOSE BY. IT'S A LITTLE LOUDER BELOW. A BIT OF CHATTER?
THAT'S SUPER CRYPTIC.
REMIND ME WHAT THAT RIDDLE ON THE MAP SAID AGAIN BEFORE IT WAS BLOWN TO SMITHEREENS?
IF EVER THERE'S A FRIEND IN NEED, TRUE ART WILL REVEAL ITSELF INDEED. THE WITCHING HOUR IS THE WAY TO SAVE THE EARTH ANOTHER DAY.
THE WITCHING HOUR... THAT'S 12 O'CLOCK.
CLICK
VOILA.
THE CHATTER. IT'S MUCH LOUDER NOW.
I GUESS WE GOTTA GO DEEPER INTO THE WORMHOLE. LET'S DO THIS...
TOGETHER.

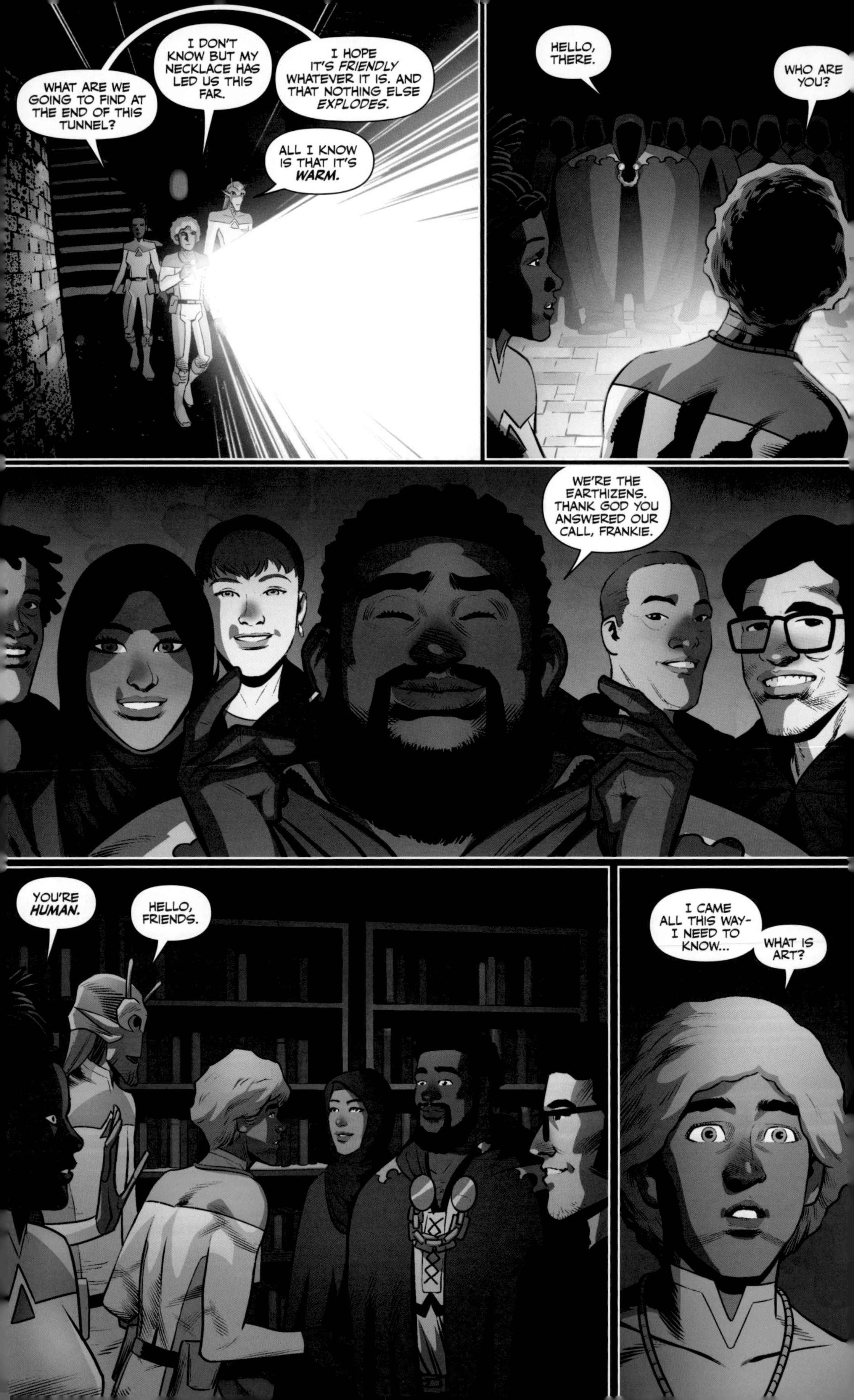
WHAT ARE WE GOING TO FIND AT THE END OF THIS TUNNEL?
I DON'T KNOW BUT MY NECKLACE HAS LED US THIS FAR.
I HOPE IT'S *FRIENDLY* WHATEVER IT IS. AND THAT NOTHING ELSE *EXPLODES.*
ALL I KNOW IS THAT IT'S ***WARM.***
HELLO, THERE.
WHO ARE YOU?
WE'RE THE EARTHIZENS. THANK GOD YOU ANSWERED OUR CALL, FRANKIE.
YOU'RE ***HUMAN.***
HELLO, FRIENDS.
I CAME ALL THIS WAY- I NEED TO KNOW...
WHAT IS ART?

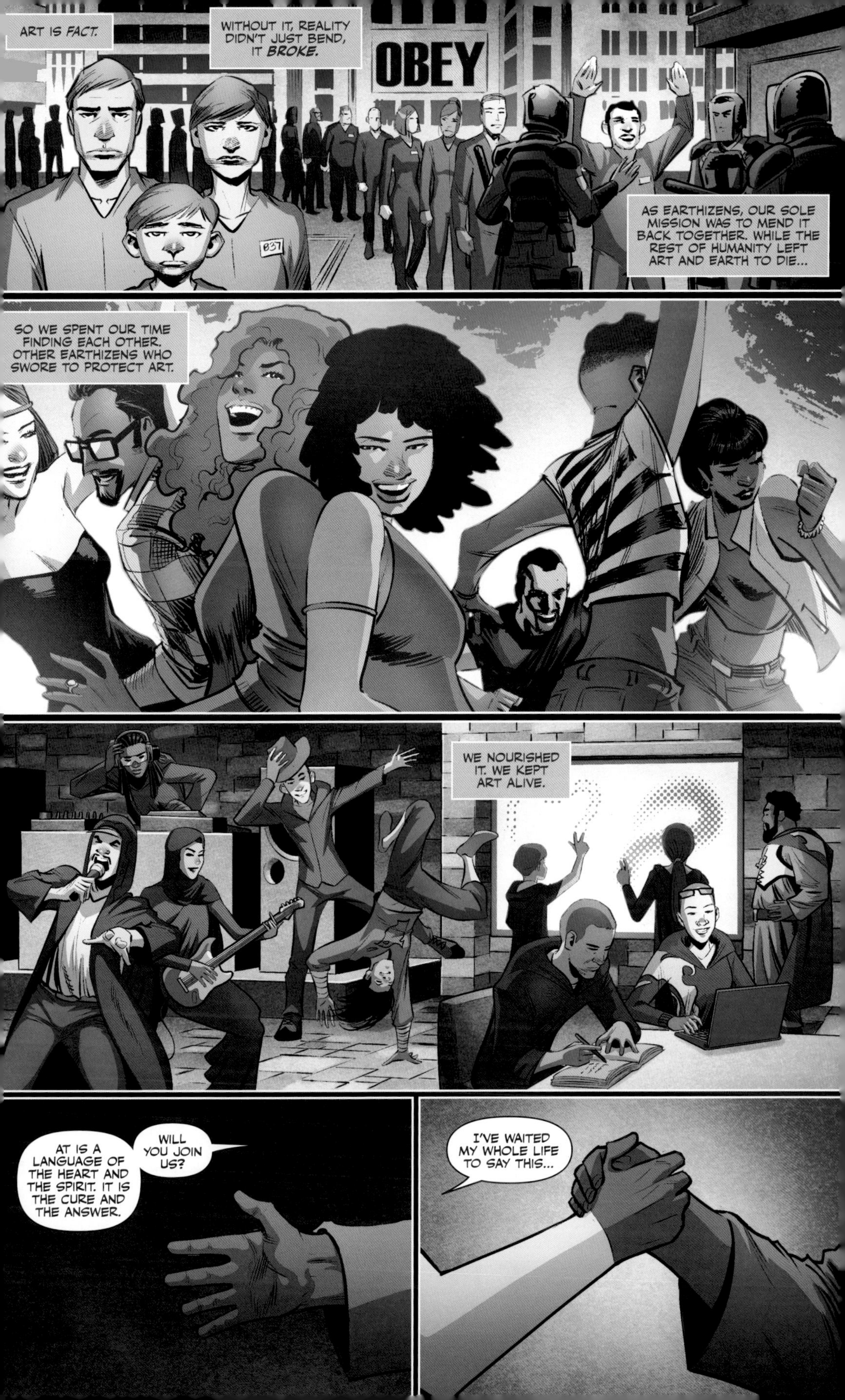
ART IS FACT.
WITHOUT IT, REALITY DIDN'T JUST BEND, IT BROKE.
OBEY
B37
AS EARTHIZENS, OUR SOLE MISSION WAS TO MEND IT BACK TOGETHER. WHILE THE REST OF HUMANITY LEFT ART AND EARTH TO DIE...
SO WE SPENT OUR TIME FINDING EACH OTHER. OTHER EARTHIZENS WHO SWORE TO PROTECT ART.
WE NOURISHED IT. WE KEPT ART ALIVE.
AT IS A LANGUAGE OF THE HEART AND THE SPIRIT. IT IS THE CURE AND THE ANSWER.
WILL YOU JOIN US?
I'VE WAITED MY WHOLE LIFE TO SAY THIS...

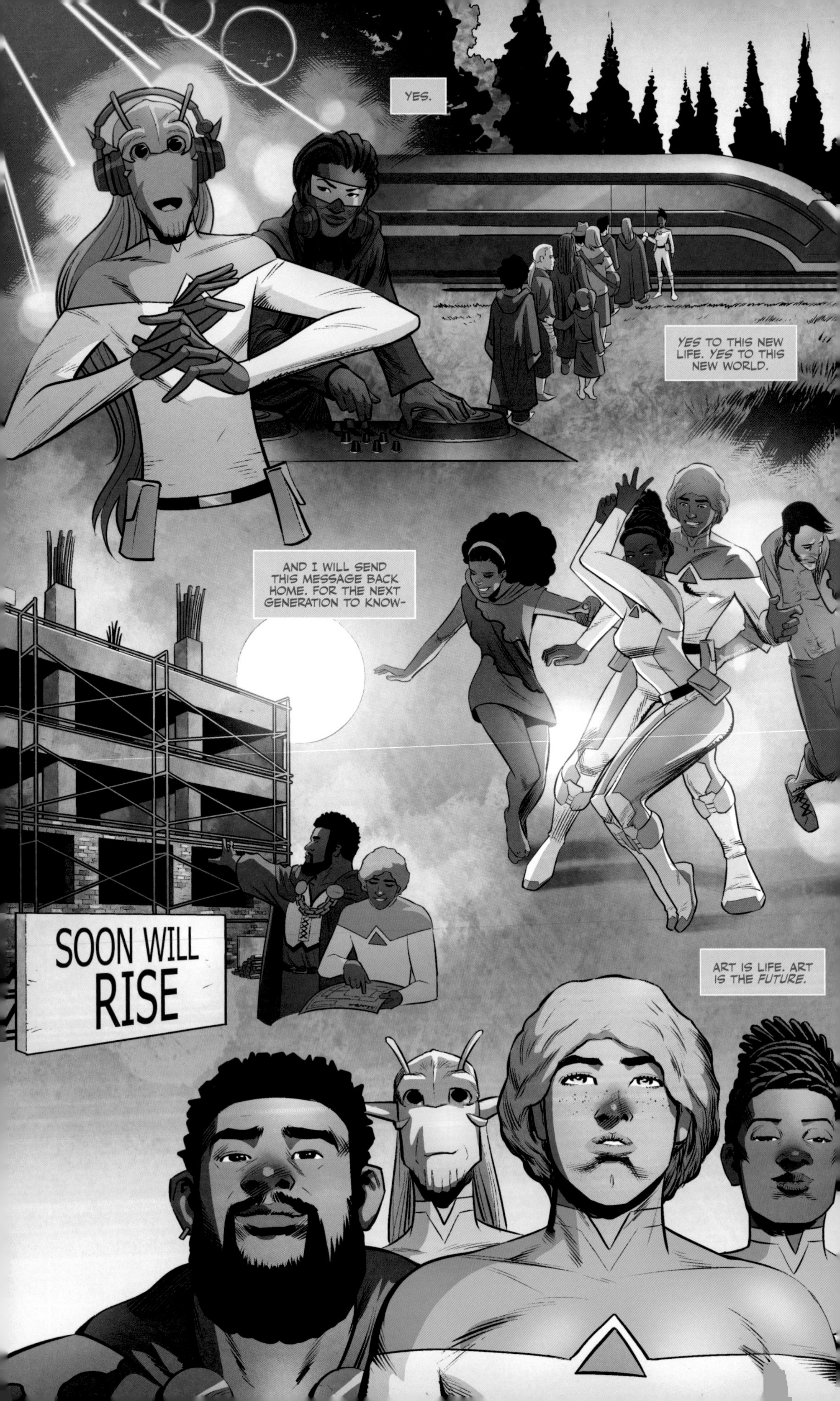
YES.
YES TO THIS NEW LIFE. YES TO THIS NEW WORLD.
AND I WILL SEND THIS MESSAGE BACK HOME. FOR THE NEXT GENERATION TO KNOW-
SOON WILL RISE
ART IS LIFE. ART IS THE FUTURE.

GALLERY

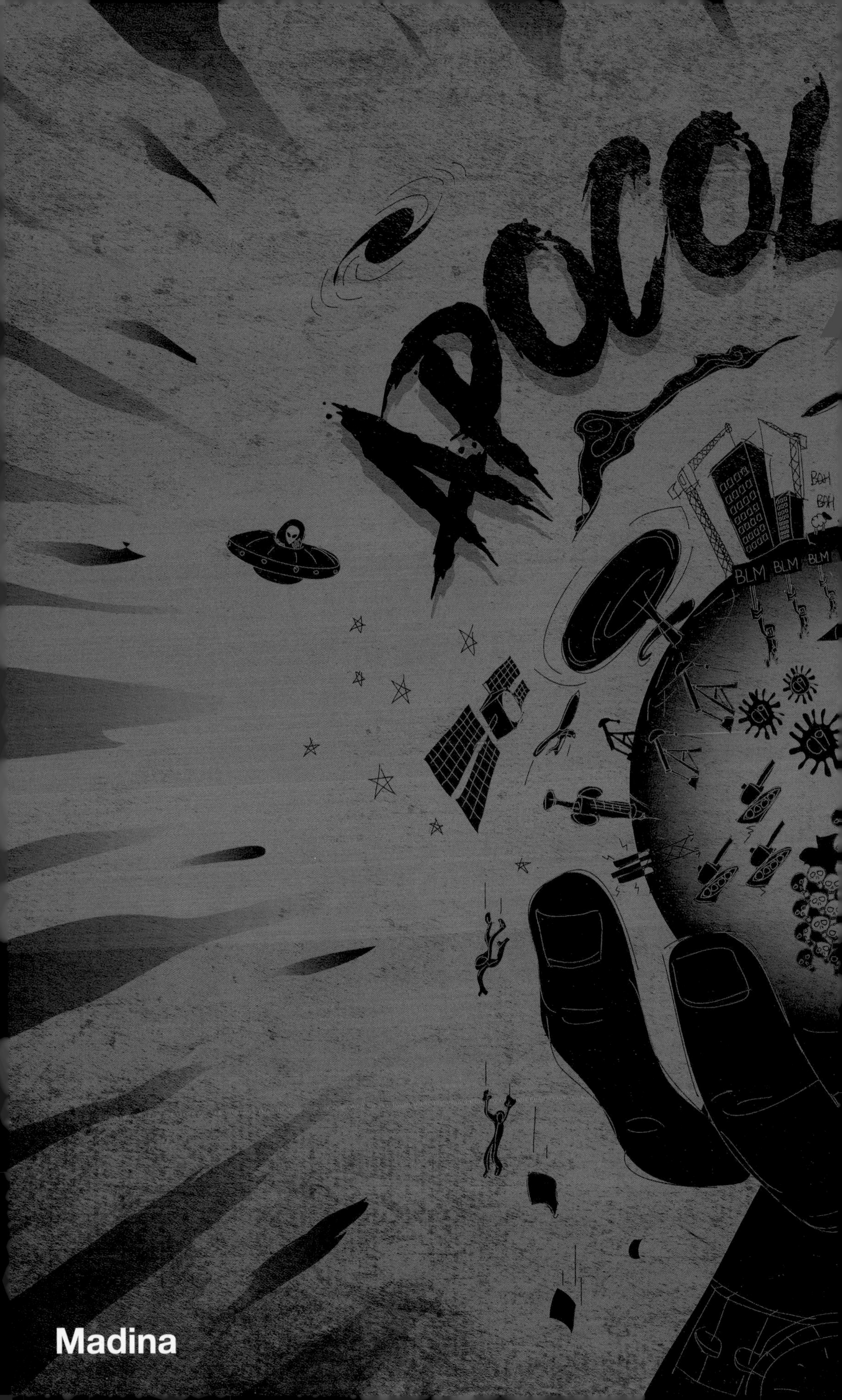
BLM BLM BLM
BAH
BAH
Madina

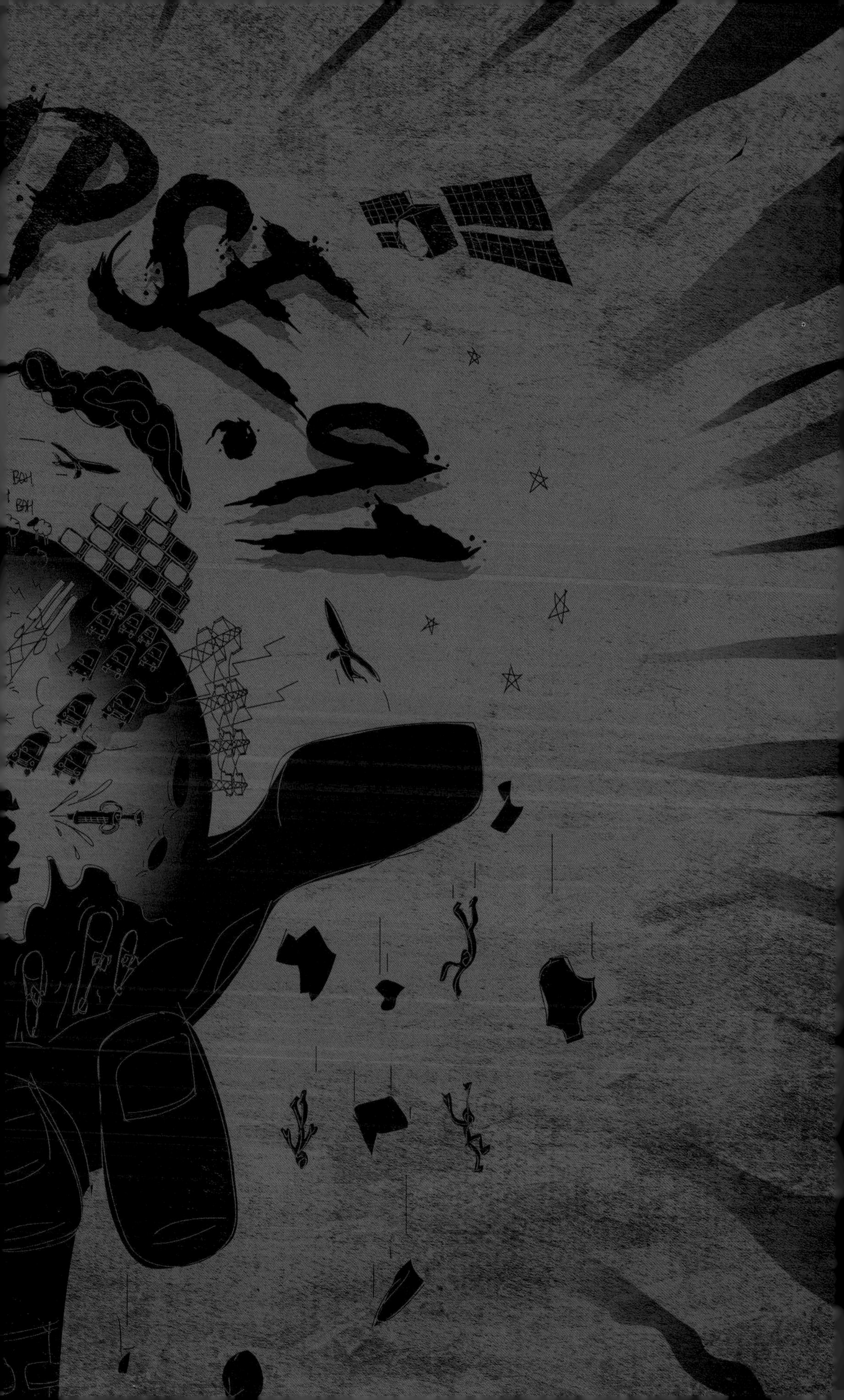
BAH
BAH

Marco D'alfonso

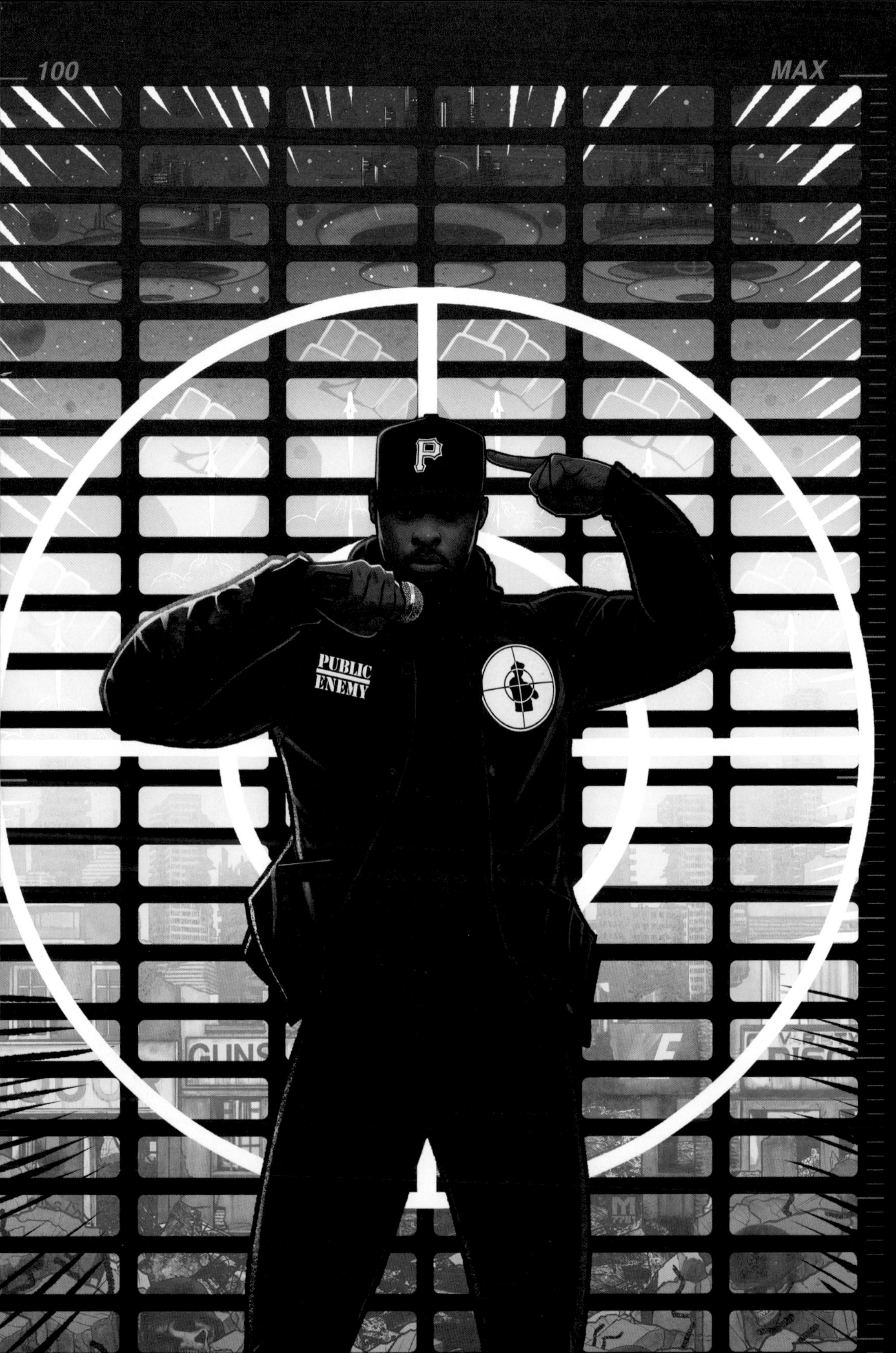
100
MAX
P
PUBLIC
ENEMY
GUNS

Mike del Mundo

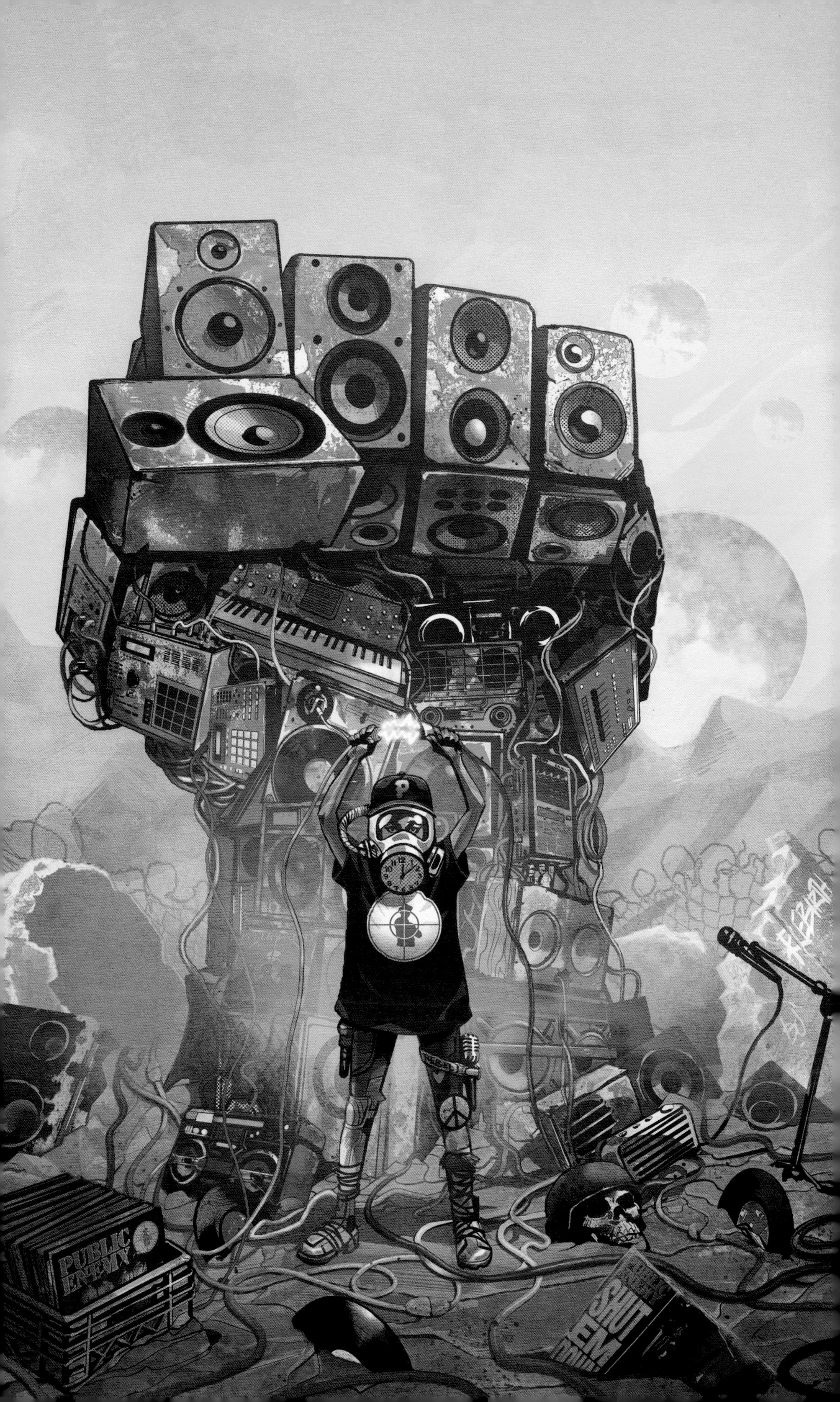
PUBLIC ENEMY

Chuck D

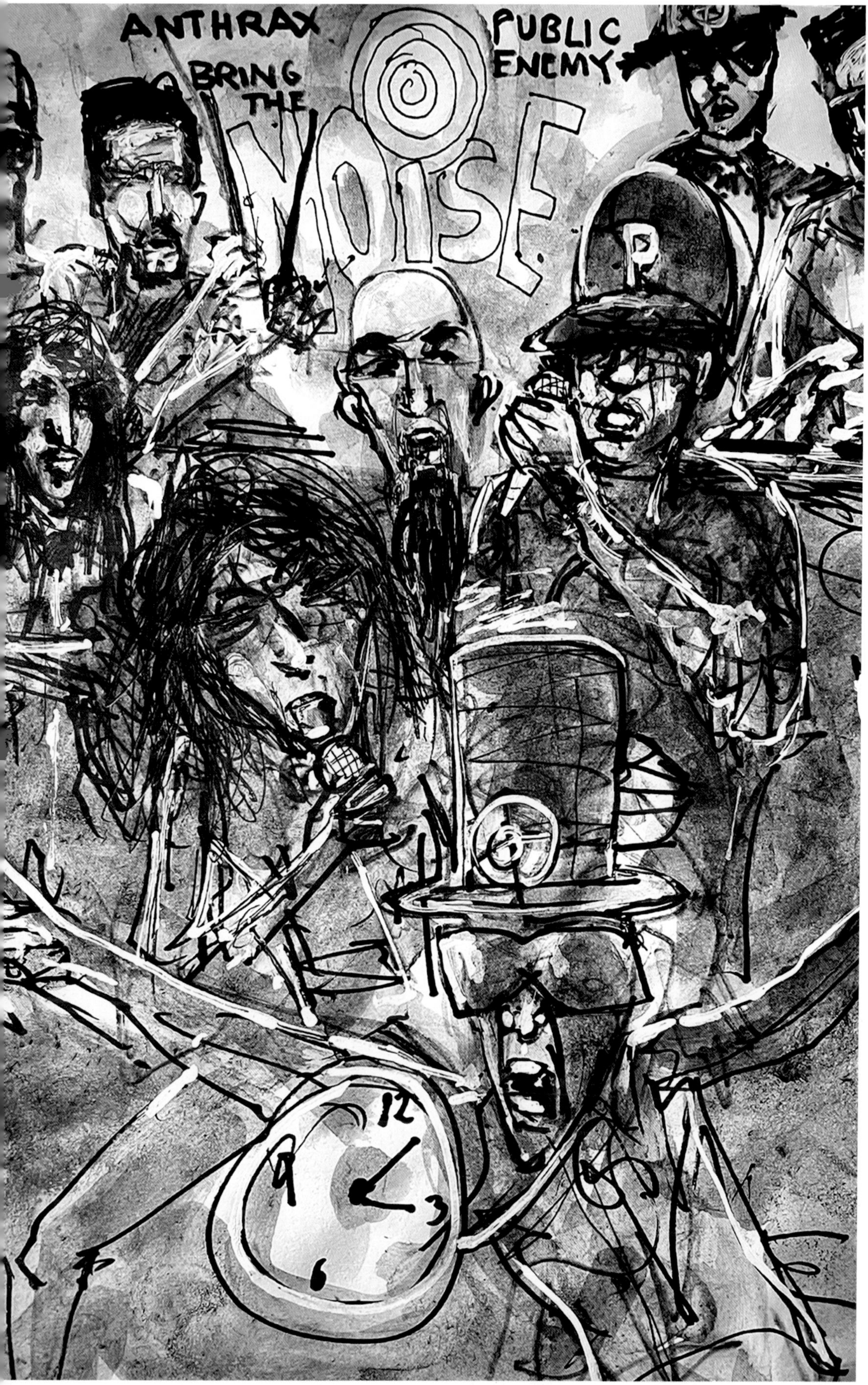
ANTHRAX
BRING THE NOISE
PUBLIC ENEMY

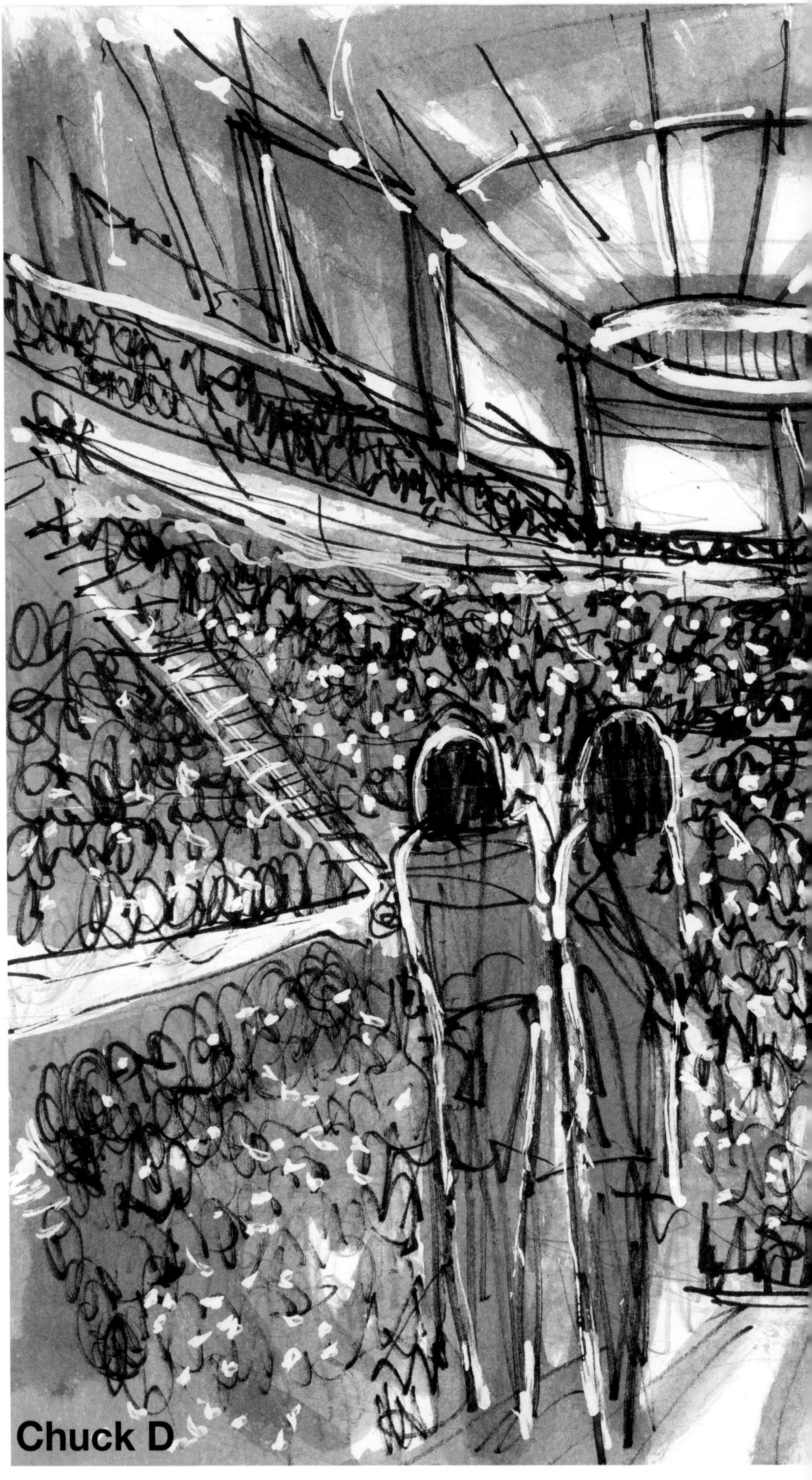
Chuck D

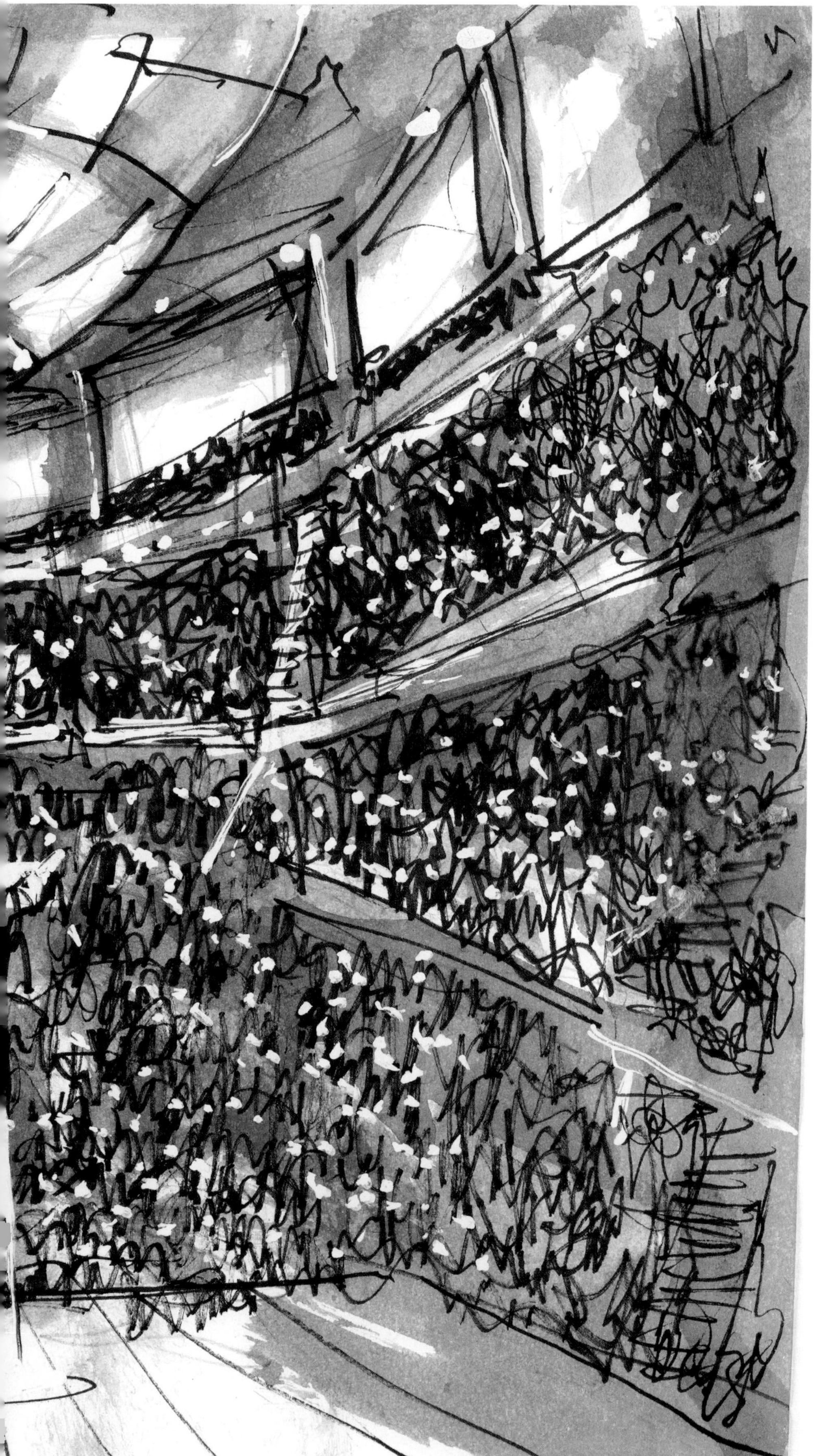

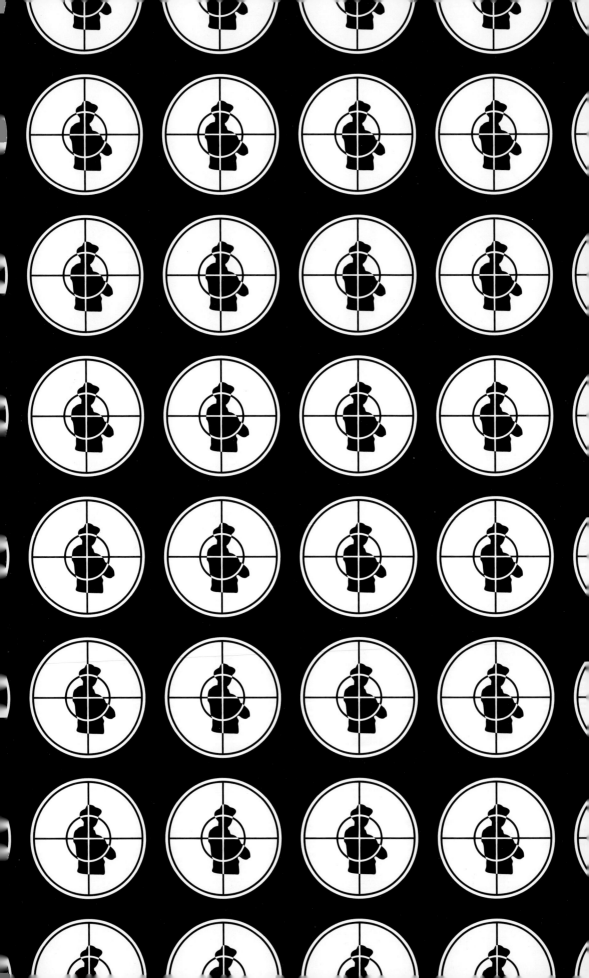